DIS(

PRAISE FOR OTHER BOOKS
BY ÓCHA'NI LELE

The Diloggún

"In this new book, Ócha'ni Lele has brought together information never before published for the education of serious students
of divination, and for use by initiated practitioners of African traditional religions, especially those who follow La Regla de Ocha.
In doing so, he has more than justified his own claim that 'one
cannot overstate the academic and scholastic value' of this work."

EDWARD BATCHELOR JR., FELLOW IN
RELIGION, YALE UNIVERSITY

Diloggún Tales of the Natural World

"Anyone interested in the folktales and oral traditions of other
cultures should snap up this book. Contained within are charm-
ing stories of personified natural forces, foolish mortals, and gods
of all levels of power and wisdom. Think Aesops' fables with a
Yoruban twist."

WITCHES' ALMANAC

Sacrificial Ceremonies of Santería

"The Lucumi faith—better known to noninitiates as 'Santería'—
has been one of the most misunderstood and maligned subjects in
Western history. The good news is that this is finally changing.
The importance of *Sacrificial Ceremonies of Santería* cannot be
overstated. Ócha'ni Lele has provided us with yet another magnum
opus in his ever growing library of Lucumi textbooks, instruction
manuals, and mystical explorations. If you study religious movements here in the West, you simply cannot ignore this book."

AARON LEITCH, AUTHOR OF *SECRETS OF
THE MAGICKAL GRIMOIRES*

"... very useful to students of religion, history, and folklore, as well as general readers eager to know more about this complex religion. It will be a welcome addition to academic and public libraries."

CYNTHIA DUNCAN, PH.D., PROFESSOR OF HISPANIC STUDIES
AT THE UNIVERSITY OF WASHINGTON/TACOMA
AND AUTHOR OF *UNRAVELING THE REAL:*
THE FANTASTIC IN SPANISH AMERICAN FICCIONES

"This book is an important work that can dispel the fears and false assumptions about animal sacrifice held by the general public. Ócha'ni Lele chronicles in great detail the struggle for Santería to be recognized as a legitimate religion by the Supeme Court. Practioners of the Yoruba, Santería, Candomble, and Lucumi traditions will better understand their common origins and practices after reading this book, and it will serve as a text for the thousands of initiates in priestly training. This book is fully researched, the information is balanced and integrated, and the writing voice is clear, humble, and humorous. It is an excellent delineation of the deeper meanings secured within the sacred Orature of the tradition."

LUISAH TEISH, FOUNDING MOTHER OF ILE ORUNMILA OSHUN
AND AUTHOR OF *JAMBALAYA: THE NATURAL WOMAN'S*
BOOK OF PERSONAL CHARMS AND PRACTICAL RITUALS

"Written in equal parts journalistic/academic style and personal account, Lele gives clear historical and political context for the development of Santería and explains how ancestor worship factors in to animal sacrifice. The account is thorough and gives the Santerían side of conflicts over sacrificial practices. He even digs in to Santerían folklore, providing a complete context for these practices. . . . Highly recommended."

FACING NORTH.NET

OSOGBO

Speaking to the Spirits
of Misfortune

Ócha'ni Lele

Destiny Books
Rochester, Vermont • Toronto, Canada

Destiny Books
One Park Street
Rochester, Vermont 05767
www.DestinyBooks.com

Text stock is SFI certified

Destiny Books is a division of Inner Traditions International

Library of Congress Cataloging-in-Publication Data

Lele, Ócha'ni, 1966– author.
  Osogbo : speaking to the spirits of misfortune / Ócha'ni Lele.
     pages cm
  Includes bibliographical references and index.
  ISBN 978-1-62055-098-4 (pbk.) — ISBN 978-1-62055-344-2 (e-book)
  1. Orishas. 2. Fortune. 3. Santeria. I. Title.
  BL2532.S5L45 2014
  299.674442—dc23

                                                              2013034605

Printed and bound in the United States by Lake Book Manufacturing, Inc.
The text stock is SFI certified. The Sustainable Forestry Initiative® program
promotes sustainable forest management.

10 9 8 7 6 5 4 3 2 1

Text design and layout by Priscilla Baker
This book was typeset in Garamond Premier Pro with Carumba, Gill Sans, and
Legacy Sans used as display typefaces

To send correspondence to the author of this book, mail a first-class letter to the
author c/o Inner Traditions • Bear & Company, One Park Street, Rochester, VT
05767, and we will forward the communication. Or communicate with the author
directly at **ochanilele@gmail.com**.

For Rebecca: you were more than a goddaughter.
You were my sister, my partner, my roommate,
my best friend, and my heart.
You were my family, and I love you.

 Contents

If we would listen to the teachings of odu, we would last like our ancestors lasted; if we would follow the teachings that odu has to offer us, we would grow old like the ancient ones did.

UNLE IROSUN (8-4), IN THE DILOGGÚN

Acknowledgments

I taught my first online diloggún divination class in February 2010. At that time there were no books written on either the Lucumí concept of *osogbo,* the word in our dialect that refers to misfortune, or the Yoruba concept of *íbi,* a modern Yoruba reference to misfortune. Although I published two books about the process of cowrie shell divination, *The Secrets of Afro-Cuban Divination* and *The Diloggún,* my work to date has only provided lists of the various osogbos mentioned in the divination system, along with their translations. Through class lectures I further fleshed out my students' knowledge of osogbo. As my syllabus evolved, I devoted several classes to the religion's *patakís,* or stories, in which the osogbos are the main characters. The more stories I taught, the more my students wanted. My first divination class forced me to dig deeper into our lore, uncovering these gems. The result was a rough collection of patakís about the spiritual creatures we know as the osogbos. I organized and presented that initial collection to Inner Traditions as a book proposal; thankfully, they contracted for it. Thus it was because of those students in that first course—Valinda Brooks, Laura Cantu, Yona Deshommes, Dr. Cynthia Duncan, Eddy Gutierrez, and Dr. Iyanla Vanzant—that this book was born. Without them I would never have written it. Our countless hours together as fellow students (for even a teacher is a student) were integral to my own understanding of osogbo in the world.

There are many others who I must thank for their involvement in my work. First, thanks to my goddaughter Rebecca Brown for letting me tell her personal story of courage and healing when diagnosed with stage 4 ovarian cancer; she fought for her life with the best of both worlds, *ebó* and modern medicine. Our faith is filled with hundreds of testimonies just like hers, and these are the stories we need to tell one another to remind us of our divine power as priests and priestesses, as we all have the healing power of *ashé,* the dynamic spiritual power of the universe. Wield it wisely, my friends; it is the greatest gift Olódumare, the supreme deity, gives us.

As always, I put my head on the floor to my godparents, Oba-oriaté Banacek Matos, oniyemayá (an olorisha initiated into the mysteries of Yemayá), and Angel Jimenez, oloshún (an orisha priest initiated to Oshún). What can I say that hasn't already been said? It is through the orishas that we create and re-create our families, and we build spiritual ties beginning in this world and carrying through to the next. The orishas brought me as godparents two men who reflect the light of heaven in all that they do. By their hands I received life's greatest gift: ashé. In this world there is no greater force, and it is a power that I wield only because they accepted me as part of their family and initiated me into the mysteries of the orishas. Words are not enough to thank them.

I am grateful to my own godchildren who encourage me to write and who give me the time and space to do the work that Oyá charged me with: Ashara Yvonne Watkins, Katelan V. Foisy, Vivienne D'Avalon, Sandy Short, Kristi Marrero, Helen, Stephanie, and others who move through our lives like the tides of the ocean. I depend on their strength as much as they depend on mine, and without their support I'm not sure how I would manage my spiritual work. A godparent could not ask for better godchildren; a man could not ask for better friends. I love each of you deeply.

For this book I also wish to make many professional acknowledgments:

I owe much of my success to a handful of college professors who took special interest in both my writing and my studies. Each of these teachers was inspirational and motivational. I would not be what I am now had it not been for their private tutelage: Webb Harris, Virginia

Magarine, Ann Refoe, and Terie Watkins, all with Seminole State College in Sanford, Florida. Words are not enough to express the love I have for all of you. Even with your insane student loads, each of you took time to guide me, and I realize what a huge sacrifice of your own personal time that was. Hopefully, each book I write honors the sacrifices you have made to nurture my raw talents. I am forever grateful.

Radiah Nuñez and the H20 Network: on her own, Dia has created a wealth of material in the form of archives and interviews with an elder Lucumí priest, oriaté Ernesto Pichardo, who has, in essence, done ebó so that each of us in the United States could be reborn through Lucumí ritual. For those who still don't know who this oriaté is, Pichardo is the *babalorisha* (father of the orishas) who, against all odds, fought for our right to practice our religion in the United States in the Supreme Court case known as *Church of the Lucumí Babaluaiye v. City of Hialeah*. If any *aborisha* (one who worships the orishas of Santería) or *olorisha* (an initiate of an orisha) is unfamiliar with this case, then you simply do not know our history. While to date he has not taught exclusively on the subject of osogbo, his archived interviews gave me much to think about when developing my own theories on the concept of osogbo. Pichardo's archived lectures made me think, and they made me think deeply. I encourage readers to get to know his work through the archives of the H20 Network.

I thank all the editors with whom I have worked, both now and previously: Susannah Noel, Doris Troy, Nancy Ringer, Patty Capetola, and Margaret Jones. They all influenced my craft, and with each book I write, something from each editor goes into it.

Laura Schlivek, my project editor throughout all my work with Inner Traditions, deserves special thanks. Somehow she is able to encourage me and motivate me when I feel powerless to complete a book. I love you, and I adore working with you. Sometimes the deadlines you give me for projects are insane, but you manage to motivate me—and with your guidance, my writing becomes art. You've also taught me time-management skills with your deadlines and instructions, and that in itself is miraculous!

Jon Graham, my acquisitions manager at Inner Traditions: I'm sure there are a thousand manuscripts that come across your desk more worthy of publication than mine, but somehow you work your magic and come up with a contract for each proposal. You told me once, "I'm going to help you share the beauty of your faith with the world; we are going to create the biggest library of Lucumí knowledge ever written!" And unlike so many who have broken promises to me over the years, you've gone above and beyond your duties at ITI to help me accomplish just that. You, along with Laura, have been an incredible team. I value both our professional relationship and our friendship. There's a special place in my heart for you as well.

Inner Traditions International: I offer my eternal gratitude to you. Every publisher wants books that will reap huge sales, and often books that need to be published because their content is important are overlooked because there are other books that will draw in vast financial rewards. You didn't have to publish any of my books. You could have spent your financial resources on other books that would have given you greater returns in a broader market. I understand that, and thank you from my heart for putting my work out there. Olófin blessed me the day he sent my work to your desk, and I offer my loyalty as an author to you. I feel that ITI is my writing home. More important than all this, however, is that I'm proud to be a part of your publishing house. Of all the publishers who work with indigenous and spiritual authors, you put spiritual principles to work in your business practices. From your voluntary participation in the Sustainable Forestry Initiative to your use of solar energy, and the way you run your business as if it were a huge, extended, loving family, it makes me proud when I say I am published by Destiny Books, a division of Inner Traditions International. If only other publishing companies would follow suit, the world would be a much better place.

There are a few personal acknowledgments that I wish to make:

Joseph Pagan, who was instrumental to my research for this book. In my private collection of notes and patakís, I had many essential stories written in Spanish, and, unfortunately, my Spanish skills are poor. It takes me a day of concentrated effort to read and understand a single page written in the Spanish language. Joseph spent countless hours translating Cuban materials, and without his kind help my book would have been much harder to write.

Steven Cherena, another friend who was instrumental in helping me translate some of the more obscure but essential stories in my collection that were in Spanish. Although his contributions are not included in this book, some of the material he helped me with will appear in future volumes.

Finally, I would like to thank each of you, my thousands of readers, who have bought my books and spread the word about them for years. An author without an audience is a lonely creature, and your thoughts, words, critiques, letters, and e-mails have helped keep me focused on the work at hand: writing about the spiritual beauty of the Lucumí faith so that the world can understand who and what we are. I thank each of you for that support.

Lucumí Spelling and Lucumí Cosmology

Please note that there is no standardized spelling of Lucumí words and terms. Yoruba scholars use standard Yoruba spellings, with all the necessary diacritical marks, while American scholars tend to take the easy route and Americanize all the spellings, leaving out the essential accent marks. Those initiated in the Afro-Cuban branch of Yoruba orisha worship known as Lucumí follow Spanish guidelines when adding diacritical marks to syllables, and even among those writers the spellings of words can differ (such as Oshún or Ochún, Shangó or Changó, Lucumí or Lukumi, ache or ashé, and yubonna or ojigbona). I have retained the same spellings that I have used for Lucumí words over the past thirteen years in my own writing; however, when quoting verbatim from other writers and scholars, I must of course use their spellings. Dear readers, please forgive me if you encounter different spellings for different words in this work; copyright law and fair use acts require that when I quote, I must quote verbatim.

Also, realize that while my writings on Lucumí metaphysics and ontology are based on sound spiritual principles from the sixteen olodu and 256 odu of the dilogún, what you read in this book is based on my personal experience and studies from fourteen years of orisha worship as an aborisha, and another ten years as an olorisha. The writings and thoughts of many Lucumí elders have influenced my views. I have been influenced and taught, either directly (through private conversations) or indirectly (through their published and unpublished writings) by Oba Miguel "Willie" Ramos (who has published some wonderful books in English over the past few years), Ernesto Pichardo (through his online reflections and BlogTalkRadio interviews on the H20 Network), Clayton Keck (through private conversations and online writings), Kola Abimbola (through published work), Hector "Tiko" Rojas (through private discussions), Banacek Matos (through extensive and intensive one-on-one training), Angel Jimenez (through extensive and intensive one-on-one training), Dr. Iyanla Vanzant (an elder and well-respected Yoruba priestess), Radiah Nuñez, and countless other olorishas who are very near and dear to my heart but who prefer to remain unnamed in my work. In the end, however, the views expressed in this manuscript are my own, and they are based on personal experience, knowledge, study, and interpretation. When privately circulated manuscripts or published works are used in my text, I have made the appropriate documentation.

Hopefully, this volume opens a wider discussion about *iré,* blessing and good fortune, and *osogbo,* misfortune, among our people and helps advance a thoughtful consideration of Lucumí cosmology and ontology in the world. Lucumí ontology and metaphysics are vast fields of study, studies gaining serious academic consideration over the past decade, and a work such as this is merely a beginning, one that demands more advanced consideration. If I've written it once, I've written it a thousand times: true spirituality cannot be taught in a book. Especially with this faith, Lucumí orisha worship, real learning begins at the feet of one's elders. Never undervalue real-world experience.

Preface

LIFE IS MESSY LIKE THAT

My years in this religion span almost three decades, with more than ten of those as an active priest. My specialty: divination. It takes an entire bookshelf to hold the notebooks containing the *itán* (readings) I have given to clients, some of whom still come to me on a regular basis, others of whom are long gone, eaten up by the very osogbos they fought against. Many moved to other states and we lost touch; others found olorishas with whom they were more comfortable, being made to their own orishas in those *ilé ocha* (houses of the orishas). Of the thousands of people for whom I have divined, a small handful remain with me; these are my family, and even though we do not share the same blood in our veins we share a proud connection through our *otás* (stones) of the orishas, and we are a spiritual family whose lineage takes us back to the days of ancient Oyó and the flourishing Yoruba empire that commanded vast regions of what post-colonial Europeans divided into the modern state of Nigeria. We are not bound by blood; we are bound by spirit, inseparable and devoted to one another. I, as their priest, am known as their godfather, their *padrino,* and I love each of them as if they were my own children.

Like any parent, when my child suffers I suffer, and there came a time in my life when the suffering was more than I could bear. You will learn about that in this book; it is here, in these pages, that I bare my soul in a way few people are comfortable doing. But if by telling this story I can save at least one life, then the awkward nakedness I feel in sharing it is worth the uneasiness. At a vulnerable time in my life, a time when a best friend of eleven years and I parted ways over irreconcilable differences, Olófin brought into my life an incredible woman named Rebecca Brown, who not only consoled me through my sorrows, but also filled the hole my lost friend had left in my life. In time, she became not only my goddaughter in this faith, but also my best friend, my sister, my roommate, my confidante, and my heart. *She* healed *me*. But soon she became sick, and no matter what I tried to do on her behalf I could do little more than relieve her suffering. My faith was strained and tested. One night while studying odu (I spend an average of two hours each day studying odu, the way a rabbi studies the Torah or Talmud) I came across a patakí long forgotten, and it helped put *everything* into perspective.

In the beginning of time, Osogbo* swathed the world with his darkness; and Unle, the eldest of the odu living on the earth, dedicated his life to the creature's destruction. Unle was a diviner, a powerful one at that, and he spent his youth learning, searching for ways to drive Osogbo back into the shadows where he belonged. But it seemed that a single lifetime of work and study were not enough to destroy Osogbo, and in his old age Unle tired; he was embittered by the battle. No matter how much good he did there was always more to do, and where he was not, Osogbo reared his ugly head and took control once more. It was in his old age that Unle found himself at the feet of Orúnmila, as many of us do in time, and there he sat, in silence, facing the wise diviner.

Orúnmila was preparing an ebó when Unle walked into his temple; he spread a thick powder over his table of Ifá in preparation for the divination ceremony to follow. Unle listened as Orúnmila chanted, tapping his tray and drawing lines in the fine sand. Finally, Unle's own odu in Ifá appeared: Ejiogbe Meji. Orúnmila stopped. "Your own pattern sits before me, Unle," he said. "Tell me, what is on your mind?"

---

*Osogbo is both the living entity or spirit of misfortune and a reference to misfortune in general.

Again, silence. The old man sat across from the young man—Unle, whose wisdom came from a lifetime of service, and Orúnmila, whose wisdom came from a lifetime of study. "We are not so different, you and I," said Unle. "For you now are as I once was, a young man devoted to his studies. I have dedicated my life as one of service, as you do now. I help everyone who comes to me, as do you. Throughout the world I have traveled, dispelling misfortunes with my work as a diviner and healer, but no matter how hard I work, no matter how hard I try, I can neither create nor discover perfection in Olódumare's creation." He sat silently, staring at the table of Ifá. "What is the purpose of this if I cannot fix the world?"

Orúnmila picked up an egg that was sitting beside his mat, quivering and shaking as it was. "I am not going to tell you what you seek. I am going to show you what you seek using your own sacred symbol, the egg." Between the lines of Ifá on the table he set the egg. "This holds the secret of Ejiogbe Meji, your sign in Ifá. Just watch."

Unle watched as the egg quivered some more, scattering the powder and ruining his sign in Ifá. Soon the shell cracked and a young chick emerged. "Life unfolding," said Orúnmila as the chick walked across his sacred board, flapping its wings to dry them, crying and defecating as it walked in random circles. After some minutes of this, with Unle watching intently for a great secret to unfold, Orúnmila lifted the chick in his hands and set it on the floor. To Unle, there seemed to be no secret, no point. "Look at the board, Unle. What do you see?"

"A total mess. My sign, your board, it is all a mess."

"And there is your answer, Unle. Life is messy like that."

Perhaps, for the first time, Unle understood what it meant to live, and to have lived.

As I teach my students in my dilogún classes, and as I so often tell my godchildren, when the world began it was like this: there was Iré, the spirit of blessings, and there was Osogbo, the spirit of misfortunes, and they took turns ruling over the earth. In time, Osogbo gave birth to the osogbos, creatures who swathed the earth with their specific forms of darkness, while Iré remained a solitary creature. Perhaps it was because

Osogbo was obedient, making ebó while Iré slept. Or maybe it was always Olódumare's design that Iré was to remain alone and lonely. No one knows. But Lucumí priests remember the story, and we tell it in the olodu Ofún:*

Iré and Osogbo were twin brothers, yet they lived as rivals. Both coveted supremacy over the earth and neither desired parity. In the beginning, they argued as friends; they chose their words carefully, each not wanting to hurt the other's feelings. Time impassioned their words, however, and they became harsh. The passage of centuries brought battles and wars for power, each epoch bringing more chaos until there was no peace on earth. Olófin could take no more, and from heaven he commanded, "Enough!"

The skies rumbled, the world trembled, and every living thing hid in shadows. Never before had Olófin raised his voice. As its sound echoed and waned over the earth, silence ensued. Even the air was still, yet thick with anticipation.

Iré and Osogbo were hushed; neither brother dared defy Olófin in his anger.

Taking form in their midst, Olófin demanded, "This war ends now!" He raised a powerful black fist, withered by age, as he gestured at both. "Brother should not raise hand against brother. Today, each of you will make ebó, and when you are done making ebó you will come and see me. I alone will decide which of you is greater on the earth."

Olófin's form wavered in the air before dissolving like a desert mirage. The twins, still stunned, looked at each other with wide eyes. Then they retreated to opposite ends of the earth.

Once alone, Iré smiled smugly to himself. He looked up at the skies and spoke into the air, "I do not need to make ebó. No one on earth desires death; no one desires sickness; no one desires any of life's misfortunes. Every living thing invites me into their homes and their lives with each prayer they offer to heaven. All of the world's hopes and dreams and desires begin and

---

*This story first appeared in my book *Teachings of the Santería Gods;* it is titled "The Story of Iré and Osogbo."

end with me." Satisfied that Olófin would make him supreme regardless of his disobedience, Iré settled into a comfortable, peaceful sleep.

Osogbo knew his brother and knew his arrogance. He thought to himself, "When goodness is away, I, misfortune, am all that remains. I am everywhere in the world—it is the natural order for things to fail and decay. I will make my ebó; I will make it twice; I will make it three times over. This I will do not because I desire to be greater, because already I am the greatest, but because Olófin himself has ordered it." And so Osogbo made ebó as Olófin had mandated, and while Iré continued to sleep, he did it again and again. Obedience was pleasing to Olófin, and obedient was what Osogbo wanted to be. Satisfied that he had done his best, Osogbo gathered himself up and flew into heaven, knocking at Olófin's door.

Olófin was surprised when he saw Osogbo so soon, and he was concerned that Iré was not with him. "Where is your brother?" he asked.

Osogbo's face cracked in an evil grin as he said, "My brother, Iré, did not feel he had to make ebó. He was tired and went to sleep after you left. He still sleeps down on the earth; he sleeps while humans and orishas alike pray for his blessings. He sleeps while I, tirelessly, do the work that I was born to do."

Olófin's all-seeing eyes scanned the earth for Iré, and he saw that it was true: Iré was sleeping, smugly convinced that goodness, despite his refusal to make ebó, would be supreme on the earth. Olófin looked at Osogbo and saw that despite all the evils he embodied, he was the one brother who was obedient and who did what he, Olófin, had asked.

With a mighty wave of his hand, Olófin conjured Iré to appear before him. Iré wiped the sleep and confusion from his eyes as Olófin pronounced, "To end the eternal warring between you and your brother, I demanded that you both make ebó. After making your ebós, I demanded that you both come before me for my final decree. Iré, you slept while the world begged for your blessings, and your brother, Osogbo, made his ebó not just once, but three times over."

A horrible expression of fear and confusion crept over Iré's face as Olófin continued, "Osogbo, because you made ebó, you are first in all things. You are not that which is desired, but you are that which fills the world. You are not that which is called on, but you are the one who will come. For being obedient you are the greatest and the most powerful. Humans will get but one chance to ask for a blessing, and if a blessing does not come you will be all that remains. Humans will get but once chance to hold on to that blessing, and if they are not obedient it will melt away as if it had never been there. You will be all that remains."

Olófin took a deep breath and looked lovingly at Osogbo, "And for your obedience, my son, know this: that although you think all you bring to the world is evil, with your misfortunes will come much good. For it is human nature to seek out blessings and to grow and evolve into something greater. Because of you, civilizations will grow and flourish as they try to banish you back into the shadows; great books will be written and art will be created. The weak will be destroyed and the strong will become stronger. Each generation will grow into something greater and more powerful because tragedy encourages human nature to grow and persevere, while undeserved blessings make the heart grow weak and lazy. You will be both the catalyst and the motivation for my creations to achieve great things."

Iré was silent. His disobedience had cost him much.

So it has been: since that day misfortunes follow humanity always, and those who hope to achieve anything great in life must do it with great suffering and through sacrifice. Osogbo became the first and the greatest, not because he was sought out by those living on earth, but because, of the two brothers, he was the only one who made ebó. This was the beginning of the world's evolution.

Introduction

LIKE IRÉ, I WAS SLEEPING

On January 3, 2010, my godchildren were at my house, each waiting for their annual reading for the coming year. Rebecca's came in a strange combination, one I'd not encountered before. The odu Oché Obara opened on the mat for her, but instead of coming with a gentle, incomplete iré (blessing) as it usually did for her, this time it came with a harsh osogbo (misfortune)—that of Aro, durative illness. The olodu Oché (represented by 5 mouths on the mat) comes with many misfortunes aimed at women, misfortunes I had carefully explained to my divination students in class, misfortunes I had carefully explained to my goddaughter Rebecca. I remember telling her, "This letter speaks of sickness in the blood, the belly, and the genitals. It speaks of decomposition in these areas. It marks infections and tumors. It speaks of problems with a woman's ovaries." I went deeper into the odu Oché Obara to speak to her about the illnesses found there. "Oché Obara is especially dangerous for you because as a composite in osogbo it guarantees issues in the womb and the female reproductive tract. It also speaks about heavy use of pain medications and alcohol; these could mask early symptoms of disease and make it more difficult for you to catch any strange symptoms early, while the problem is still small." Of Obara, which was in the second position of her odu, I told her, "It speaks of problems in three areas: the kidneys, the stomach, and the ovaries. This odu leaves you open to severe illness in any of these areas."

1

Rebecca stiffened. She'd never had a reading this bad. I continued: "The osogbo Elegguá marks on you is Aro, durative illness." I reminded her that she already had three durative illnesses tormenting her: multiple sclerosis, rheumatoid arthritis, and fibromyalgia. I reminded her that she had beaten breast cancer once already. Because of her coinciding pain symptoms from all three chronic diseases, she was taking large amounts of pain medication. With Oché Obara on the mat, this had me worried. "The pain medications you're on can mask new symptoms. And this disease predicted by Oché Obara is something new coming for you, Rebecca. You need to be proactive with your health." I marked several cleansings for her but told her that the ultimate resolution was to be found with the physicians and both medical and surgical intervention. Her osogbo was marked by the odu Ogundá, which always speaks of surgery; and the osogbo came for her *elese otonowa* (from heaven), witnessed by the odu Unle (8 mouths), which meant she brought this part of her life with her from heaven—it was a part of her destiny. She took notes on this reading; as a matter of fact, she took copious notes—pages that I would later obtain for my private archives, determined that should this odu ever fall again, I would make sure that no woman would ever suffer as she did. Oché Obara in the osogbo of Aro—it's a combination I hope to never see again.

More than a year later, like Iré, I was sleeping; I was unprepared when osogbo came for me, for our *ilé*, for my goddaughter Rebecca. Early on the morning of April 12, 2011, not much after 2 AM, my phone rang. The voice was raspy and shaken. "I'm scared," it said. "The pain got so bad tonight my son had to drive me to the emergency room. I couldn't take it anymore. They're running tests." It took me a moment to clear the fog from my head, to glance at the caller ID and actually see *Rebecca Brown* on the display before I knew the person to whom I was speaking— my own goddaughter. I rolled over and shook Bryan; he groaned, his hand flopping back on my face to push me away. I sat up.

Rebecca described the emergency room activity, and the doctors, nurses, and patient-care technicians who were running in and out of her room, drawing blood, palpating her swollen abdomen, and wheeling her to various parts of the hospital to administer tests. Her voice was dreamy and faraway; I could hear the morphine mixed with her words. My own mind was wandering to a *misa* (a spiritual mass) we had had at my house just a couple of weeks earlier. One of the mediums had a spirit dedicated to healing, and the spirit came to visit us that night. It took control of the medium's body, and, shaking like a newborn testing its legs for the first time, it walked to Rebecca. Gently, using the medium's hands as if they were her own, she touched Rebecca's stomach. "There is something there," she said, using the medium's voice. "There is something there."

"It's not hurting anymore." My mind snapped back to the moment. I could hear Rebecca's voice fading away; the morphine the nurses had given her for her pain was doing its job, putting her into a gentle twilight where the fire in her belly no longer burned. She told me the excruciating pain was gone. "It can't be that serious if it's not hurting anymore," she said. Her voice sounded hopeful.

"Do you want Bryan and me to come down?" Now he, too, was sitting up, silently mouthing, "What's wrong?" I was the one waving him away now with a hand on *his* face. He shook it off.

"No. There's nothing you can do. I need to rest."

"Call me back when you get your results," I told her, reassuring her that everything would be okay. But dread made me shiver; my blood was like ice water in my veins. Something told me that everything was *not* okay, but Rebecca was frightened, and she needed reassurance. At least I could give her that. I hung up the phone with the words of that medium's healing spirit still ringing in my head: "There is something there."

Back in October 2010, ten months after her reading of the year, Rebecca had been admitted to Winter Park Memorial Hospital in Winter Park, Florida, for severe abdominal pain. The physicians ordered several tests, one of them a CT with and without contrast. Despite all the tests they ran, their diagnosis was an ovarian cyst. "No treatment is needed," the doctors reassured her. "It will resolve on its own." They ascribed her pain to her previously diagnosed conditions of multiple sclerosis, rheumatoid arthritis, and fibromyalgia. They sent her home and told her to rest. Over the next few months she continued to feel pain and experienced occasional bloating. She went to one doctor who told her that the issue was not in her ovaries, it was in her colon, and she was diagnosed with Crohn's disease, an autoimmune disorder causing chronic inflammation of the gastrointestinal tract. Because she was already suffering from one autoimmune disorder, multiple sclerosis, a disease causing both bowel and bladder symptoms such as bloating and constipation, fatigue, muscle spasms, and pain such as what she was experiencing in her abdomen, to the physicians this diagnosis made sense. But for Rebecca it wasn't the answer. She had no relief from her pain or her symptoms.

I put diloggún on the mat for her one night when she was feeling most desperate. The odu that opened for her came with osogbo, specifically the osogbo of Aro, durative illness, and the sign itself pinpointed her reproductive tract as the cause of her issues. "You have to be proactive with this," I told her. "You have to stay on top of the doctors and convince them that their diagnosis is wrong." Aro is an osogbo that plagues its victims until our eventual demise, while her sister, Ano, is that which can kill us but is fleeting and, often, curable. Of the two sisters, Rebecca had the most powerful on her. Ebó was offered: weekly and monthly cleansings of her abdomen to the orisha Érínlè, our divine physician, until the earthly physicians could pull themselves together to discover the root of her issues. Rebecca performed these ebós frequently and flawlessly.

But she fought with the doctors.

Her symptoms continued. There were days the pain was harsh; there were days the pain was almost nonexistent; still, she felt something out of whack inside of her, something broken, something growing. Each physician she went to confirmed the previous diagnosis of Crohn's disease combined with her multiple sclerosis symptoms. No one listened to her as she told them what her body was saying; not a single doctor would revisit the issue with the ovarian cyst. She tried to go back to the first hospital physician, the doctor who first found the cyst, but he refused to see her; he had discharged her from his practice, and she was unable to get an appointment. Because of her continued attempts to see various doctors for the same symptoms, insurance issues got in the way, and it took her weeks to find a doctor who would take her. Finally, just days before the pain in her abdomen exploded into something that felt like fire, she found a doctor who would see her and consider the ovarian cyst. That appointment, unfortunately, was a few weeks away. During that time the pain got so bad that she went to the emergency room before ever making it through that physician's office door.

Later in the morning Rebecca called again. This time her voice was fragmented and worn. Some of her words were unintelligible. A palliative care physician had just walked out of her room. His first and only question to her was, "So how far into your cancer treatments are you?"

Suddenly, that *something* about which the odu had warned and the spirits had spoken had a name: cancer. Not just any cancer. Her cancer markers were off the charts, immeasurable; the CTs and MRIs showed a spreading ovarian cancer, and it was stage 4. When the palliative doctor realized this was a new diagnosis for her, he reassured her but offered her little hope. "We're admitting you to hospice care. We'll make you as comfortable as possible. You won't suffer." His expectation was that she would never leave the hospital; she was there to die in a matter of weeks, if not days. As quickly as he came in he walked out, shaken. *What doctor wouldn't be shaken,* I had asked myself, *if he had wrongly assumed that she already knew she was dying?*

Rebecca called me immediately after he left the room. "Do you want me to come?" I asked. "No," she said. "Rest. I'm exhausted. Come see me tomorrow after I'm settled in." After hanging up, I threw the phone across the room in anger. A goddaughter was dying, and for all my spiritual gifts I was unable to wrap my fingers around the cancer and pull it from her belly. I went to bed and cried myself to sleep. I felt . . . helpless.

That afternoon when I woke up, Bryan surprised me by having coffee made. He was about to make a late breakfast, but I wasn't hungry. "Rebecca's dying," I told him. "Why didn't she listen to the spirits when they told her there was something there? I feel so powerless." I had to turn my head away from him; I was crying.

"Ócháni Lele is powerless?" Bryan laughed and rolled his eyes, a habit of his that annoyed me to no end, but one he did every time he thought I was being pathetic. "You? The diviner? The one who studies odu like a rabbi studies the Old Testament? *You* feel powerless? Put Elegguá on the mat and see what he has to say about that. Use your ashé. Isn't that why you have it?"

Of course; as always, he was right.

Later that afternoon, after calling Rebecca to make sure she was settled into her hospital room and comfortable, and after Bryan had left to run errands, I put my mat on the floor. I drew a careful chalk circle on the mat using *efun,* powdered chalk made from crushed eggshells, and marked the four cardinal points with two lines each: north, south, east, and west. On the white plate with the gourd of fresh water I placed five cowrie shells from Elegguá's diloggún, the shells some know as *adele,* the witnesses. With the remaining sixteen shells of the diloggún inside the chalked circle I prayed to Olófin, Olorún, and Olódumare; I prayed to the ancestors one by one, and I prayed for all the crowned heads of my elders. I prayed to Elegguá, Ogún, Ochosi, Oyá, Oshún, Yemayá, Shangó, and Obatalá, the main orishas of our faith. Finally, I prayed to Elegguá again and there, on the mat, told him about Rebecca and how powerless I felt. With his shells clutched tightly to my heart, I cried into them for what seemed an eternity; I let my tears fall from my eyes like rain. I was so choked up I could barely get out the words, "*Ocháreo* (we join to the orishas)!" and the response, "*Adaché* (of our own free will)!"

There, alone, I divined for my goddaughter.* The letters that fell reminded me of a conversation I had had with my godfather more than a decade ago.

We had been on the phone late one night after a mutual acquaintance had died, and we were discussing the Lucumí views on death. I remember my godfather's voice, both somber and soft, and I was silent, listening to him speak. "We think of death as something final, the end, the annihilation of life," he told me. "And while that is true, Ikú, the spirit of death, is not an evil creature. It is the nature of all living things to die. The only

---

*For more information on the process of casting the diloggún, see my book *The Diloggún.*

misfortune is to die before one's time." I remember him going silent, listening, waiting for me to respond. I didn't. "My point," he said, "is that until someone is in the actual grip of Ikú, and until it is truly their time to go, there is always something a diviner can do to save that person, to extend that person's life. You just have to trust your knowledge, your ashé, and the orishas. In the end, though, it is in Olófin's hands. If he has sent Yemayá Ibú Achabá* to make the cross of *efun* on one's forehead, there is no way to prevent that death. It is their time."†

It was late the next evening when Bryan and I arrived at M. D. Anderson Cancer Center in downtown Orlando, Florida. Bryan carried a large wicker basket, while I pulled a small suitcase packed with eggs, coconuts, cocoa butter, rolled cotton, pears, bread rolls, and a single white sheet—all things that both my godfather and Elegguá (through his diloggún) had dictated as essential for the ebó I needed to do. When we got to Rebecca's room she was with a nurse, seemingly pain-free and in good spirits. The nurse was checking her I.V., and when she was done we told her, "We need some time alone to pray." M. D. Anderson is well known in the central Florida area for supporting and advocating both spirituality and alternative healing in its treatment of cancer, and the nurse left us alone.

---

*In Lucumí ontology, the avatar of Yemayá known as Yemayá Ibú Achabá is responsible for directing Ikú's work responsibly. If it is someone's time to die, Olófin sends her from heaven to make a cross on the forehead with *cascarilla,* a chalk made from powdered eggshells. While invisible to us, Ikú has the ashé to see this cross, and when she sees it on the forehead, she knows it is part of Olódumare's design to take this person's life. Nothing done by an olorisha can remove this spiritual mark. Simply, it is the nature of all things to die.
†Yemayá Ibú Achabá and the orisha Oyá are sisters, spiritually speaking. Yemayá Ibú Achabá marks a person's forehead (under Olófin's direction), and when Ikú moves to take that person's life, Oyá captures the last breath and moves the body to the cemetery gates. In natural death (as opposed to an untimely death), Oyá accompanies the body to the graveyard and puts it in the hands of the orisha Oba. Oba then turns the body over to Orishaokó, who is the hole opened in the earth, and once the body is put to rest in that hole, beneath the earth, both he and the orisha Yewá rise up and consume its material components. For a lifetime, the earth feeds us and gives us ashé (a concept discussed in chapter 1 of this book), and at the end of life, we feed the earth and return our ashé to it. In this role, Ikú is no longer an osogbo; it is a natural part of life.

"Are you ready to do ebó?" I asked Rebecca.

"As ready as ever." She smiled. I was hopeful.

Bryan set the wicker basket at the foot of her bed, bowing his head in prayer to his own spirits. He is a *houngan,* a priest of Vodun (i.e., Voodoo), initiated in Port-au-Prince, Haiti, and although in that tradition they don't refer to their essence as *ashé,* he had ashé of his own. Gently, I covered Rebecca with a white sheet, wrapping her like a corpse, and began to pray to our God, known in Lucumí as Olódumare. With Olódumare are Olorún and Olófin, Olorún being the aspect of God who spreads ashé on the earth, and Olófin the aspect who can come down and touch the earth, and I prayed to them as well. Libations and prayers followed—to the ancestors, to all the living priests and priestesses of our religion, and to the orishas themselves. Finally, I prayed a secret prayer I knew for the odu that had fallen for her that afternoon in my home, a restorative prayer to banish osogbo and call life back into her body. When I was done, I slowly pulled the funeral sheet back; it lay in the basket, a lining for the remainder of the ebó.

With one coconut on either side of her head, I repeated the same litany of prayers, and when I was done I rubbed the coconuts down her body, focusing on her belly before rolling them down her legs and into the basket. The coconuts were used to capture and remove as much of the illness as possible. I oiled eight eggs with cocoa butter, wrapped them in rolled cotton, and repeated the ritual once more. I oiled eight pears with cocoa butter, wrapped them in rolled cotton, and again repeated the entire prayer. Finally, I buttered eight bread rolls with the cocoa butter, wrapped them in rolled cotton, and cleansed Rebecca with those. Bryan helped me tie up all these things inside the white sheet. When we were done, as much of the osogbo as I could capture was, in theory, wrapped inside those items.

The ebó was almost complete. "We have to go," I told her. "We have to take this somewhere and finish the ebó. But I'll come back tomorrow."

We hugged, and Bryan and I left.

We drove to the church. Even though most olorishas do not go to just *any* church (for our homes become our temples), we see Olódumare,

Olorún, and Olófin in all religions. We believe that every faith has some spark of the truth and its own ashé. To us, a church holds a high concentration of Olófin's ashé (but the same could be said of a mosque, a synagogue, or even a mountain), and sometimes we go there to pray to Olófin. It was late and the doors were locked, but with the wicker basket beside me I knelt in front of the doors to the church and prayed to Olófin. "I'm leaving Rebecca's illness with you," I said. "And I trust you will do what's right."

So often had I left ebós at this church that there was now a trash can by the front door. I put the ebó there, and I slipped a small *derecho,* a religious fee or monetary offering, under the front door. We left.

So how does Rebecca's story end?

Instead of deteriorating, Rebecca suddenly "felt better." The palliative care physician decided to look more deeply into her illness. The day after her ebó, the physician at M. D. Anderson agreed to do a biopsy and another scan. To make her medications easier to administer, he decided to insert a port, a medical implant giving direct access to a vein, into her chest. Rebecca died during surgery, but fortunately she was resuscitated on the table. In itself, the doctor agreed that was a miracle. When the biopsy results came back, her ovarian cancer was restaged to 3B, which, unlike end-stage 4, is treatable but rarely curable. As well, her insurance agreed to pay for chemotherapy instead of hospice care. After her first regimen of chemotherapy was complete, to support the healing process I gave her the orishas Olokun (the owner of the ocean), the Ibeyi (the divine twins of Oshún and Shangó), and Ideu (the child of Oshún and Orúnmila). Olokun was to be her foundation, her strength; the Ibeyi were to heal her ovarian cancer; and Ideu was to restore joy to her life. After three months of chemo treatment, a total hysterectomy, and extensive surgical interventions, a woman who was once resigned to hospice care was in full remission. By November 2011, her CA125 levels (a specific ovarian cancer marker) were down to normal.

Still, Aro is constant torment; it is said that once she has us in her grip she never lets go.

Early in 2012, Rebecca was out of remission; her cancer markers were rising, and while they were not as high as when she was first diagnosed, the physician prescribed another round of chemotherapy. Before starting treatment, however, Rebecca wanted to receive Orishaokó, an orisha whose ashé can, and often does, keep the earth from feeding on us before our time. Determined to have Orishaokó before starting her treatments, we went to New York, where my godfather presided over the ceremony. When we returned home she felt stronger, healthier, and she was ready to fight her cancer with a renewed vengeance. Her determination was inspirational; her closest friends and family rallied around her as she began her second series of chemotherapy treatments. Everyone . . . was hopeful.

This book investigates the subject of osogbo and its Lucumí ontology through individual layers of understanding. Chapter 1 provides an overview of the philosophy of orisha worship and identifies the concepts of God through the trinity of Olódumare, Olorún, and Olófin, along with the myriad diffused faces known as the orishas. Chapter 2 introduces the reader to the concept of osogbo: what it is and what it is not. Chapter 3 investigates the connections between *orí,* the spiritual consciousness of humans, and one's personal responsibility when dealing with osogbo. Chapter 4 investigates the role of Elegguá, the personification of fate, in the governance of osogbo.

The major osogbos are presented in chapters 5, 6, and 7, but I only tell you, the reader, a little about who they are. Mostly I allow them to speak directly to the reader through their own stories, the patakís. Chapter 5 deals with the sacred stories about the osogbo known as Ikú, the spirit of death; chapter 6 deals with Arayé, the senior osogbo who is the spirit of wickedness; and chapter 7 presents a selection of patakís about the other osogbos. Sacred stories, indigenous mythology and folklore, and oral history—all these teach us what it is to be Lucumí, and they teach us about the essence of osogbo in the world and how to overcome its grip.

If all these patakís were to share one theme, it is this: Osogbo, the spirit of misfortune, sees itself as a vile creature, one who stands against life and all that is good in the world. But in truth it is misfortune that strengthens us, misfortune that motivates us, and misfortune that brings great evolution to the world. Lucumí ontology is neither fatalistic nor defeatist; it is healing and life-affirming. In their own ways, the osogbos of Lucumí belief serve life and its continuation. As we learn in the olodu Oché (represented by 5 mouths on the mat): "Without bitterness, one could not know sweetness." Likewise, without misfortune in our lives, we would never know blessing or what it means to be blessed.

The Philosophy of Orisha Worship

Teach me how to divine so that I may know how to divine;
teach me how to appease the orishas so that I may appease
the orishas; teach me how to prescribe sacrifices so that I
may prescribe sacrifices; for wisdom is all that I am seeking,
and this wisdom will be my wealth.

FROM THE OLODU UNLE

The Lucumí faith, often known by the pejorative Santería,* came from the Yoruba territories of what is now southwestern Nigeria during the transatlantic slave trade. As early as 1501, traders brought Africans to Cuba as slaves for cheap labor. Initially, the Yoruba were a small ethnic presence on the island, a mere fraction of the total slave population, but as the centu-

---

*Santería was the term applied by Cuban slaveholders when Yoruba slaves seemingly focused on the Catholic saints instead of the Christian God. The terms *santero* (a male practitioner) and *santera* (a female practitioner) were applied to the men and women who practiced this form of "saint worship." Although many modern initiates refer to themselves as Lucumí (the true name of the faith) or olorishas (the true name for priests and priestesses), many practitioners embrace those racial slurs proudly, as different people have different feelings regarding those terms in modern practice. So, for example, I am an olorisha, but I embrace the power that comes from being called a santero.

ries progressed and Cuba's economy grew, it needed more labor to produce sugar, and so the numbers of Yoruba on the island steadily increased. By the early to mid-1800s, with the fall of Oyó, the capital of the Yoruba empire (established in the fourteenth century and the most politically important state in Africa from the mid-seventeenth to the late eighteenth century), traders had forced hundreds of thousands of natives through the diaspora, thrusting them into the lower rungs of Cuban society. The Yoruba slaves in Cuba managed to maintain their spiritual heritage by hiding the worship of their orishas behind the facade of Catholic saints in the ever-growing cabildo societies, African ethnic clubs based on the fourteenth-century Spanish *cofradía,* or guild system. It was during this time that the religion grew and evolved, inventing and reinventing itself. A religion as ancient as it was unique coalesced on the island, and the Lucumí—the term that refers to the Afro-Cuban descendants of the original Yoruba slaves—codified their faith despite colonial efforts to Europeanize them.

By the time of the Cuban Revolution of 1959, the religion had grown exponentially, although hidden underground, and the trickling exodus of Cubans to the United States that had started as early as the 1940s had become a flood of refugees escaping the iron grip of Fidel Castro's new Communist government. The Mariel boatlift, a mass emigration of Cubans between April and October 1980, sent another new generation of priests and priestesses into the United States. Soon the religion traveled beyond the borders of both Cuba and the mainland United States, as olorishas (priests and priestesses) and aborishas (unconsecrated worshippers) found their way to Puerto Rico, Canada, Alaska, Mexico, Europe, and even farther, into Newfoundland, Finland, Germany, Russia, and other countries where there are no travel restrictions to Cuba. Thus a localized faith, orisha worship, became globalized.* Some estimates put the numbers of Lucumí adherents worldwide well into the millions. Still, it is a faith veiled in secrecy. To understand the globalized worship of the orishas, one must begin with an understanding of the ultimate deity, Olódumare, and the concept of ashé in the Lucumí faith.

---

*For more information on the history and globalization of the Lucumí faith, see my book *Sacrificial Ceremonies of Santería: A Complete Guide to the Rituals and Practices.*

ASHÉ AND OLÓDUMARE, THE ULTIMATE DEITY

According to Lucumí belief, before creation there were only two great forces in the universe: Olódumare, who is the ultimate God, and ashé, the primal life force. Ashé is creative potential, and Olódumare is the creator. As Olódumare became self-aware, ashé spread with his awareness. Its first manifestations were in the sacred containers known as the *olodu,* the sixteen primal containers of existence, followed by their composites, the *odu,* which are the 256 patterns of creation. Filled with ashé, each expanded, creating a number of limitless spiritual principles and potentials. Each odu is an individual in heaven; however, ashé spreads through them all, forcing them to create and re-create spiritual patterns. In time, these patterns resulted in the forms we know as the material universe.

If one had to choose a term to describe the Lucumí faith, *diffused monotheism* would be accurate. This world, and everything that came before it, began with Olódumare and his ashé. It is difficult to write about the ultimate deity of the religion in English-language terms; indeed, it is difficult to write about God at all, since language puts limits on that which is, in essence, limitless. Furthermore, the English language has no gender-neutral pronouns, and Olódumare is beyond gender. Formal English has rules, and therefore when writing about Olódumare I am forced to use the pronouns *he* and *him.* Realize, however, that I could just as easily use *she* or *her,* for Olódumare contains the spark of both genders. If something exists in creation, it began as a spark of awareness somewhere within Olódumare's mind. Simply, everything in nature is an extension of God's thoughts and dreams.

In the Lucumí faith, the discovery of the powers and attributes of a spiritual force begins with a disentanglement of its name, Olódumare being no exception. Names are carefully chosen for everything, and the names often comprise shorter root word clusters hiding that being's essence within their letters. Within God's name are many sentences revealing his nature. Olódumare is, therefore, Olódù, the "owner of odu" (the container for the potentials of creation). He is *má ré* (the final four letters found in the name), that which "does not go" or "does not proceed" without us. He is *mà iré,* or "truly blessed." Finally, he is *ārekanfò,* a word contracted as *āre* (the final three letters of the name): Olódumare is "that which sees." A more extensive study and breakdown of the word structure shows that the name Olódumare means "the owner of all possibilities," "the one who sees all things," and "the one who sees the possibilities in all things." It can also mean "the owner of all possibilities" and "the supreme head among heads." He is the owner of the actual world (this world) and all possible worlds (alternate worlds that exist simply because all possibility exists within him). Olódumare contains fullness, the fullness of all creation, and is perfect in his existence.*

Part of Olódumare's perfection rests with his ashé; the divine is the primal generator of this force. Indeed, ashé and Olódumare are inseparable. Still, Lucumí mystics believe that as the olodu and odu formed, taking shape as the containers for future existence, ashé continued to grow and move. Ashé became a primal intelligence existing both within and without Olódumare's nature. For eons it remained a primal intelligence, a potential, but eventually ashé congealed; no longer just a potential, it became a possibility. Primal intelligence became actual intelligence, and another divine force, Olorún, took shape within Olódumare. Between Olódumare and Olorún, all ashé flowed, and the possibility of creation became manifest.

OLORÚN AND THE CONCEPT OF ASHÉ

Unraveling the name Olorún is simpler than unraveling the name Olódumare. Here, gender is stable: Olorún is male. The name contains two words: the prefix *ol,* which means "owner," and *orún,* with two variations of meaning. Spelled *orún* it means "heaven"; spelled *ōrùn* it means "sun." Thus, Olorún is the owner of heaven, and Olorún is the owner of the sun. As I wrote in *Sacrificial Ceremonies of Santería,* "It is difficult to separate the concept of Olódumare as the ultimate godhead

---

*For a more extensive study of the names Olódumare, Olorún, and Olófin, see pages 25–29 of my book *Sacrificial Ceremonies of Santería.*

from the concept of Olorún as the ultimate creative force. Olorún owns the invisible realm of creation, heaven, and is the aspect of God guiding evolution."[1] While the odu are primal divisions of Olódumare containing his direct essence, as we will see later in this chapter, the orishas are primal divisions of Olorún containing his ashé. Born as concepts in the mind of Olódumare, they are embodied and enlivened by Olorún and continually recharged and replenished by ashé. The orishas, as extensions of both Olódumare and Olorún, are streams of consciousness by which a person comes to understand primal deity.

Olorún is best known as the dispenser of ashé on earth. His symbol is the daytime sun, and just as it provides warmth and energy to support life on this planet, so does it provide the ashé to sustain life on this planet. Basically, the concept of ashé is similar to the vitalizing force described by other ancient and indigenous religions. The Hindu know it as *prana,* a cosmic energy flowing from the sun and vitalizing the universe; it is their vital principle, often described as one of the five breaths cycling in the human body. Some who practice the discipline of Reiki know it as intelligent energy, a vibrant, healing force channeled from one's hands to bring balance and health back to an ailing body. The Chinese know is as *qi,* "the breath," "the air," or "the gas." Likewise, the Japanese call it *ki,* "the life force" or "the life essence." Native Americans know it as *medicine,* anything in nature that embodies healing or spiritual evolution. Finally, perhaps the most similar comparison to ashé would be the Hawaiian concept of *mana,* "power"; Hawaiian beliefs regarding mana closely parallel the Lucumí concept of ashé. To us, however, it is ashé, and ashé is at the core of everything the Lucumí priesthood and laity work with in this faith.

OLÓFIN

Within the name Olófin are two smaller word structures: *olo,* which means "owner," and *ofin,* a word designating "laws," "prohibitions," "commandments," or "disciplines." The concepts of sovereignty and sovereign rule are within the word *ofin.* Olófin is masculine in gender;

priests envision him as an elderly man, infinitely wise, who is the owner of natural and divine law. Some branches of the Yoruba religion still found in modern-day Nigeria differentiate between Olófin Ayé and Olófin Òrun. Olófin Ayé is the "supreme ruler on earth," while Olófin Òrun is an alternative title for Olódumare, the "supreme ruler in heaven." The Lucumí faith, which derives from its Yoruba progenitor, makes no such distinction; simply, Olófin is the part of Olódumare that can incarnate on earth, and he is the part of Olódumare transcending heaven. With such a wide range of sovereign rule, Olófin is the king of all the orishas.

OLODU AND ODU, CONTAINERS OF POSSIBILITIES

At the heart of Lucumí ontology are sixteen sacred principles known as the *olodu*. In books published previously for an English-speaking audience, I referred to these as both the parent odu and the root odu; they were the first emanations of Olódumare as he became self-aware, and they form the basis for the 256 potentials of creation known as *odu*. I referred to these 256 potentials as *omo-odu*, "the children of odu" (or the children of the olodu). In truth, each olodu is the head of a spiritual family; each gives birth to sixteen sacred patterns. Lucumí priests have knowledge of these sacred containers and their contents, and in ritual these are accessed during divination. *Babalawos*, the male-only priests of Orúnmila (an orisha often known as the witness of creation), access the olodu and the odu through the ritual of Ifá, their form of divination. Ifá is an oracle accessed by palm nuts (known as *ikin*) or by means of a sacred divining chain known as *òpèlè*. Orisha priests, on the other hand, access both the olodu and the odu through the process of diloggún, a ritual using consecrated cowrie shells to discern these patterns. Because I am an orisha priest, I cannot write with authority on the process of divination used by babalawos; I can only write about the process of divination used by olorishas. Realize, however, that there are differences in how the two oracles work.

The diloggún is the spiritual basis of orisha worship; it is the divinatory mechanism by which orisha priests communicate with the orishas. It employs sixteen cowrie shells to access both the olodu and the odu. In its natural state, a cowrie shell has on one side a smooth, rounded back, and on the other side an elongated, serrated opening resembling a mouth. Unaltered, a cowrie shell cannot be used for divination; therefore each shell must be prepared, or opened, to create the cowries used in the oracle. With a knife or file, the priest removes the rounded back of the cowrie, popping off the hump to give it a flat back. He files down the new surface so it has no ragged edges. Almost all the orishas in the Lucumí faith have eighteen of these shells in their possession, and with these they speak. The exception is the orisha Elegguá; he has twenty-one cowrie shells. Because orisha priests believe Elegguá was a witness to creation, most diviners use his diloggún for divination. Elegguá saw the world begin; Elegguá knows everything in it; and this being so, Elegguá knows what will happen. His knowledge is flawless.*

To cast or read the diloggún, the diviner selects sixteen shells at random from the set of eighteen or twenty-one consecrated cowries. The priest keeps the remaining shells to the side, with the natural mouth of each shell facing down. Diviners refer to the cowries left to the side as "witnesses," and while present for divination, as observers (they represent the *egun,* or ancestral forces, of each odu's earthly incarnation), they remain unused. The mechanically opened side of the shell has a value of zero; the natural mouth has a value of one. When a diviner casts the sixteen shells on the divination mat, he obtains a number from zero to sixteen by adding the values of the shells. The number corresponds to a particular odu in the divination system, and the orisha uses this odu to speak to the priest.

To employ this oracle effectively, one must know all sixteen names and their numerical equivalents. They are:

---

*The diloggún of other orishas are accessed by the *oriaté,* the priest with the skill and knowledge to put any orisha on the divination mat to speak.

1 mouth	Okana
2 mouths	Ejioko
3 mouths	Ogundá
4 mouths	Irosun
5 mouths	Oché
6 mouths	Obara
7 mouths	Odí
8 mouths	Unle
9 mouths	Osá
10 mouths	Ofún
11 mouths	Owani
12 mouths	Ejila Shebora
13 mouths	Metanlá
14 mouths	Merinlá
15 mouths	Marunlá
16 mouths	Merindilogún

Comparing the oral tradition of the sixteen parent odu to the written tradition as exemplified by a library, one can envision each olodu as a book in that library; just as books are divided into chapters, each of these individual books has smaller divisions. We know these "chapters" of olodu as *odu*. Each odu is a part of a spiritual family linked by the parent giving it birth, just as each chapter of a book is part of the book's whole.

In casting the diloggún, a diviner accesses one of these odu, or chapters of the book, on behalf of his or her client. Initially, the diviner does not know which section of the book to read. Therefore he must first gently awaken the orisha whose diloggún he uses by chanting an invocation, paying homage to Olódumare, the earth, the ancestors, and the orishas. After this series of prayers, the diviner makes two initial castings, recording the numbers of each. With these numbers, the orisha identifies the odu applying to the diviner's client. The first casting names the olodu, and the second establishes the actual odu, narrowing the reading down to one of 256 possible combinations. For example, if the first casting of the diloggún results in a pattern of 10 open mouths on the mat, the olodu is Ofún. Casting the cowries a second time, if the diviner counts 6 mouths, the resulting odu is Ofún Obara (10 mouths followed by 6 mouths), and the diviner can then search his memory for the meanings of that particular composite letter.*

Each of these odu forms a spiritual organism, a complete entity that foretells various blessings, known collectively as *iré,* or misfortunes, known collectively as *osogbo.* After casting a composite letter, the diviner uses various *ibó* (auxiliary divination tools such as white chalk, a black stone, a spiral cowrie shell, or a bone†) to extract from it the qualities of iré and osogbo. Depending on the question asked, the diviner uses the ibó in a number of pairings. Together, the diviner and client manipulate the cowries and ibó in tandem to determine the orientations of the odu. From these are the predictions of any one letter drawn, and from this the ebós, or sacrificial offerings, needed to placate volatile essences are determined. In this way one creates harmony, and evolution unfolds.

It is important to understand that the diloggún is both a system of divination for Lucumí adherents as well as a system of categorization for Lucumí lore. In the past thirteen years I have written two volumes dealing with the diloggún as a system of divination: *The Secrets of Afro-Cuban Divination* and *The Diloggún: The Orishas, Proverbs, Sacrifices, and Prohibitions of Cuban Santería.* In addition, I have written three other volumes dealing with diloggún as a system of folkloric categorization: *Teachings of the Santería Gods, Diloggún Tales of the Natural World,* and *Sacrificial Ceremonies of Santería.*

And it is here, as a system of folkloric categorization, that we arrive at the diloggún's main importance to Lucumí adherents, for while divination is a practical application of this knowledge, at its heart the diloggún is a library of oral literature, a series of books containing the sum total of

---

*For more information on this process, see my previous work *The Diloggún: The Orishas, Proverbs, Sacrifices, and Prohibitions of Cuban Santería.* Chapter 1 gives complete directions for manipulating the diloggún safely and completely, from its opening to its closing.
†Those who come from branches of the Lucumí faith with Arara influence have additional ibó used in divination. Among them might be a broken pottery shard, a small doll's head, a seed, two cowries tied back-to-back, et cetera.

Lucumí spiritual knowledge. Therefore, as another definition of dilogún I would like to add that it is, simply, a holy book, oral though it may be. My life's work is this: to preserve the oral traditions by bringing them into the world of printed literature, a task that, unfortunately, cannot be accomplished in a single lifetime, as the dilogún is too vast to be captured in the scope of a single man's existence.

Since the earliest Yoruba people sought to make sense of the world around them, they created sacred stories and proverbs that brought sense to what seemed to be chaos. As the centuries progressed, they added these stories to each of the many chapters found in the odu of the dilogún. Sacred lore, magic, sacrifices, proverbs, myths, histories—all this became a part of the system. From the composite signs of Okana (1 mouth) through the final letters of Merindilogún (16 mouths), they used the 256 patterns as mnemonic devices to remember the ancient stories, and they used this same system when passing the lore from priest to priest, or within the confines of their own families. This is why, of all the religions in the world, Santería's complexity surpasses all, even that of the Vedas of the Hindu faith. And it is within these 256 massive chapters that one finds the mandates, restrictions, prohibitions, sacred duties, recipes, songs, chants, invocations, life stories, and ebós that fight osogbo in the world and help each of us live a live filled with iré.

THE ORISHAS, RIVERS OF CONSCIOUSNESS

While the dilogún represents the core of Lucumí knowledge, the orishas are the focus of worship. After acknowledging God in all three forms—Olófin, Olorún, and Olódumare—Lucumí priests and aborishas focus their worship on the orishas. Most anthropologists who study Yoruba-based faiths translate the word *orisha* into "goddess" (as some are female) or "god" (as some are male). Yet this simple translation does no justice to the concept of an orisha. As with the names Olódumare, Olorún, and Olófin, the word itself has smaller divisions and deeper meanings describing the true nature of these earth-based deities. Most scholars fall back on the work of John Mason and other writers like him who break down the original Yoruba word structure, *òrìsà,* into two smaller Lucumí/Yoruba words: *orí,* which means "head" or "consciousness," and *sà,* meaning "to select with reflection." This is a legitimate breakdown of the word, over-used though it may be, and it defines each orisha as a carefully selected head; each is a spiritual force representing the height of some specific state of consciousness. Keeping this breakdown in mind, an excellent definition of the word *orisha* would be: a selected aspect of consciousness in the mind of Olódumare. In other words, Olódumare, being too vast to be known by humans, is made approachable through smaller divisions of his divine essence—the orishas.

In his book *Orin Òrìsà,* John Mason carries this etymology of the word one step further. He believes that the word *àsà* is buried in the word *òrìsà.* Through a process known as elision, whereby vowel sounds are dropped and words put together, he believes that *òrìsà* can be pulled apart into two words, *orí* and *àsà.* When brought together, the letter *a* is dropped to give more strength to the *i* sound. *Àsà* translates as "tradition," and the traditions referenced are the religious foundations and protocols of the Lucumí faith. Orally transmitted for centuries, the foundations of the religion are embedded in the minds and hearts of each generation's priesthood and laity; carefully, through practical and theoretical instruction of their godchildren, they lay new foundations in the psyche of the new priesthood. This means that the orishas are both traditions of the head and selected heads. They are more than just goddesses or gods. A more accurate definition becomes this: they are selected heads, spiritual beings chosen by Olódumare to represent the first and highest manifestation of certain special skills, faculties, or talents. In other words, they are the primal *personified* manifestations of both Olódumare's existence and Olorún's ashé. Each is a vessel of perfection.

However, this is still a somewhat shallow study of an orisha's nature.

There is another word buried in the word *òrìsà* besides the words *orí, sà,* and *àsà.* Just as elision can cause one vowel to drop in favor of a stronger sound, so can elision bring the last vowel of a word together with the first vowel of another word, blending them into a continuous sound. Pulling the word *orí* out of *òrìsà,* and then maintaining the letter *i* with the final two letters of the name, the word *ìsa* is pulled from the cluster. *Ìsa* denotes a container for carrying water. It also refers to the ebb tide, the movement of water away from land toward the sea. Two other words related to *ìsa* are *ìsàn* and *ìsàn-omi*. *Ìsàn* denotes a current, and *ìsàn-omi* is the river's current, a tide. Rivers always flow from higher ground toward the sea. The orishas, then, are orí ìsa, spiritual currents of the head; they are tied to water, and the orí itself becomes a container of water. Their action in the world is that of orí ìsàn-omi, "the head that is a container of water flowing to the sea." They are always in motion until the water finds itself at the mouth of the sea, at which point it merges to become one with the ocean.

When one pulls all these meanings hidden in the word *òrìsà* together, a macrocosmic force with no equivalent in the English language is uncovered. The orishas are heads selected by Olódumare to represent the highest trait of a special skill or faculty; each is a special container of ashé, a direct emanation of some small part of Olódumare's being. They are containers for water, and once brought down to earth they become tides that flow, always, to the sea. Just as each river in the world has its own distinct flow, so do all the orishas in the Lucumí pantheon have their own distinct flow in the spiritual world. However, just as all the rivers in the world end up in the ocean, so do all the spiritual currents of the orishas end up at Olódumare's feet.

Still, even with this detailed description a huge mystery remains: what is so important about the concept of the orishas flowing through life, to the sea? To answer this question, we turn to the odu of the diloggún. In the corpus of Oché (5 mouths), we find the following story:

It is said that when creation stood at its final threshold, Olódumare looked down on the earth from heaven and wondered, "What more can I give the world?" He looked at its vastness and beauty. His love poured forth, a sacred river of blessings that began with his heart. As the blessings gathered throughout the land, they formed the mighty, coursing rivers; sources of fresh water swelled across the globe, and Oché was born. God smiled, for only then were all things complete.[2]

If the odu Oché teaches that the first rains on earth were emanations of Olódumare's love for the world and all creation, it follows that the rivers created by that rainfall, flowing to the sea, carry God's primordial love back to the ocean; then, when the light and heat of the sun (the symbol of Olorún in the sky) cause that water to evaporate, form clouds, and travel across the earth, the rains that subsequently fall back down to earth are Olódumare's love and ashé spread over the land again. Rain nourishes us, rain refreshes us, and rain renews creation, just as love is essential nourishment for the soul. Metaphysically it is said, "As above, so below": the earth's natural forces are a reflection of the spiritual world's ashé.

When describing the nature of Olódumare, there is a metaphor used by Lucumí priests comparing God to a great primordial stone. This stone rests at the bottom of a heavenly ocean, a sea of ashé spreading throughout the universe. Stone, of course, is a symbol of that which does not die. It is the earth's most durable material, never destroyed but instead transformed through natural processes into the various forms of metamorphic, igneous, and sedimentary rocks. The odu Metanlá Ejioko (13-2) alludes to this as being the nature of God—that he/she is a great indestructible stone resting at the bottom of the heavenly sea of ashé. From that, odu priests incant a song when creating *omiero,* the herbal water used both to bath a new initiate and to give birth to the orishas themselves; this sacred elixir cannot be consecrated without the ashé, the power that these words bring forth:

Oriaté and Chorus: Oyigiyigi ota lomio! Oyigiyigi ota lomi. Oyigiyigi iya okuma. Oyigiyigi ota lomi.
God in heaven is the immovable stone resting in water! God in heaven is the immovable stone resting in water. God in heaven is the mother who does not die. God in heaven is the immovable stone resting in water.

Oriaté and Chorus: Oyigiyigi ota lomio! Oyigiyigi ota lomi. Oyigiyigi baba agbado. Oyigiyigi ota lomi.
God in heaven is the immovable stone resting in water! God in heaven is the immovable stone resting in water. God in heaven is the father of all who goes to the river. God in heaven is the immovable stone resting in water.

THE METAPHYSICAL SIGNIFICANCE
OF THE RIVER

Olorishas know well the mysteries of the river and the ceremonies that happen at its edge. While the ceremonies themselves are secret, an understanding of the metaphysics and the odu behind them reveals more about the nature of the orishas as rivers of consciousness carrying the olorishas back to Olódumare and the primal ocean of ashé. To fully illustrate the metaphor of water and the place of humans in the world, we need to examine the metaphor of a single human life as a pool or a pond of water. An aborisha, and, by extension, any living being in this world, is much like a pond; since water is a conduit of ashé in the world, and since our bodies themselves are mostly water, all of us in the world are like small ponds. An Ifá verse in the odu Oyekun Oché (known as Ejioko Oché in the diloggún) states:

> The wise ones assembled and invited some babalawo to interpret the teachings of Ifá on death.
>
> They asked, why it is that death kills people and there is no one who does not die?
>
> The babalawo said that it is good that Amuniwaye* created death.
>
> Water, which does not flow back and forth, becomes a pond of polluted water.
>
> A pond of water that causes disease.
>
> Water takes people away freely and water brings them back freely.
>
> Let them go home to receive a new body; let the corrupt go home to receive new character so they may return to the world.
>
> Then the babalawo asked: "What is unpleasant about this?"
>
> The wise ones prostrated in respect for Ifá, saying: "Iboru; iboya; ibosise" (the offering has been made; may it be accepted; may it be blessed).

---

*A praise name for Olódumare: "the one who brought us into the world."

Then they went away and they no longer considered death a matter of sorrow.

A living creature is like a pool of water; it lives for a number of years, and as time passes it becomes polluted. In time, water must dry up or be poisoned; to remain fresh, it evaporates and returns from the skies as rain. This is the cycle of life and reincarnation taught by the Lucumí faith.* When one takes one's first faltering steps into the priesthood, that cycle is changed; through the act of initiation it is interrupted forever. For those of us who have taken initiation, our lives become part of something greater. We go to the river as a normal human being, a pool of water separated from the greater source of all things. There at the river's edge we make ebó to the orisha Oshún so she can fly to Olódumare to tell him what is about to happen—that a priest is about to be made. We find that story in the odu Irosun Unle (4-8) in the diloggún. It is the story of how Oshún, in her avatar of Oshún Ibú Adessa (whose sacred bird is the peacock), became the avatar known as Oshún Ibú Ikolé (whose sacred bird is the buzzard):

The orishas became vain, proud, thinking themselves greater than even Olódumare. Olódumare, grieved by their arrogance, withdrew from the world. So far away did he go that the earth became unbalanced, and without Olódumare, there was no rain. Plants withered, animals suffered, and soon even the humans and the orishas were weakened from heat and hunger. Without Olódumare's ashé in the world, there was only misery on earth. No longer did humans sacrifice to the orishas because animals were too scarce, and without worship the orishas themselves knew suffering. All of them, even the mighty Obatalá, wanted Olódumare's forgiveness. And as all do in time, each sought out God.

Every orisha used his remaining strength to rise to heaven and beg God's forgiveness, but so far removed was Olódumare that no one had the power to make the ascent. After the most powerful orishas had tried

---

*Of course, this is a simple metaphor; there is much more to the belief than this.

but failed, the weaker among them made the attempt. Finally, Oshún Ibú Adessa came before her brothers and sisters in her sacred form, that of the peacock, and she told them, "I will make the flight to heaven. I will be the one to save the world."

There was laughter. Everyone loved Oshún for her beauty and sweetness; they loved her because the gifts she gave the world made life bearable and worth living. But the gentle peacock was known for its beauty and not its strength. No one believed she could fly higher than a treetop, and heaven was far beyond that; it lay beyond even the sun and stars. One by one, the orishas tried to talk sense into Oshún. But she stood firm. "I will make the flight and save the world. I will go to Olódumare's feet and beg forgiveness for us all, or . . . ," she grew silent, looking at her feet, ". . . or I will die trying. If we cannot save the world, we will all die anyway. I will be the first to sacrifice my own life for the world."

Before another word was said, Oshún Ibú Adessa spread her wings and sailed to the skies.

Everyone was in awe.

The door to heaven lay through the sun, and before she broke the clouds Oshún Ibú Adessa was exhausted. Still, she pushed herself harder and higher. Breaking the clouds, she felt the sun's scorching heat and her feathers singed. Soon her body was covered in flames, and those feathers that did not burn melted against her soft skin. She screamed; every nerve in her body was exposed, her skin scorched and blackened and sore. Oshún took one last look at the sun to make sure she was headed toward heaven's gate; the light blinded her, it melted her eyes, but she flapped what remained of her wings even harder, throwing herself through Olorún's domain. Burning, she screamed, her screams fueling her desire to arrive at Olódumare's feet or die trying. When finally the pain became too much, when all she knew was agony, she went slack and fell in a faint.

Unconscious, Oshún had not a clue that she lay at Olódumare's feet.

When she awoke there was pain; she remembered being on fire, burning, and she was weak. Oshún spread her blackened wings as far as they would stretch before trying to stand. She was too feeble.

"Don't try to move," said a voice that was as ethereal as it was powerful. "Rest." Oshún felt like she was falling into herself. Mercifully, she was locked in a dreamless sleep, free from the fire, free from the pain.

She awoke to find herself in a soft bed. Oshún tried to lift her arm, but there was no arm, only a blackened wing. She tried to focus, to shed her avian form for that of a human shape, but her flight had left her too drained, and she was locked in the form of a bird with burnt feathers and scorched skin. The pain, however—it was gone.

"Why did you do such a foolish thing, Oshún?" She turned her head. Sitting beside her bed was a man whose skin was so dark that he seemed a black marble statue, perfect and unmoving. "Why did you fly through the sun? You know your form, the peacock, had not the strength to withstand such a journey. You are lucky to be alive."

"The world is dying," she said, surprised the power of voice still existed in her withered form. "I came to beg you to save us."

"I tried to heal you, Oshún," said Olódumare. "I tried to restore you to your beauty, but your ashé has changed. The beauty of the peacock is gone. Now your form remains withered and blackened, but you are stronger. You are no longer as you were, no longer Oshún Ibú Adessa. You are now Oshún Ibú Ikolé, and your sacred form is now that of the buzzard." Oshún sat up as best as she could in her bird form; she shook when she saw her once beautiful peacock feathers replaced by those of a buzzard. But she felt the new strength in her body. She concentrated, bringing all her ashé to bear with one purpose: returning to her human form. Even that was different. She was older, stronger.

"I came to beg your forgiveness, Olódumare," she said, carefully rolling out of the bed and putting her head to the floor in obeisance. "We were wrong to become so proud and vain, to think we could manage the world without you. We are forever your servants. Please, don't destroy the world. Come back to us." Tears stained her black cheeks. "We need you. There can be no world without you, no world without God."

Oshún's innocence touched Olódumare's heart the way his heart was touched when she was first created, an afterthought born from the first stirrings of love. He closed his eyes and with his inner vision saw the earth. His love for his creation was still there. He opened his eyes and saw Oshún with her head on the floor to him; his love for her was even greater. Gently he touched Oshún's shoulders and bid her to rise. They embraced. Strength flowed from Olódumare; it filled Oshún; it healed her.

Still holding her, but at arm's length, Olódumare told her, "For your bravery and self-sacrifice I will spare the world, Oshún. I will become a part of it once again, and the rains will fall to save creation from extinction." It was at that moment that the rains fell again, and the water locked up in heaven was set free on the earth. The rivers began to flow once more, all rushing toward the sea. "Because of your own selflessness, the plants will grow and the scorching heat on earth will cool. And as it was before, all of you will exist as spiritual rivers on the earth, always flowing to and seeking me, and always carrying those who worship you back to me, back home to heaven and to me, Olódumare."

Oshún cried; she embraced Olódumare. And while they embraced Olódumare made one final decree. "Because you were able to reach heaven by your own strength, your own ashé, you, Oshún, in your new form of the vulture, as Oshún Ibú Ikolé, will forever be my messenger on earth. You will tell me of everything that is about to happen in the world. And whenever a new aspirant is brought to the river to become an abokú, and then an iyawó, it will be you who brings that name and the nature of that aspirant to me as he submerges himself in your waters, my waters, and begins his true journey back home to me, with his orisha as his guide."

And this is why we bring those who are about to be initiated into our faith to the river before the rites of ocha can be done. There, beside Oshún's flowing waters, the yubonna tells her what is about to happen so that she, in the shape of a vulture, can fly directly to heaven to tell Olódumare what is about to occur. It is Oshún Ibú Ikolé who tells God that yet another human has begun his journey, with an orisha as his guide, back home to the creator of all life.

Once a postulant is taken to the river and a secret ebó is made to Oshún, she announces to Olódumare the sacred ritual about to occur. With this, the spiritual nature of the river changes. No longer is it just running water; instead, it becomes a current of ashé containing all the possibilities locked up in Olódumare's mind. It is a flowing stream of limitless potentials, and the postulant is immersed in this. His small pool of water, his simple human life, is washed away and he merges with something greater; that pool that he once was, the water that has grown stagnant over years of living on the earth, is refreshed and renewed. No longer separated from the stream of consciousness represented by his orisha, he is now a part of it. To do this, however, he dies there in that river; symbolic though that death might seem, spiritually it is a true death, and the aspirant is no longer human. He becomes what is known as *abokú. Abó* is the Lucumí word for "one who is free." *Ikú,* the second word found buried in the word *abokú* (the letter *i* is dropped through elision), is death. *Abokú* is also a contraction of a longer sentence: *abó lowó ikú,* which means "one who is free by death." It is also *àbò lowó ikú,* or "one coming back from death." The postulant immersed in the river hangs in limbo; he is freed by death, and he is coming back from death.* He does not have life again until going through the rites of the *asiento,* the initiation ceremony, to become an *iyawó,* a new initiate of an orisha. Once he enters the river he dies, and he awaits rebirth the following day.†

While the iyawó is in the river, the flow of life's ashé is interrupted by secret ritual actions, and part of that divine ashé returns

---

*The concept of abokú is taught in the odu Obara Unle (6-8) in the diloggún. It is this odu that speaks of the postulant dying, willingly, when he makes *ebó de entrada* and goes to the river, and it is this same odu that speaks of him returning from death when he emerges from the river, having obtained a "secret" in its waters.

†Before going to the river, the aspirant undergoes a ritual in his godparent's home known as *ebó de entrada,* or "the ebó of entrance." It is both a divination and a cleansing done by either an oriaté or a babalawo, and with that cleansing, his old life is, literally, locked up in a brown paper bag (biodegradable!) that is thrown into the river's currents before the postulant is immersed. Once that bag is thrown into the river, his old life is gone; he is dead, and the bag travels with the current back to Olódumare. After making the secret ebó to Oshún, the postulant himself goes into the river to find his new life and its new potentials.

to the *igbodu,* the sacred room where the orishas are born and where the initiate is reborn, crowned by his titular orisha, and there all this ashé is forever locked into the *orí,* the head or consciousness of the iyawó, and in the sacred stones and shells of the newly birthed orishas. While there in the river, the iyawó finds one *otá,* a smooth black pebble through which the ashé of the orisha will be connected to his orí. Then the *yubon,* the priest or priestess who assists one's godparent in the ritual, puts the stone in the river pot, filling it with the river's water, and the stone goes back to the initiate's igbodu, where it is surrounded by the ashé of God's love and the ashé of the new spiritual current in which the abokú has been immersed. Once the abokú and the other congregants return to the godparent's home, another special set of songs are canted to acknowledge the great ashé that he carries back from the river in the calabash balanced on his head—an ashé that will soon be a vital part of the new initiate's own life force.

All these odu—Oché (5), Metanlá Ejioko (13-2), Irosun Unle (4-8), and Obara Unle (6-8)—reveal the massive powers involved when a simple human seeks initiation in an orisha, and all give us clues as to the true spiritual nature of the orishas. They are spiritual beings whose sole purpose is to take us back home, to heaven, to the primal ocean of love and to the immovable stone in the water that is Olódumare. The orisha, as a vessel of this spiritual current, is installed in the iyawó's orí, both his physical and his spiritual head; it then guides the new priest back to Olódumare, the primordial sea from which all emanates. Once installed in the iyawó's head like a crown (hence the term *crowning*), the orisha carries the new priest's orí with it as it travels through life, seeking God. When interpreted this way, one can truly comprehend that the orishas are, indeed, containers of heaven's ashé, and one understands that they are more than mere "goddesses" or "gods"; they are the roads to spiritual enlightenment and fulfillment, and they are the core of Lucumí worship.

2

The Concept of Osogbo

There is gain, and there is loss; from one the world was born, and from one the world is lost.

FROM THE OLODU OKANA (1 MOUTH)

Life is complicated, and as the olodu Unle learned late in his life, it is, quite frankly, messy. Misfortune fills our world. Unfortunately, in modern orisha worship many adherents fall back on a Eurocentric worldview that describes absolute good versus absolute evil when discussing *ibi* (as osogbo is known in modern orisha worship variants); university-trained philosophers and professors are no exception to this bias. When describing his theory of evil in the Yoruba ontology, no less of an authority than Dr. Oladele Abiodun Balogun, professor of philosophy at Olabisi Onabanjo University in Ogun State, Nigeria, writes:

> Several responses (theodicies) have been put forward by theists . . . to explain the philosophical problem of evil. . . . The Augustinian response, which hinges upon the concept of the fall of man from an original state of righteousness; the Ireanian response, hinging upon the idea of the gradual creation of a perfected humanity through life of a highly imperfect world; and the response of modern process

32

theology, hinging upon the idea of God who is not all-powerful and not in fact able to prevent the evil arising either in human beings or the process of nature."[1]

Further in his paper Dr. Balogun translates the word *ibi* as "evil" and not "misfortune," and while his discussion of ibi is in many ways valid, its Eurocentric swathing makes it difficult to separate the wheat from the chaff. He does focus on the nature of evil and human wickedness in traditional Yoruba religion; unfortunately, while his descriptions are valid, he veils them in European and Christian concepts. Still, many of his observations and arguments are useful to understanding the Lucumí concept of osogbo, misfortune, and we will revisit those that are useful later in this discussion.

When explaining the Yoruba concept of good and evil, Dr. John A. I. Bewaji, the senior lecturer in philosophy at the University of West Indies, comes closer to a pure Yoruba ontology than his peer, Dr. Balogun, yet he still misses the mark. In his paper "Olódumare: God in Yoruba Belief and the Theistic Problem of Evil," he writes:

Nothing is intrinsically evil. We call something evil because it does not favor us or because it causes us distress. We may not know or understand the reason for the event or action, but ultimately it forms part of the overall design of Olódumare. His attributes do not preclude the device and use of evil for the betterment of society. God is the creator. He created everything, both positive and negative. Why? We cannot know. His ways are incomprehensible. God is the most powerful being, hence, He does and can do anything, including good and evil."[2]

Bewaji begins with a core Yoruba concept—that nothing in our world is intrinsically evil—and then deviates to attribute the working of good and evil to the whim of Olódumare; this too is a Eurocentric notion. Still, he tries to separate himself from the ingrained Judeo-Christian mind-set when he writes, "This is unlike the Christian God, who after having endowed Satan with powers second only to his own loses control over Satan."[3] Even though he tries to separate Judeo-Christian theology from his own arguments, and even though he criticizes the writings of other Yoruba philosophers who confuse Olódumare with the Christian or Muslim God, and Eshu (i.e., Elegguá) with Satan,[4] in his work he too does not wash out the Eurocentric stains from his personal ontology. But as with Balogun's work, many of his arguments and theories concerning osogbo in our world (specifically the workings of Eshu) are relevant to our discussion, and these will be addressed later in this book.

Despite prevailing theories coming out of universities abroad, which tend to frame Yoruba beliefs in dualistic terms, the reality is that ancient Lucumí cosmology does not teach absolute good or absolute evil. There is rather a holistic view of iré (blessings) and osogbo (misfortunes), and between these two extremes one can have balance, which the Western world calls *good,* or one can have imbalance, which the Western world calls *evil.* Promoting iré and goodness in the world are the orishas, the *egun* (ancestors), and the *araorún* (the ancestors of all faiths) who inhabit *orún reré,* the "good" heaven. And promoting osogbo in the world are the *ajé* (witches, birds of the night) and the negative forces known as the osogbos (also known by some, collectively, as *ajogún*) who inhabit *orún burukú,* the "bad" heaven.*

To really understand this concept, however, one must abandon the Western tendency to see things in black and white terms and instead see good and evil relatively, as symptoms or degrees of balance or imbalance. Perhaps the dualism that characterizes Eurocentric thinking evolved out of a cursory examination of creation's divisions between male and female, night and day, hot and cold, et cetera, but the world is not so easily divided. Besides, Eurocentric concepts of balance are easily refuted simply by observing the natural world: a tree might create 1,000 seeds, with each seed scattered to the four corners of the earth, but only one or two will

---

*The concept of ajé is not discussed in this book; it is a core teaching of Ifá, and its discussion lies in the hands of Orúnmila's priests, the babalawos. Diloggún does not access the spiritual concept of ajé; therefore, as an olorisha and not a babalawo, I am not qualified to comment on this subject.

settle in soil loose enough and fertile enough to grow without intervention. This is not evil; this is nature, and it happens as a result of the interaction of iré and osogbo. The earth revolves around the sun, with nights growing longer and days growing shorter (and vice versa), with both sunrise and sunset upsetting the balance between night and day. This is not evil; this is nature, and, again, it happens as a result of the interaction of iré and osogbo. Natural law is Olódumare's law, and natural law supersedes everything, especially human desires, in Lucumí spirituality.

An indigenous, nature-based spiritual system such as that of the Lucumí conceives of good and evil *not* as spiritual absolutes, but rather as symptoms of balance and imbalance. And while nature is self-correcting, humans are not. Eventually, the lengthening and shortening of the days and nights results in an equinox; in this, nature corrects itself. The one or two seeds that find soil in which to root grow into trees creating 1,000 more seeds; again, nature corrects itself. Between the temperatures of too hot and too cold are various gradients of comfort; nature, once again, corrects itself. This is not so with human nature. Self-correction is a product of our intelligence and free will; instead of being buffeted or nurtured by cosmologic forces, we move within them and manipulate the world around us according to our skills, abilities, and desires. The more we manipulate our lives and our environment, the further out of alignment with the natural world around us we become. Eventually, a person or a society can fall so far out of alignment or veer so far off the spiritual course that only a radical intervention brings balance. Until achieving that balance, one can fall victim to the forces that the Western world labels "evil"; indeed, one can become, by society's standard, an evil creature.

But such a concept of evil is not a part of the Lucumí worldview. Aborishas and olorishas seek wholesomeness, balance. Nature inevitably achieves this balance, one way or another, but humans must work to find balance. We do this in a world suffused with iré, blessings, and osogbo, misfortune.

When a human being lives in balance with both nature and individual destiny she lives with iré—what in Western terms is called "good." When she is out of balance with nature or her destiny, she lives with osogbo—what Western thinking calls "evil." Still, Lucumí initiates do not spend much time concerning themselves with evil; instead, they try to go to the root of the cause, which is osogbo itself. While it is true that the world must strike a careful balance to continue supporting life, the initial balance and imbalance begins in the spiritual world. In Lucumí (as in all esoteric systems) there is no separation between the spiritual and the physical realms. Spirit suffuses the material world; its power, known as *ashé,* is in every part of this realm. In this conception, evil is not a quality nurtured by a simple spirit or being; evil is a symptom of the imbalance between the spiritual and the physical—it is an adjective describing the end result, not the process. Dilemmas are an extension of our unbalanced spiritual and physical natures. Thus an olorisha faces a difficult task: bringing the spiritual and the material worlds into balance. Balance between the mundane and the sacred restores harmony, and it takes hard work to promote this. At the core of our work is ashé—we manipulate ashé, its ebb and flow, to harmonize both worlds and our world. The greatest tool at the olorisha's disposal for this is divination, with its ritual access of odu and ebó. It is through divination that our ashé manifests and moves most strongly.

THE SIXTEEN OSOGBOS

Remember that the spirit known as Iré is a solitary creature; he is a blessing, and that is the extent of his nature. Osogbo, however, is legion, and in the Lucumí cosmology we acknowledge sixteen creatures or entities known as the osogbos. In brief—we will revisit this list of sixteen osogbos in greater detail later in this chapter—they are:

Ikú	the personification of death
Ano	the personification of fleeting, curable illness
Aro	the personification of durative, terminal illness
Eyo	the personification of tragedy
Arayé	chaos and the personification of wickedness
Iñá	the personification of war

Tiya-Tiya	the personification of gossip
Ona	the personification of afflictions
Ofo	the personification of loss
Ogo	the personification of maleficent sorcery
Akoba	the personification of all things not good
Fitibo	the personification of sudden death and cardiac arrest
Égba	the personification of paralysis
Oran	the personification of moral or legal crimes
Epe	the personification of curses
Ewon	the personification of imprisonment, especially false imprisonment and kidnapping
Eshe	the personification of general afflictions*

Yoruba scholar and leadying contemporary authority on Yoruba spirituality Kola Abimbola writes, "Unlike Judeo-Christian thought, no single entity can be held responsible for the occurrence of evil . . . evil does not emanate from one source . . . evil emanates from the supernatural forces called 'Ajogún,' that is, the powers on the left."†5 Abimbola further asserts that "these forces (Ajogún) are all separate and distinct entities and as such they are individually responsible for a specific type of evil. The Ajogún have eight warlords: Ikú (Death), Arún (Disease), Ofo (Loss), Egba (Paralysis), Oran (Trouble), Epe (Curse), Ewon (Imprisonment), Ese (Afflictions)."6

Lucumí cosmology knows and names more than eight of these forces; we have a total of sixteen that come to us from the ritual beliefs of ancient Oyó, the major source of modern Lucumí rituals and cosmological beliefs. In some ways our views on osogbo are more complex

---

*Eshe takes a bit of his ashé from the previous sixteen osogbos, and although his inclusion in the list makes for seventeen osogbos, his ambiguous nature makes him but a shadow among their ranks. A bit of Eshe exists in each osogbo, and a bit of each osogbo exists in Eshe. We count him as an osogbo, but he is so minor that he is not given a ranking of importance among the others in the list.

†This is a reference to the left of heaven as we face it, which lies to the right of Olódumare as he faces us and is known as orún burukú in Lucumí cosmology.

and detailed than those of our modern Yoruba counterparts and their beliefs on ibi (the modern Yoruba word for the osogbo). And many of our sixteen Osogbos have spiritual children who do the work of their parents, and although they are osogbos too, we olorishas deal with the parents and not their children.

Note that these entities are real; they are neither abstractions nor spiritual concepts. Just as the olorisha believes Obatalá, Yemayá, Oshún, and Shangó are actual spiritual entities, so does the olorisha believe that Ikú, Ano, Aro, and Arayé are spiritual creatures. Just as the orishas and the odu once had mortal lives, so the osogbos once lived on the earth in mortal form as well. As spiritual beings, they move freely between the spiritual realms of heaven and earth, and, yes, olorishas do believe that this world, the material world, is a spiritual realm. Lucumí cosmology believes in *ayé,* the world of materiality, and *orún,* the realm of pure spirit. Olorishas strive to bring balance between ayé and orún, between iré and osogbo, and between ourselves and the orishas. Balance creates the state known as goodness, while imbalance creates the state known as evil. This is the wholesomeness underlying Lucumí spirituality.

To really understand the Lucumí concept of misfortune, one must understand the spiritual entities that promote misfortune in our world, the spirits known collectively as the osogbos. One must know their names, for knowing their names is the first step to having power over them; then one must know their spiritual nature, for by understanding their ashé one understands how to overcome them. Know that there was a time when the entity known as Osogbo was a lonely creature; however, because she* made ebó, she did not remain lonely for long. Osogbo is the matriarch of a powerful family, one that plagues both mortal and immortal creatures in their quest for evolution and meaning. We learn of misfortune's growth in the world through the odu Ofún Unle (10-8) in the diloggún:

---

*The gender of Osogbo is problematic, as are the genders of many osogbos. Gender is fluid according to the role each misfortune plays in nature. It is for this reason that understanding and subduing osogbo can be difficult.

After Osogbo attained supremacy over Iré, she birthed many children: Ikú, Ano, Aro, and Eyo. Soon she conceived and nurtured Ona, Ofo, Akoba, and Fitibo. Chaos came to the world, and from that chaos sprang the creature known as Arayé. She found wickedness in the hearts of humans and fed off not only that, but also the malicious deeds the osogbos created in the world. Content with her powers, which were extreme, Arayé left her brothers and sisters and wandered throughout creation, but everywhere she went, the children of Osogbo followed and fed off her waste. Arayé was powerful, the primal cause of dissent and disorder on the earth, and she led the osogbos in the world.

Iré was content with his place in nature, and often he slept while the osogbos did their work. He remembered Olófin's decree that humans would always pray for him first, but rarely would he answer. "If I cannot be the first and the greatest," he thought, "then I will make the world work for me. Through trials, through tribulations, through suffering, they will beg me, again and again, to come." Humans prayed; priests divined; orisha worshippers made ebó. Wherever the osogbos went, Iré soon followed, but only if they were obedient to Olófin's demands. Iré resigned himself to the way things were; he was satisfied.

By their nature, the osogbos were never satisfied.

Soon war rose among them; the osogbo Iñá was born from their conflict. The elder osogbos in the world—Ikú, Ano, Aro, and Eyo—acquired superiority complexes, each believing himself greater than all the others, while the minor osogbos born in the world—Ona, Ofo, Akoba, and Fitibo—acquired inferiority complexes and wanted to rise to greatness. The spirit of war moved among them; they fought among themselves, and the war was bloody.

Iré woke up, so loud was their battle.

"Enough!" he said to his nephews. "Your war is ripping apart the very world in which we live. You should go to Olófin as I and your mother once did. He is the only one in heaven with the wisdom to mediate your war. Only he can give each of you your proper position in life." Never before had Iré addressed them, and although the osogbos wished he would die and cease to exist, they knew he was wise.

They went to heaven; they stood before Olófin and asked for his advice.

To the elder osogbos Olófin said, "You are all equal. The misfortunes you cause humans and orishas alike are unparalleled in the world. I cannot change your birth order. I cannot make one of you more powerful than the next. But I can insist that you do ebó and learn to work together, to help one another in all situations." And this is why sickness, death, and tragedy seem inseparable in the world. Tragedy brings sickness. Tragedy brings death. Sickness causes tragedy. Sickness causes death. Death leaves behind tragedy in its wake, and when she walks the earth there is sickness as well. The four elder odu are equal and dependent on one another.

Olófin addressed the younger osogbos, Ona, Ofo, Akoba, and Fitibo. "I cannot change your birth order, and for the sake of the world I cannot make you more powerful than your elders. For you there is no ebó beyond my mandate: support the work of Ikú, Ano, Aro, and Eyo in the world. This is my word; this is my law." Afflictions, loss, bad things, and sudden death—they follow Ikú, Ano, Aro, and Eyo in the world. Find one of the elders, and the minors are not far behind.

So what happened to Iré?

While the osogbos were with Olófin making ebó and listening to his mandates, Iré was sleeping on the earth. Some say his sleep was so deep that for centuries nothing could wake him, while others say Iré's sleep was so deep it led him to his death. And this is why, when the odu Ofún Unle falls on the mat, diviners will often quote the proverb, "Iré was the only osogbo who did not make ebó, and for this reason he died." For as we can see, blessings do not last forever, and when they are gone, misfortunes are all that remain. Misfortune's numbers are legion, and Iré . . . he is a lonely creature indeed.

The names and individual natures of the sixteen primary creatures (and one secondary creature) known as the osogbos are:

IKÚ: A literal translation of *ikú* is "death"; however, Ikú is the personification of death, not a theoretical abstract. Note that this osogbo's gender is problematic; in the odu of her birth, Ikú is envisioned as female, but there are several patakís referring to Ikú as male. Gender fluidity is an issue with many of the osogbos, Ano, Aro, and Arayé being other examples. In Yoruba belief, death in itself is not a misfortune; however, untimely death is undesirable. In chapter 5 Ikú and the concept of death is revisited through her patakís. What is important to know here is that through a series of spiritual occurrences, Ikú became disempowered to take human beings before their time as long as they had lived in accordance with their destiny, living wisely. Not everyone comes into the world with the promise of a long, full life. There are some who agreed before Olódumare and Ajala (an avatar of Obatalá) to die young, just as there are some who agreed to hard, meaningless lives. Destiny is a personal thing; never is it easy to divine or figure out. While it is possible to extend one's destiny and grow beyond what one was promised in heaven, this is not the only goal of divination. The ability to change one's destiny is an exception, not a rule. What is promised is that each of us, if we listen to the orishas' advice and make ebó, will live the full amount of time that we were allotted by Olódumare and Ajala before our descent to earth. And if a hard life is our lot, to some degree that too can be lessened; this, however, is never guaranteed.*

ANO: Ano is the osogbo controlling fleeting illness; however, in those with weakened bodies, even a fleeting illness can be a doorway to death. There are those who believe she is Ikú's wife (and in this example, Ikú's gender is male), and there are those who insist Ano is Ikú's child, born in the odu Ogundá Meji (3-3) of the diloggún. Others believe that Ano is the mother of Ikú, and that pataki is told in Ejioko with the birth of Ikú on the earth.

No matter who she is or is not a child, daughter, or wife of, she *is* a mother herself; her children are contagion, infection, lunacy, fever, and

---

*For those familiar with the process of divination, when ikú comes *elese otonowá* (from heaven) or *elese omotorunwá* (a variant that means "I brought this with me" from heaven), it is referring to ikú as a natural misfortune, the eventual end to one's life. In these divinations, however, at the moment the diloggún rolls out on the mat, the client is putting in motion the forces that will create and determine his eventual demise. Living unwisely presents ikú as a true misfortune, while living wisely and gently on the earth presents ikú as a natural and blessed occurrence.

deformity. Those children grew up to give Ano a total of 603 grandchildren and 1,206 great-grandchildren. Whenever Ano afflicts humans, one of her many descendants (symptoms of disease and disease itself) latches on to the human body.

ARO: Sister to Ano, she is durative or terminal illness. As a force in nature she is born in the odu Ejioko Meji (2-2), not long after Ikú was born in the world. She became one of the ways for Ikú to feed; humans contracted an incurable illness, and in their suffering they prayed for Ikú to come. Another pataki places this osogbo with the odu Osá (9); in that odu it is said Babaluaiye brought the constant torment of Aro to the world so that Oyá would be forced to bring Ikú down from heaven. No matter its odu of origin, it is a dangerous misfortune. While Ano can be a fleeting affliction, such as a cold or flu (with the power to kill those who are weak), Aro is a chronic illness whose end result is always death. HIV, cancer, diabetes, and other degenerative illnesses are examples of Aro. Also, Aro can be genetic. It predicts chronic illnesses suffered through the duration of one's life.

Keep in mind that while Ano and Aro are sisters, Aro is the one most feared. Ano is passing and fleeting, although she is the older of the two and is said to be the mother of death (Ikú) in some patakís. Aro is constant torment and forces us into Ikú's hands. From Ano there is freedom and redemption; from Aro there is no such thing. Some say that Aro and Ikú are husband and wife, for terminal, durative illness always ends in death. There are many olorishas who combine the concepts of fleeting illness and durative illness under one name, Arún, and the odu Ofún Meji (10-10) in the diloggún is specific in its pronouncement that the sisters Aro and Ano made a pact to walk and work together. Some olorishas use this as their rationale for combining Ano and Aro into one name, Arún, relying on the odu itself to identify the type of illness, whether fleeting or durative. However, in my work as a Lucumí diviner I make sure to differentiate between the two spirits for my clients. Each has its own existence and consciousness in our world, and the illnesses they control are often fluid. What was incurable sixty years ago (syphilis, for example) is curable today with antibiotics; however, what is curable today can again become incurable in the future as the disease changes and mutates to become drug-resistant. This is the nature of the sisters Aro and Ano—their realms are fluid and interchangeable as the world evolves. This makes their presence in the world more difficult to manage, understand, and overcome.*

EYO: At its most basic meaning, Eyo is the osogbo of tragedy. Even though it is autonomous, as are all the osogbos, almost always tragedy is followed by sickness (Aro or Ano), Ikú (death), Arayé (wickedness and chaos), or Eshe (general afflictions). Eyo has no defined gender, and in the odu of the diloggún there are few patakís told about this osogbo. He was born in the odu Ogundá Merindilogún (3-16) as the twin of Tetura (the mortal incarnation of that odu); when the townspeople tried to lynch him for the great tragedies he had caused in their land, Ikú recognized him as one of his own, lifted him from the flesh, and gave him the ashé of an immortal. He grew in strength in the odu Odí (7) and Odí Meji (7-7) in the diloggún.

ARAYÉ: Arayé is the senior of all the osogbos; she is the most powerful, and she is the most feared. She is first mentioned in the odu Ofún Unle (10-8); she rose from the chaos created by the birth of Osogbo's first eight children in the world (Ikú, Ano, Aro, Eyo, Ona, Ofo, Akoba, and Fitibo). Her next appearance is in the odu Unle Odí (8-7); this is the sign in which her existence was revealed to the world. In the odu Owani Meji (11-11) she gained ultimate power, and even now, her power grows. Ofún Unle and Unle Odí refer to her as chaos, and Owani Meji

---

*Of all the concepts mentioned in relation to Aro, that of *constant torment* is essential. When Aro comes, she does not like to let go, and in most cases, unless the orishas choose to work a miracle, once Aro has humans in her grasp it is difficult to unwind her fingers from their bodies. Cancers, especially those that go in and out of remission, are an example of this. During divination, the osogbo of Aro demands immediate, extreme, thoughtful action from both the diviner and the client. Any laxity in dealing with Aro commits the client to a life of suffering. Of course there are times when the client has come to see the diviner too late, and in those cases, when Aro is already on the person, all we can do is support the healing process and hope for the best.

adds extreme wickedness to her nature. She became a multifaceted, multilayered creature, and each generation on earth feeds her and strengthens her with the wickedness lying dormant in their hearts. Those who argue against Lucumí cosmology and point out historic figures that were, in essence, truly evil (e.g., Hitler, Jack the Ripper, Osama bin Laden) are referring to people we believe were consumed by this osogbo, Arayé. Writing about human wickedness, Dr. Balogun says, "A great attention is paid to the kind of pain and affliction which are inflicted on men by men. The Yoruba strongly believe that it is possible for men to inflict pains and afflict fellow human beings. This kind of evil is what the Yoruba would refer to as human wickedness . . . nefarious acts perpetrated by man in order to subject his fellow man to torture and all forms of pain."[7] He names those who perpetrate Arayé qualities of chaos and wickedness in the world as *ika eniyan,* "wicked people"; he also refers to them as *onise ibi,* "workers of ibi" (workers of osogbo in the Lucumí dialect). Onise ibi and ika eniyan are human embodiments of Arayé; they are not, however, proof that absolute evil exists in our world.

He continues his discussion of human wickedness:

> Among the Yoruba, human wickedness towards another fellow human being may be perpetrated for several reasons. It might be done to revenge an evil that was already done by another human being. Human wickedness may be pursued to punish an offender or to even test the efficacy of a supernatural power on those who doubt the potency of such power. Some people undertake the act of human wickedness in order to force others to fear them or to show that they are more powerful than others.[8]

Arayé feeds on all these things and returns them many times over in our lives. She devours the human spirit. She is often accompanied by Aro's child, Lunacy. Lunacy follows and craves unadulterated power, and she finds that at the heels of Arayé. Keep in mind that Arayé can be the precursor to other osogbos, paving the way for them to be active in the world. Any osogbo can find as its source in the world Arayé.

Those well versed in the mechanical process of the diloggún can recall many examples of an osogbo such as Ikú (death) coming *elese Arayé,* "at the feet of Arayé." This too can denote wickedness worked by the hands of *onise ibi,* "workers of osogbo," or *ika eniyan,* "wicked people." The human element is always present when Arayé is active as either an osogbo or as a source of osogbo.

IÑÁ: Iñá is the spirit of war said to be born in two odu: Ofún Unle (10-8) and Marunla Osá (15-9) of the diloggún. In the odu Ofún Unle, Iñá was born when the osogbos began to fight among themselves, and in that manifestation he afflicted only his brothers and sisters, the osogbos. In Marunla Osá, Iñá was born into the world, causing entire nations to rise up against one another. Again, the existence of war is not proof of absolute evil, according to Lucumí ontology. Rather, war is considered an osogbo; it is the creature known as Iñá that drives humanity to war. Acts of terrorism such as the 9/11 attacks and subsequent military actions (declared or undeclared war) are influenced by the activity of this osogbo in the world. Note that Arayé's influence can be assumed in Iñá's working, even if the source of war is not Arayé herself. What Balogun says about Arayé is also applicable to Iñá: *onise ibi,* "workers of osogbo," or *ika eniyan,* "wicked people," are at the core of Iñá. Simply put, war arises in response to wickedness in the world; Arayé and her human minions are the source of this wickedness.

TIYA-TIYA: Tiya-Tiya is the osogbo creating and controlling gossip, and although many attribute gossip to women, this osogbo's gender is male. He was born when the odu Metanlá Okana (13-1) opened in creation. He creates not only idle gossip, but also libel and slander. Often, Tiya-Tiya walks in the world before the osogbos of Eshe (general afflictions), Arayé (wickedness and chaos), and Iñá (war). He is their precursor and creates environments in which other osogbos may thrive. Tiya-Tiya, like Arayé, can be the source of osogbo. As an example, one can have iñá elese (war at the feet of) Tiya-Tiya (gossip, libel, and slander). False words or false beliefs create a hostile environment in which the human agents of Arayé, onise ibi (workers of osogbo) and ika eniyan (wicked people), incubate Iñá on a grand scale. There are those who will lie for the sole purpose of creating war between friends, families, tribes, religions, and nations. The world is a complicated place, and osogbo feeds and nurtures itself off human misery and suffering.*

ONA: Ona is the spirit of afflictions, and his ashé is general and vague. Broken roads and lost paths in life (his most common manifestation), chastisements, beatings, general losses—all these are brought about by the action of Ona in one's life. Ona was born in the odu Owani Ejioko (11-2) in the diloggún. That letter's symbolism speaks of both the roads we walk in life and the crossroads we must enter and pass; it also speaks of the broken roads we face and false turns we make when wandering without direction. These are manifestations of Ona in our world.

OFO: This osogbo is the spirit of loss. When Ofo appears, it creates losses in one's financial, personal, marital, and familial life. There is no part of the world that Ofo cannot touch, and often when it comes it afflicts large geographic regions at one time. Economic recessions and depressions are created by Ofo's work in the world. It was born when the olodu Okana (represented by 1 mouth in the diloggún) opened in creation. There is an essential proverb found in the olodu Okana speaking about Ofo's power in the world: "There is gain and there is loss; from one the world was born, and from one the world is lost." The concept of loss and the osogbo Ofo gained power in the odu Okana Meji (1-1) of the diloggún; it was there that loss was first spread over the earth.

OGO: Ogo is witchcraft, the product of maleficent sorcery. Sorcery

---

*At this point readers should understand that the workings of osogbo in our world are no simple matter. Misfortune feeds misfortune, and once osogbo, any osogbo, has infiltrated one's life, it becomes a complex cycle. Ebó, morals, ethics, and personal responsibility must all be taken into account when battling osogbo. Divination, carefully conducted, is the key to identifying these complicated relationships and putting the world back into balance. It takes the development of good character and careful judgment to bring a person, a tribe, a culture, or a nation back into alignment. Still, while the effort to overcome osogbo might be great, and while the personal or collective sacrifices might be huge, the rewards that come are immeasurable. Once osogbo is defeated, iré, blessings, are all that remain. The ancient Lucumí and Yoruba were masters of this process, and their modern descendants on both sides of the Atlantic retain the wisdom and ashé to lead us from darkness into light.

shares many odu when speaking of its birth and evolution. The odu Ogundá (3) gives birth to maleficent witchcraft due to Ogundá's association with Arayé; they were husband and wife, and she taught him much of her wicked witchcraft. Also, there was a time in his life when Ogundá had a wandering heart, and it led him into the land of the Congo. There he learned the secrets of *nganga* (shamanism and medicine) and *nfumbe* (spirits of the dead), and he brought both back to the land of the Lucumí. Congolese practices are neutral, used to harm or heal according to the character of the *palero* (the adherent of Palo Mayombe, an Afro-Cuban spiritual system originating among the Congolese). The olodu Oché (5) gives birth to sorcery in the form of powders blown to a person or spirits sent to a person; it is said that when she became bored living among the Yoruba, Oché wandered into the Congo kingdoms to learn about powders, nfumbe, and nganga, concepts originating in Palo Mayombe. Owani (11) was a mistress of magic; because of her deep associations with Eshu she was able to manipulate the osogbos into doing her bidding. Thankfully, most of her manipulations were beneficent; she used her knowledge to hold them at bay in her life. Ogo, as an osogbo, exists in the world because those with ashé learn it is neither good nor bad; it simply is, like electricity, and if properly accessed can be used to harm or heal. In our modern Western world, blaming one's ills on witchcraft may seem superstitious; however, Ogo is a very real spiritual force.

AKOBA: This is a general osogbo denoting things that are not good in our lives. While it is an osogbo in itself, Akoba works in conjunction with other osogbos to promote an environment of weakness and destruction. It can lead to sickness (Ano or Aro) and death (Ikú) if it is not fought. Iñá (war) can arise among people, tribes, and nations in times of economic loss or failure, and Tiya-Tiya (gossip) often runs rampant when things in life are not good. Akoba is an osogbo drawing much strength from its brothers and sisters. Rarely does it act alone in the world, and often it is caused by the actions of the other spiritual principles. In my own study and research I have not found a direct source in the diloggún that gives birth to this osogbo, but that does not mean it does not have an odu of origin; simply, in all my years of study I have not been able to pinpoint its origin in our oral literature.

FITIBO: This is the osogbo of sudden death, in contrast with Ikú, which can be an eventual, natural death (since it is the nature of all things to die). Fitibo was born in the odu Irosun Ogundá (4-3) in the diloggún. In that odu, Fitibo's first manifestation was a sudden cardiac death. With this osogbo, death is close, almost on the client, as opposed to Ikú, which predicts eventual death. In our own house we have seen the differentiation of these two misfortunes thus: When Fitibo opens on the mat, the client is in danger from violent acts or accidental death from the moment he walks out the diviner's door. When Ikú opens, death may be accidental; the accident, however, is far into the future. Ikú also points out death from slow, wasting diseases, while Fitibo marks more sudden illnesses such as a heart attack. Fitibo is also known as the "widow maker," and in my experience as a diviner it speaks of the asymptomatic blockage of the left coronary artery, which is also known in medical literature as the widow-maker because it comes with no physical warnings or symptoms. Literally, one drops dead of cardiac arrest, although stress, anger, and severe fright are precursors to this.*

ÉGBA: Égba means "paralysis," and it signifies the loss of all that is good in the client's life. Although this orientation will never be specific

---

*In my one experience with a client who drew Fitibo, I marked ebó for him and told him, "You need to go immediately to your doctor and get a physical. You need a complete workup, including cardiac." The client, who was in his early forties, mocked me at the mat, claiming to be in perfect health. And honestly, his appearance was one of perfect health; however, I've learned that Elegguá's words never "fall on the floor" (they are never without meaning). Three days later, he died. His wife called me, heartbroken, because it was a complete blockage of the left coronary artery. Please: if Fitibo comes as osogbo, the danger to your client is so severe that as a diviner you must insist that your client go to his doctor immediately, as his life is in that much danger. Also, keep in mind that an accident or sudden fright can cause a person's heart to stop, and often it will not start again. If the client chooses not to listen, well, in the end everyone has free will. As diviners and olorishas, we deliver the orishas' words and hope our clients listen. What they do or don't do with what they're told is up to them.

as to what is to be paralyzed, depending on the odu opened, paralysis of the body, or part of the body, is always a possibility. Note that in the elderly it is not unusual to suffer Égba through a stroke or a broken bone. Égba almost always speaks of bodily paralysis through the break-age of the spinal cord. In my practice as a diviner, I have noted that it warns also of wasting diseases that lead to contractures and the loss of one or more limbs' usage. It also refers to mechanical loss due to illness; chronic pain in a limb might force a person to use this limb less and less until its range of motion is severely restricted. This, too, is a form of Égba. In the diloggún, Égba is born and acquires its ashé from two odu: Unle Meji (8-8) and Merindilogún Meji (16-16). Unle Meji, in extreme manifestations, speaks of complete decapitation, while Merindilogún Meji, in extreme manifestations, speaks of internal decapitation (e.g., severing the spine from the brain stem while leaving the head attached to the body). Less harsh manifestations of these two odu speak of general spinal damage.

ORAN: Oran is the osogbo personifying both moral and legal crimes. While he does not refer to moral and legal crimes specifically by the name Oran, Dr. Balogun writes about them:

> The Yoruba . . . take cognizance of the existence of moral evil. Moral evil is taken to mean . . . disorderliness and chaos that occur when one contravenes the norms of society. The Yoruba believe in the smooth running of the society and any contravention of the moral norms on the part of the individual may result in disorderliness, which is evil. Thus among the Yoruba, it is not only the contraven-tion of moral norms that brings evil, but the repercussion of such contravention will also result in moral evil. In other words, the Yoruba believe that when one deliberately contravenes the moral norms of society, the divinities, ancestors, and other theoretical enti-ties that are ensuring the smooth running and governance of both "aye" (earth) and "orún" (the world beyond) give out punishment and torture to such individual, which also results in moral evil.[9]

Forgiving Balogun for his focus on evil, a Eurocentric, Judeo-Christian concept as previously discussed, note that he does separate the human desire to commit moral crimes from the influence of Oran himself. He also notes that when humans skirt moral and ethical norms, the orishas allow punishment. In Lucumí cosmology, this punishment comes through the action of Oran. Often Oran leads to Ewon (the osogbo of imprisonment).

Many who argue against the Lucumí concept of iré and osogbo and instead refer to absolute good versus absolute evil usually refer to "evildoers." They cite the heinous crimes of humanity, using these as examples that absolute evil exists in our world. The osogbo Oran is the personification of what many might consider to be absolute evil: here one finds both moral and ethical crimes of a heinous nature such as rape, arson, child abuse, and murder. Evil, as a crime against humanity, is created and espoused by the osogbo Oran; however, Oran in no way denotes a Judeo-Christian or Eurocentric dichotomy of absolutes. These are concepts contained in the spirituality of Oran itself.

EPE: Epe means "curse," and Epe is the name of the osogbo under whose directions such things are done. We differentiate between Epe and Ogo (sorcery, witchcraft) for many reasons, the most obvious being that a curse is a direct, malefic attack, whereas Ogo can be sent with good intentions by another yet still have destructive effects on a person. Also, Epe can denote "generational curses." These are curses that follow an entire family's bloodline. When writing about misfortunes wrought through supernatural means, Dr. Balogun states:

> The Yoruba believe that through the use of supernatural means it is possible for a man to inflict and afflict fellow man from afar with evil even without physical contraction. This type of spiritual wickedness is more grievous than the physical type of wickedness in that it might not be easy to trace the cause and oftentimes the sympathizer may even be the cause. . . . Someone can summon a supernatural power to inflict another person with leprosy, blindness, and even kill

the fellow through the use of "apeta" (spiritual arrows).* . . . Events in nature *can have their causes traced outside of nature* [italics mine].[10]

It is possible for the osogbo Epe to have, as its root cause, the osogbo Ogo (sorcery or a sorcerer). This is seen in diloggún divinations where Epe is marked *elese ogo,* "at the feet of a sorcerer (or sorcery)." I cannot emphasize enough that once osogbo infiltrates the human heart, there are times it can generate another osogbo under its influence, and diviners are warned to think seriously about these implications. Often they reach far beyond the person sitting on the diviner's mat. Remember, in the Lucumí worldview misfortunes are interconnected, and succumbing to one creates a domino effect whereby others become prevalent in one's life.

The concept of a curse was born in the olodu Ofún (10), and we say that Epe itself was born with the first curse cast in the odu Ofún Meji (10-10). The patakí is simple: A powerful diviner, a babalawo, was jealous of the orisha priests' divination skills.† The babalawo's ashé was great, and he cursed the diloggún, hoping to bring all the cowrie-shell diviners' clients to his own door. His curse rendered diloggún useless in the hands of the orisha priests, and the cowries of each newly washed orisha suffered Epe. Obatalá broke the curse by washing all the orishas' cowrie shells in rum. For a while, the babalawo was powerful. The ashé of the rum was enough to destroy the curse; however, it left a great

---

*Apeta, spiritual arrows, are a concept found in the olodu Ejioko (represented by 2 mouths on the mat in the diloggún) and in its resulting composites. There are many proverbs in the corpus of Ejioko in which arrows are the central symbol: there are arrows between brothers; a palace guard is not struck in the back by arrows, he is always wounded in the front; there will be arrows between friends. Ejioko also speaks of Olódumare's punishment of those who abuse apeta. Those who cover their heads with mortars (heavy stone bowls) and shoot arrows into the sky, God's eyes encompass them all. Nothing escapes the ever-watchful eye of Olódumare.

†By sharing this patakí I do not intend to dishonor Orúnmila's priests, the babalawos. Osogbo is a powerful thing, and once it gets a firm hold on any of us it moves us to do horrible things. Babalawos are human; olorishas are human; and as humans all are capable of both excellence and malevolence. Throughout the corpus of Ifá and diloggún are stories about babalawos and olorishas who abused their ashé, and we are to learn from these stories and not repeat the mistakes of our ancestors.

spiritual heat on the shells, and the diviners were unable to promote the freshness and coolness needed for divination. Olokun provided the final solution: being the owner of all the water on earth, he used fresh water to rinse the essence of rum off each set of diloggún. This revitalized the diloggún, and the olorishas reclaimed the power of divination.*

In Ofún Meji was the world's first curse, the first manifestation of Epe, and it is for this reason we say, "The curse was born" when Ofún Meji opens on the diviner's mat.[†]

EWON: Ewon is the spirit of imprisonment. It's true that Obatalá created the justice system along with its jails, and it's true that Obatalá gave Ochosi, the orisha of divine justice, the crossbow, while Olófin gave him the arrows (i.e., apeta, spiritual arrows). However, the imprisonment spoken of here is not that of divine punishment and retribution. Ewon is human justice, and even though we may think of our laws as being divorced from emotion and based on reason, such is not the case in our world. There is no divine justice by human hands; true justice comes only by decree of the orishas and Olódumare. Ewon, as an osogbo, speaks of those unjustly imprisoned. Ewon is human justice, and human justice is often unjust for that reason—its human nature and human logic. Jails are filled with innocent people, just as they are filled with guilty people. The laws themselves that define crimes are

---

*Since this time oriatés follow the custom of *lavatorio* in the igbodu: a rinsing of rum and fresh water for each newly washed set of cowries. When an orisha is born, its shells contain the curse spawned by Ofún Meji; the oriaté removes it with a generous washing of rum and fresh water. This is a ritual action to break Epe; it is also a reminder that the most powerful sorcery is broken by the simplest things. As a side note to this pataki: once the curse was broken, the babalawo who cast it lost the power of divination himself. Wickedness never goes without punishment, and malevolence returns to its origin like a river flowing to the sea.

†After breaking the curse, an avatar of Obatalá known as Alabalashe made the trip from heaven to earth for one purpose: to teach the olorishas the secrets of the odu and to enhance their power of divination. Alabalashe is referred to as the Obatalá of the diviners, and olorishas who specialize in divination receive this orisha to strengthen their ashé with diloggún. This illustrates another concept of osogbo: if one has faith and makes ebó, when the osogbo is lifted something happens to bring balance and a blessing. The more extreme the osogbo, the more extreme the blessing when one overcomes it.

written by men and driven by political agendas. Take, for example, the woman with breast cancer whose only relief comes from the use of medical marijuana. She is arrested and convicted, and she must spend time either on probation or behind bars. Take, for example, the child who goes to juvenile detention because he shoplifted a new shirt; perhaps the child had neither adequate clothing nor money to buy what he needed, and he needed a shirt. Consider the woman forced to sell her body in the sex industry to feed herself, her parents, or her children. Take the father forced to steal to feed his family, or the mentally ill person whose psychosis drove him to commit an act of violence. Is it truly justice to punish these people when in fact there were other factors that drove them to commit these crimes? Sometimes people are forced to do what they do because they have needs they cannot fulfill in any other way. Where, then, is the real crime?

The orishas teach us that when a human being lacks basic needs because resources are unevenly or grossly divided, the true crime lies with society, not with the person forced to break a law to fulfill a need. Even our final ebó of priestly consecration, the ebó at the marketplace done under Oyá's watchful eyes, teaches us that there will be times when people need to steal to eat. Eating is essential to life, so it is our collective responsibility to make sure everyone has food. In an ideal world, an ideal espoused by Olódumare and the orishas, no one should go hungry, no one should go unclothed, no one should go without love and compassion. Yet all too often these are the people we put behind bars.

We can be imprisoned in other ways as well: We are imprisoned by our unfulfilled needs and imperfect psyches. We are imprisoned by our own greed. We are imprisoned by the society we live in, one that values wealth over wisdom. Simply, we are all imprisoned. Ewon afflicts all of us.

Ewon denotes other types of imprisonment beyond inhumane "justice" delivered through the hands of humanity. It denotes more than physical incarceration for crimes committed for the sake of survival. Ewon can denote imprisonment of the mind; it can denote imprisonment by life's cruel circumstances; it can denote imprisonment by unhealthy emotions, thoughts, circumstances, and habits. It can denote kidnapping, and it can speak of a man, woman, or child imprisoned in an unhealthy, abusive environment. Ewon encompasses all these, and the appearance of Ewon in one's life demands careful consideration and contemplation on the diviner's part. It is one of the most dangerous and difficult osogbos to sort out in our lives, and even though we might *think* we live with iré, blessings and goodness in our lives, every man, woman, and child alive lives under the influence of Ewon. We are all imprisoned by something, and the bars are of our own making.

ESHE: Eshe translates as "general afflictions." This is a very dangerous osogbo. It encompasses anything and everything bad the world has to give, and the diviner needs to impress this on the client. A little bit of every osogbo from this list exists in Eshe, and it can be a precursor to more intense onslaughts by the other osogbos. Eshe eats away at us until, little by little, everything is lost. If any osogbo can be said to result in desperation, depression, despondency, or despair, it is Eshe.

HOW CAN WE GIVE LIFE MEANING?

The dualism of the Western, Eurocentric, Judeo-Christian mind-set is rather too simple; a thing is either good or evil, it is either black or white. The philosophy underlying orisha worship is far more complex and acknowledges that life is many shades of gray—it is not simple; it is messy. Goodness arises when we respond to osogbo with good character and seek to overcome adversity. Evil is a symptom of a deeper dis-ease—an imbalance in our character or an outside spiritual influence that causes us to falter and stumble in the darkness instead of turning toward God's light. Lucumí spirituality asserts that a life of constant blessings offers no chance to learn, no chance to grow, no chance to become stronger. Just as the entity we know as Iré is inherently lazy, sleeping while the world pleads for his presence, so would humans become lazy and life pointless if it took no effort at all to grow and evolve.

Still, each of us asks: *What is the meaning of life?* Perhaps we are asking the wrong question; perhaps instead of asking what the meaning of life is, we should be asking *How can we give life meaning?* Not long after her initial diagnosis of stage 4 ovarian cancer, Rebecca asked me this question. I never answer spiritual questions with simple answers; instead, I prefer to answer such queries with patakís that give us not so much an answer as more to think about . . .

As I put my final edits on this chapter, I was remembering a time when Rebecca's cancer diagnosis was still new, her chemotherapy barely begun. To take her mind off it, we went away for the weekend to the beach, to Ashara's little pink house in Ormond Beach. It was almost midnight. The air felt cold and tasted salty; our breath was vaporous as Rebecca and I made our way to the beach. Through the dark back-streets of Ormond Beach we walked away from Ashara's until we came to the main road through town, and then we ran across the boulevard as drivers drove sloppily, weaving, college kids and young adults either too tired or too inebriated to drive safely. We were like schoolkids ourselves, jaywalking when the light was only a block up the road, but I'd had one or two rum and cokes too many (Ashara makes them strong), and it's more fun to make a drunken dash through traffic than wait at the light. Rebecca, who was sober, followed me. The weight of her cancer brought life's mortality to bear down on all of us in our ilé, and maybe that night we both felt like taking a risk. Ashara was worried. "You shouldn't be out after drinking," she nagged, but Rebecca and I shared a smile. "You shouldn't be trying to get your godfather drunk," I chided her, and then we were off into the darkness. We found the spot we wanted—it was between two hotels and over the boardwalk, rising above a steep sand dune before plunging down into darkness. It was turtle nesting season, and all lights beachside were turned off. There was only darkness—deep, velvet, almost crushing in the waning moon, and a darker ocean whose surf crashed and roared with the wind. Above were millions of stars, more than could be seen in landlocked Orlando. No words. We stopped; we sat; we rested.

"It makes me feel so small," Rebecca whispered.

"What does?" I was lying back on the boardwalk stairs, staring into the sky.

"All this," she said, holding her arms out to the ocean, to the stars. I nodded my head; wordlessly, I agreed. For the first time since coming home from the hospital her mood was light, almost upbeat; the Rebecca that I'd come to know and love over the years was back. And our silence, it was long but fragile. It broke when she asked me, "What's the point of all this?" For a moment I thought she was asking about her cancer, the reason for her suffering. Instead, she added, "Why is there so much out there? Why did God make so much because we're so small? And what's the point of life, anyway? We live only to die. It makes no sense."

I can never resist the chance to tell a story. "We find the answer to that in the odu,"* I told her, "because there, the orishas asked Olófin himself the same question."

The orishas were, for lack of a better word, bored, almost listless, when they went to Olófin to complain. They had worked for eons in heaven, and then they had worked for eons on earth. More or less each orisha knew just about everything—or so they each thought: eons of work in the spiritual world; eons of work in the material world; eons of knowledge stored in their heads. No one knew, however, the reason for it all.

Obatalá himself led the orishas before Olófin, and with them at his back he put his head down in obeisance. Olófin blessed him, lifted him, embraced him, and asked him, "What troubles my children?"

"Why?" Obatalá asked Olófin. "We know everything in these two worlds, heaven and earth, except for why."

It was then that Olófin revealed the great secret to the orishas—they were not alone in creation. He told them that at the beginning of time, Olódumare created life not only on the earth, but throughout the entire universe. Just as the continents are separated by great oceans, so are the galaxies and solar systems separated by great distances in space. When

---

*Odí Merindilogún (7-16).

the orishas were created, they were not created as single entities: Olófin revealed that when Obatalá was created, he was created many times over; when Yemayá was created, she was created many times over; when Olokun was created, he was created many times over; and so on. These "duplicates" were sent to govern the other planets that exist throughout space. And Olófin taught the orishas this: at the end of days, when even the universe ceases to exist, Olódumare would judge the orishas and humans who populated each world and would decide which planet had evolved the most and had done the most with what he had given them.

In short, Olófin taught the orishas that we are not alone in the universe, and even though we might feel lonely or think that we are the epitome of existence, we are not. Simply said, we are the inhabitants of one planet among many. And it is our job, if we can be said to have a job in the greater scheme of things, to be the best stewards of the resources Olódumare provided.

"Are we doing well? Are we winning the race?" I asked Rebecca rhetorically. "I don't think we're doing well. But then again, who knows? We have no idea what's out there. We don't know who's out there. And we don't know what civilizations might have already destroyed themselves with their own osogbos. There's too much we don't know, and it's probably for the best."

Rebecca stood up and took one last look at the ocean; she sighed, deeply. She let out something with that breath: sadness. She smiled, and without asking me if I was ready to go back, she turned and climbed the boardwalk stairs. I followed her. The darkness gave way to the light of the streets, and the ocean's roar was lost in the sounds of cars dashing down the main road. This time, we walked to the crosswalk and waited for the light to change. No more chances; now both of us were living deliberately and carefully.

Still, we were silent as we walked back to the little pink house.

3

The Concept of Orí and Destiny

Remember, it is the head that rules your body, so do not lose your head.

FROM THE OLODU UNLE (8 MOUTHS)

Lucumí cosmology teaches that there are two major realms of existence: *orún,* heaven, and *ayé,* the material world. There was a time when the two worlds existed side-by-side (or, more properly, one within the other), and passing from one to the next was as easy for humans as walking between rooms in a home. The original human bodies were made directly from the earth. Our essence, known as *eemi* (the force causing us to breathe), gave us *emi* (breath), and it came directly from Olódumare's own breath. As perfect beings made from the earth and infused with Olódumare's essence—for breath is life—we could not defile the essence of either world with our presence. Because the odu Odí taught us how to procreate in the flesh instead of by means of Obatalá's hands molding the body from the mud of the earth, and with the birth of earth's first human child (a child born not from the earth, but from a human mother's body using the ashé acquired from her connection with the earth), human nature changed.

The odu Okana Meji (1-1) tells the story of earth's first human child; it defied its parent's wishes and tried to cross from ayé to orún, from the material world to the spiritual world, while still in the flesh.* Reality's rules had changed, and to save orún from defilement, a gate, a spiritual chasm, formed. Only that which is perfect—the immortal soul, the orí of human consciousness—can cross that gate. To move between worlds, humans had to die or be born; there was no other way. Of course, as a spiritual principle, Ikú, the spirit of death, was not born to the world until Ejioko (2 mouths) became active on the earth.†

THE CROSSROADS OF HEAVEN AND EARTH

As an odu, Okana stresses balance and teaches that everything in nature is self-correcting. In his book *Obi Agbón,* Lucumí oriaté Miguel Ramos writes, "For there to be good, there must be bad. . . . Okana upholds the basic philosophical and scientific principles that assert there is no positive without a negative; no action without a reaction. These same notions are reflected in the Yoruba conception of life in orún and ayé. Each plane brings harmony to the other by reflecting upon the other's nature."[1] Our first hint about the true spiritual nature of our world comes from one of Okana's proverbs: "There is gain and there is loss; from one the world was

---

*There are two patakís in the oral corpus of Okana Meji (1-1) supporting this theoretical rift. One is titled "The Separation of Heaven and Earth," and the other is titled "The Separation of Sky and Earth." The theme of separation is central to Okana Meji. For a written version of these two stories, see my book *Diloggún Tales of the Natural World: How the Moon Fooled the Sun and Other Santería Stories.*

†The physical gate by which we come into this world is the mother's womb, and the physical gate by which we leave this world is the earth's womb. There is no religion, indigenous or otherwise, that refers to "Father Earth." The collective unconscious of all faiths intuitively knows that the earth is female. Many women may feel disempowered in this religion because of a limited understanding of only the outer forms of its rituals. In truth, the female body is considered sacred, and Lucumí ontology acknowledges that women embody the forces of life and death. Those who study and understand the workings of Ifá (another sacred body of lore in the Lucumí faith) would do well to compare and contrast this with the sacred principle known as Odu, who is woman. Ultimately, Odu represents all the powers of creation. Women are sacred simply because they are women.

born, and from one the world is lost." There are other proverbs in the corpus of Okana that also refer to this mystery: "The world was created by
one; and because of one, the world began." The proverbs found in that
olodu also tell us: "From a good thing was born a bad thing, and from a
bad thing was born a good thing." What is this mysterious "one" to which
Okana alludes?

Simply stated, in universal terms, it is the mind of God, Olódumare.
In mundane terms, it is the mind of man. Between these two extremes—
mortal and divine—ashé flows. Orún interacts with ayé, with the orisha Elegguá controlling the crossroads between heaven and earth.

A crossroads implies a four-way intersection, while a division between
heaven and earth implies only a straight line. But note that there are
other divisions in orún and ayé. In orún, there is *orún reré,* known as
the "good heaven," and there is *orún burukú,* the "bad heaven." Ayé, the
earth, has divisions as well; there is *ayé reré,* the "good earth," and there
is *ayé burukú,* the "bad earth." In heaven these are distinct and separate
spiritual realities; however, on earth the good and the bad are as blurred
as the concepts of blessings and osogbo sometimes are. There is the nur-
turing side of nature and there is the destructive side of nature. These are
themes developed and deepened throughout the 256 odu of the diloggún.

Regarding orún reré and orún burukú, good heaven and bad heaven,
Ramos writes:

The forces that inhabit the superior side of the sphere are separated
into two separate realms: positive and negative. . . . There is the
"good" side of the sky . . . where the orishas and the ancestors reside
along with iré, the provider of good. Orún's other side, orún burukú
(the "bad" sky), is the abode of all the osobo and other negative entities. Like earth, orún has its good side and its bad, an idea that is
totally distinct from the Judeo-Christian notions of two manifestly
separate realms, heaven and hell.[2]

While it is the olodu Okana and the odu Okana Meji that teaches and
enforces this separation, when those divisions meet and form a crossroads,

the ashé of the olodu Owani (11 mouths) comes into play. Eleggúa (also known as Eshu) guards both the heavenly crossroads and the mundane crossroads. And as Ramos notes, "Residents of orún . . . descend to ayé and participate in the affairs of the world, even when their primary abode is orún. This is why iré and osobo interact so often with humankind and ayé."[3] This is why the good part of earthly life is often mistaken for the bad side of earthly life and vice versa; this is why nature is both punitive and rewarding. The orishas, as well, interact with mortals, and likewise, iré and osogbo interact with the orishas. Ramos notes that human beings no longer have the right to cross heaven and earth at will; however, despite what the oral literature says, Ramos attributes this to the lore of Unle Meji, identified in his work as Ejiogbé.[4] This is a huge deviation from my own lineage's teachings; still, it is a valid one. To come to ayé, humans must suffer the trauma of birth, and to go to orún, humans must suffer the trauma of death. This is our only passage between the worlds.

While the concept of birth and death is a theme in many of the diloggún's odu, it is integral to the ashé of Unle Ogundá (8-3). In this odu, the beliefs attribute both sublime and traumatic events to occurrences before, during, and after birth. Before investigating this multidirectional trauma, one needs an understanding of the Yoruba and Lucumí ontology regarding humans, known as *eniyan,* and their physical/spiritual components. Yoruba scholar Oladele Abiodun Balogun writes, "A person, according to the Yoruba, is made up of three elements: 'ara' (body), 'emi' (the life-giving element) and 'orí' (that which is thought to be responsible for human destiny)."[5] He states that humans have two basic elements: the material and the immaterial. The body, *ara,* is the material element. Anything that is tangible, any part of the human that can be known through any of the five senses, is said to belong to ara: head (*orí*), neck (*orun*), hair (*irun*), trunk (*iyoku ara*), the extremities of the hands and feet (*apa* and *ese*), and the nails (*eekanna*). If it is tangible and has an anatomical definition or placement, that part of the eniyan, the human being, is a division of ara.[6] Dr. Balogun goes on to define the immaterial elements of an eniyan (human) as being *emi* (the life-giving element) and *orí* (that which is thought to be responsible for human destiny). Yet he insists that concrete divisions cannot be drawn between material and immaterial components of the human being. Note that *orí* refers to the physical head yet also carries the connotation of a spiritual head. Orí is visible (the head we are able to see) as well as invisible (the spiritual head that cannot be seen with human eyes). In both Yoruba and Lucumí ontology, the physical and spiritual are so deeply intertwined that separating the concepts is difficult.[7]

The physical essence might be the bulk of what our senses take in, but it is a small part of the human being, according to Lucumí ontology. Going deeper into metaphysics, both the Lucumí and the Yoruba believe in *emi* (breath; the life-giving element) and *okán* (the heart). "*Emi* is invisible and intangible," writes scholar Babasehinde Ademuleya. "It is closely connected with breath, which may be thought of as residing in the mouth and nose. But breath is not *emi,* which in Yoruba is *eemi. Emi* is that which breathes in man, and it can be best described through its causal functions as that which gives life to the body."[8]

About emi, Dr. Balogun says,

> As far as the Yoruba are concerned, "emi" is the life-giving entity. It is the life force of a person. It is believed that the "emi" (life-giving entity) is the mysterious vital principle which distinguishes a living person from the dead. "Emi" is closely associated with the breath and the whole mechanism of breathing is its most expressive manifestation. The Yoruba believe that "emi" is the causative of breath and so it is "breather," that which breathes in man.[9]

He defines *emi* as a kind of human essence that Western metaphysics refers to as the *astral body,* an ethereal presence that can leave the body and inhabit other bodies or even animals. He believes that it is the emi that is responsible for the phenomenon of dreaming and astral travel in both the physical and the spiritual realms.[10] The cessation of the breath results in the loss of eemi, with *eemi* defined as the enlivening essence that causes the body to breathe. Loss of eemi, the enlivening presence, causes cessation of emi, the ethereal breath, and this deprives the body of life. Emi and eemi are thus the essence of a human being's physical life.

Okán, the heart, is both a physical part of ara (the body) and a spiritual center of activity for ara. Of okán, Balogun writes that it is "the seat of emotion and psychic energy. . . . [It] performs psychic, psychological as well as intellectual functions."[11] Ademuleya writes, "In a physical sense, the heart is closely connected with the blood. But for the Yoruba, the heart is more than a blood machine; it is the seat of the emotions and psychic energy."[12] Important to both descriptions is this: Both Lucumí and Yoruba ontology ascribe spiritual principles to the heart and to the breath, and while the heart is the seat of emotions and psychic activities, and while emi (breath) and eemi (enlivening force causing breath) are the life forces in the human body, Lucumí ontology confuses neither of these with the concept of the human soul. These are only the spiritual engines that keep the body running, and they keep the soul connected to its human form.

THE ORÍ, THE HEAD

To understand Lucumí ontological beliefs about the soul, we return to the concept of the head, orí. The connotation is that of a physical head, the main sensory organ; however, the meaning of this word goes much deeper. *Orí* refers to the sacred center of every human; for this reason it is the essence of the eniyan, the human being. Balogun refers to the orí as the seat of the human soul; the rest of the human body (ara) is simply life support for the head.

Inside the orí is *opolo,* the brain. Balogun affirms that this is the organ of thought, human intelligence, and sanity. He describes basic human nature as being divided. Either a person is *olopolo pipe,* meaning someone with a complete or "good" brain, or someone with intelligence, or a person is *opolo re ti da ru,* an insane person with a disorganized brain.[13] Of course, an eniyan with a good brain, or olopolo pipe, is someone well equipped to make good choices; such a person is not easy prey for osogbo and can therefore promote iré, goodness, in the world. A good brain, however, does not necessarily equate with a person of good character; even those with intelligence can choose to be agents of osogbo in the world.

Contrast this with an *eniyan opolo re ti da ru,* an insane person, who is easy prey for osogbo; varying degrees of insanity can make people unwilling agents of Arayé (the spirit of chaos, wickedness) in the world—the concepts of *ika eniyan* (wicked people) and *onise ibi* (workers of osogbo) that we examined in chapter 2. Realize, also, that lunacy is one of the children of Ano, fleeting illness, and those who are insane might not have an organically disorganized brain; instead, they could be suffering the afflictions of osogbo, and while under lunacy's influence, Arayé, the most powerful of them all, could step in and take control. Finally, there is yet another possibility: those who are *eniyan opolo re ti da ru* might have disorganized brains and organic mental illness, but nevertheless, even the most mentally ill among us can have a good heart, and because of that good heart, they can do good works in the world despite organic brain issues. In the material world, the spiritual possibilities are endless.

In Lucumí ontology, no part of the human being is more complex than the orí. Our beliefs provide many subdivisions for the spiritual head, subdivisions that correspond to various points on the physical structure. First, there is *iporí,* which some Lucumí know simply as Orí (spelled with an uppercase *O*). Iporí is our perfection, our spiritual pinnacle of existence; it is the highest, most essential spark of self that cannot incarnate in the flesh because there is nothing in this realm to hold or mirror its ashé. Never does iporí seek to incarnate; instead, it sends pieces of itself into the material world throughout successive lifetimes, and in each life lived we try to attain our highest potential through divination, ebó, behavior modification, and priestly initiations. Iporí could be compared to the concept of the higher self found in Western mysticism and spiritual traditions, with this difference: there is no limit as to how many incarnations iporí can provide in one generation—a concept difficult for many Westerners to understand.

Iporí can, and often does, send out multiple rays of itself into the physical world concurrently; each of these generates a spark that infuses a single body of flesh. The idea of soulmates in Western thinking comes closest to this concept, the idea being that every person is said to have a "twin soul" wandering the world in loneliness, and part of our destiny is to find that soul and reunite as lovers. Still, the concept of soulmates is limiting when it come to the potential inherent in the concept of iporí; we cannot impose our limits on that which is, in essence, limitless. Many of us walk this earth connected spiritually because we all come from the same essence we know as iporí. Ultimately, each iporí in heaven is subject to an orisha known as Orí. This is the source of all spiritual heads in our world and is an orisha born in the odu Ogundá Meji (3-3) of the diloggún. Although there are some oriatés in the United States who claim this orisha was lost to the Lucumí faith generations ago—and they may have even traveled to Yorubaland or Brazil to reclaim it for our modern practice of the faith—my lineage of orisha worship has retained the mysteries of Orí; it is alive and well in our tradition.

In Lucumí belief, next comes the *orí* (spelled with a lowercase *o*). This term denotes the physical head; however, as a spiritual entity orí is also said to refer to one's guardian angel, an energy that hovers just inches above the crown of the head (the crown of the head is known in Lucumí as *atarí*).* If one were to draw a comparison with Eastern mysticism, the orí would refer to the crown chakra. Note that the orí is a spark of iporí, our spiritual pinnacle, with ashé flowing between the two. Each human being is continually in touch with the higher self; we are no more disconnected from iporí than the toe is disconnected from the body.

Note that orí, as a spiritual principle, extends and connects throughout the entire body. In the ritual of consecration, when an *abokú* (one freed by death) becomes an *iyawó* (a newly born olorisha, or initiate), orí's energy extends and forms a connection with the left big toe on the human body; orí then encapsulates the entire human energy matrix (the full implications of this mystery are only for the priesthood and not the

---

*In Lucumí terminology it is common to refer to one's titular orisha as the guardian angel; however, in Lucumí cosmology it is more proper to refer to *orí* as the guardian angel. It's not that the orishas aren't angelic in nature (because they are perfect beings, emanations of Olódumare), and it's not because they don't guard us, because they do. But there are times when the orishas aren't entirely focused on us as individuals—they have other tasks in creation beyond guiding their human adherents. Of all the orishas in heaven, only our personal orí follows us and guards us at all times and in all places. This, too, is a concept born in the odu Ogundá Meji (3-3) of the diloggún.

laity). Just beneath the orí and resting with the atarí (the crown of the head) is *eledá,* the spark of God, Olódumare, enlivening the heads of all living creatures. Every eniyan, every human being, contains a tiny spark of Olódumare's ashé.* With consecration into the priesthood, the orí and the eledá of the person become more intimately intertwined and perfected; they are bound together by the *gbogbowan olodó* (a secret artifact that the postulant brings home from the river ceremony before consecration) and the essence of one's orisha. When all these elements come together in the consecrated olorisha, perfect and inseparable, it is defined as *elerí*—the union of iporí, orí, eledá, gbogbowan olodó, and orisha. It is a special ashé that binds them all together and strengthens them, and that ashé is, quite simply, the ashé of priesthood.

THE ENERGY CENTERS OF THE HEAD

On the physical head itself are special energy centers that are a part of the spiritual orí: *atarí, iwajú, ipakó,* and *ajagbalá* (also known as *beborún* by some). Atarí has already been mentioned; it is the crown of the head, the place where eledá, the spark of the Creator, resides in each of us. Atarí is an important energy center because this is where consciousness connects with orún, heaven, and it is the place where we receive impulses from iporí, our perfect selves still residing with Olódumare. Atarí maintains ties between orí and iporí as well as ties between eledá and Olódumare.

Iwajú occupies what Eastern mysticism knows as the third eye in the human body; it is in the center of the forehead, slightly above and between the two physical eyes. As an energy center, it links our conscious thoughts with the world around us, and it connects with a region inside the brain known as *ogbón,* our unconscious self. Lucumí belief attributes psychic abilities to iwajú; therefore there is a connection

---

*Even animals have eledá, although neither the animal's orí nor its opolo are advanced enough in the material world to express consciousness equal to that of a human. This is why Lucumí priests respect all life, including animals offered in sacrifice. They have divine consciousness, and Olódumare feels what they feel at some deep level.

between that energy center and the spirituality of okán, the heart, in which true psychic power resides.

Ipakó sits at the back of the neck; many say it is the base of the brain stem controlling the body's animal functions. Through it we connect with not only our past but also our family's past, and we connect with not only our past mistakes but also our family's past mistakes. An entity known as Eshu ni Pacuó lives in ipakó; this is an individual avatar of Eshu connecting our orí with the orí of each ancestor.

Ajagbalá (known as *beborún* by some) lies at the front of the neck, at its base, just above the dip between the collarbones. Just as ipakó connects us with our past, our family's past, and the mistakes of both, ajagbalá connects us with the future—our future and our descendants' future—and it leads us to possibilities that lie before us. In many ways, intuition about the past and the future comes from ipakó and ajagbalá, and iwajú gives us the ashé to sort them all out.*

THE ORÍ-INU, THE COLLECTIVE UNCONSCIOUS

Within all the aforementioned divisions of the orí is an important concept known as *orí-inu*. My godfather, Banacek Matos, an oriaté, refers to orí-inu as the inner self, consciousness within consciousness. And while it does denote what modern psychology terms the *subconscious mind,* more correctly it connects us with the level of being that Carl Jung referred to as the *collective unconscious*. Within orí-inu there is no fear; there is no hatred; there is no anger; there is no apprehension about the future. Orí-inu has a special connection with both orí (our guardian angel, which hovers just above the head and eledá) and iporí (the perfect self

---

*Although it is beyond the scope of this work, it is worth mentioning that ipakó and ajagbalá have much to do with the shadow, or literally, the body's shadow cast upon the earth. Some believe the shadow itself is a manifestation of Eshu ni Pacuó, who is envisioned as a very young avatar of Eshu. It is noteworthy that children become preoccupied with their shadows at anywhere from four to six years of age. Lucumí rituals involving Eshu ni Pacuó and the feeding of the shadow strengthen our ties with *egun* (family or ancestral spirits) and heal the often damaged inner child of every person. Sometimes these rituals are integral to overcoming osogbo in our lives.

in heaven). Orí-inu is the inner head chosen in heaven before the orisha Ajala, the avatar of Obatalá known as the carver of heads, and it is orí-inu that contains perfect knowledge of our destiny. When a client sits at a Lucumí diviner's mat for a consultation, when the auxiliary divination tools known as ibó are used, it is orí-inu that guides the process in tandem with the orisha consulted; it is a divine dance, a sacred movement between the client's head and the orisha whose cowries are cast. Orí-inu is the perfect knowledge and essence of our current incarnation. It is also the true equivalent of a human soul.[14]

Orí-inu is chosen in the house of Ajala, the carver of heads, and is the main concept spoken of in the odu Unle Ogundá. It is for this reason that the participation of orí-inu in divination is essential. Orí-inu contains perfect knowledge of the following Lucumí concepts: *iwa, akunleyan, ayanmo, akunlegba,* and *apere.*

Ìwa is character, our natural tendencies in life. Our goal is to promote a concept known as *iwa pele,* gentle character. Orí-inu knows our propensity for or against violence, laziness, greed, anger, and other psychological qualities. It helps us overcome the negative and promote the positive.

Akunleyan is free will. Even though we come to this world with a goal, a destiny (the concept of *ayanmo*), by using free will we can alter the course of our lives in ways that bring us closer to attaining our ayanmo, or further away from what it is we were meant to do and be.

Akunleyan creates changes in our lives; these changes are known by the term *akunlegba.* Some of the changes might be for the good, while some might create chaos in our lives. Orí-inu knows and understands the choices we have made, and through the process of divination it can help us correct the bad choices and promote good ones.

Apere is perfection, and only orí-inu knows if we are on the road to perfection. Perfection is attained by cultivating a gentle character. Perfection is attained by making the right choices, moving closer to our chosen destiny. Perfection is that which allows us to rest, permanently, at the feet of Olódumare.[15]

Returning to the concept of the human as a holistic being, the scholar Babasehinde Ademuleya breaks down the Yoruba word for human, *eni-*

yan, into two more words that help us understand our sacredness: the root words *eni* and *ayan.* In essence, humans are eni-ayan; each is a chosen one. Much as the orishas are selected heads, chosen by Olódumare to be the pinnacle of any talent, skill, or natural function, each human who lives is a chosen one, a chosen head, charged by Olódumare to live and fulfill a specific function on the earth. This function is known as one's destiny, one's apere; it is one's perfection in this life. As we have seen, orí-inu contains that destiny, and, in Ademuleya's own words, it is the "umbilical cord" connecting us to Olódumare at all times. Indeed, in Lucumí belief it is known that each orí is so vast that not all of it can be contained in a single human form. Part of each orí resides in heaven, with Ajala, the avatar of Obatalá who carves heads and crafts our destinies, and with Olódumare.

HUMAN DESTINY

The preceding brings us to the odu Unle Ogundá (8-3) in the diloggún and the concepts of orí, human destiny, iré, and osogbo. Ademuleya cites two scholars of Yoruba spirituality in discussing the concept of orí (the spiritual head) in connection with the oral literature regarding creation. Of Wande Abimbola's version of the Yoruba creation pataki he writes:

> *Obatala,* who is equally referred to as *Orisa-nla* (the arch divinity), . . . is said to have been charged with the responsibility of sculpting the human being *eniyan* and designing only the physical features: hence his appellation *a-da-ni bo ti ri* (he who creates as he chooses). This portrays him as one who creates as he likes, making man shapely or deformed in his features. After finishing his work, Olodumare (the Deity-God) would give the body *emi* (life). The *eniyan* then proceeds to *Ajala—Irunmole to o nmo ipin* (the divinity who moulds *ipin*) to select for himself his *ipin* (portion), also referred to as *orí-inu* (inner head)—that which he so desired to be on getting to the world. In Abimbola's explanation, this *oriinu* or *ipin*—means destiny.[16]

Ademuleya then narrates a variant of this story as given by the Yoruba scholar E. B. Idowu:

> [Idowu] paints a picture of a "complete person" kneeling before Olodumare (the deity) to have his destiny conferred on him. In this, man obtains his *ipin* (destiny) in one of three ways: by kneeling down and choosing his destiny *a-kun-le-yan* (that which one kneels to choose), by kneeling to receive *a-kun-le-gba* (that which one kneels to receive), or by having his destiny apportioned to him *a-yan-mo* (that which is apportioned to one).[17]

Not only Ademuleya but other scholars of Yoruba cosmology agree that it embraces the notion of predestination, softly deterministic though it may be, in which one is said to choose the orí-inu, the inner head, that will be a part of the eniyan's life on earth. Before the orisha Ajala and with Olódumare's consent, a head is selected, and within that head one receives ipin, a special portion of identity that is not truly a part of the eniyan's personality in heaven but becomes an integral part of the personality on earth. A Yoruba proverb found in the odu Unle Ogundá states that in heaven we receive *akunleyan ni ad'aye ba,* "a chosen destiny that we must pursue and meet on the earth." As part of our spiritual destiny and evolution, we may have to choose one or more osogbos to accompany us as companions during important segments of our journey. Thus osogbo becomes a catalyst for spiritual development, an agent of growth by which we learn to make wise choices and develop good character. As eni-ayan, chosen ones, we are also the choosers of our major life events, including both triumphs and losses. In itself that would seem straightforward enough, but in orún (heaven), something amazing happens: once we choose our orí-inu and ipin, we "forget" our choices.* Of this Ademuleya writes,

> When man comes into the world at birth, he forgets everything about heaven and his destiny. It is only his *ori* [i.e., orí-inu, the inner head

---

*This is a teaching of the odu Unle Ogundá (8-3) in the diloggún.

and, in many ways, the subconscious mind] that remembers the course and content of his chosen destiny, and pursues [it] accordingly. It directs a man's affairs in this world. To the Yoruba people, the *"ori"* is invisible, and is therefore referred to as *ori-inu* (the inner head), destined to become the person's instructor, his "guardian angel," which is equally referred to as "a semi-split entity," the "man's double." This is further established in the Yoruba saying: . . . "One's *Ori-inu* makes his life for him. The creature that accompanies one to the world is his *ori.*"[18]

Ifalola Sanchez, a traditional Yoruba babalawo who maintains a blog on Ifá practice and beliefs, writes often on the subject of orí in Yoruba beliefs. In a blog post published in 2008 Sanchez wrote extensively on the odu and on destiny from the perspective of Ifá in Ogbe Ogundá. He began his discussion with the concept of orí:

Let's start with the Yoruba concept of Orí. While its literal meaning is "head," there is also a more esoteric meaning for the followers of the Orisa tradition. Orí is in fact the closest equivalent in Orisa theology to one's soul, as evidenced most clearly by the idea that Orí chooses one's destiny. When one's Orí is in Orún, awaiting to make its descent to Earth, it goes before Olódumare to receive its vocation and pick the destiny it (Orí) will fulfil on Earth. . . . During the process of choosing one's destiny at Ajala's castle, one has the opportunity to pick from a variety of pottery heads, but not all are equal, some are deformed, some are fragile and weak, some are half-baked, and some are well made. It is quite difficult to discern the differences in heads, and we are told to look to Ifá for guidance in our choice before and eventually afterwards on Earth. . . .

After incarnating on Earth, one's destiny is forgotten, and our lives are spent attempting to find and fulfil it while on Earth. . . . There is an assumption that one will choose a destiny that is befitting of the ideals of ìwa pele and ìwa rere (cool character, gentle character) which can be seen in the Odu Irete Ofún. It can also be safely assumed that picking a destiny that is positive and fulfils many of the ideals set forth in Odu Ifá (helping those less fortunate, helping one's community, bettering oneself, etc) is best.[19]

All of these concepts—choice, agreement, destiny, companions, accomplishments, and the ultimate forgetfulness of all these things when we take the journey to earth—are summarized in a pataki found in the corpus of the odu Unle Ogundá in the diloggún. This story, which I have titled "Blood, Weeping, Laughter, and Patience," examines, by means of metaphor, many of these teachings.

After making the first humans from the mud of the earth, Olódumare decreed that the mortal race would repopulate itself, male and female; no longer would they be molded by Obatalá's hands from the clay and given Olódumare's own sweet breath. Instead, they would be molded in the mother's womb and would take their first breath from the air around them. Spirits waited in heaven for the new gate of life to be opened; none knew, however, that the gate lay between the legs of women.

Olódumare unfolds all mysteries in his own time.

When the time was ripe for the first soul to incarnate, there was both fear and excitement; patiently, Ajala and Olódumare waited for the first brave soul to ask to make the journey. After days of waiting, it was a woman with a heart brave enough to kneel before Ajala and ask, "I want to be born on earth; what must I do?"

So important was this first-born child-to-be that Olódumare himself came to counsel her. "Choose, choose your destiny wisely," he cautioned. Still kneeling before Ajala, who was busy carving heads, and with Olódumare watching, she pondered the life before her and what she wanted to accomplish. Finally she said, "I do not want to go alone. May I have four companions to take with me?"

"And who might those companions be?" asked Olódumare. Ajala was molding her head in silence.

"Blood, Weeping, Laughter, and Patience. Those are the four companions I want in the world." Olódumare considered this, and with a

smile on his face he accepted her request. A great cry of triumph could be heard on earth—the first child was on its way.

All the spirits of heaven watched as the mysteries of conception and pregnancy were revealed. They watched the woman's orí descend into the mother's womb, sleeping; they felt her memories of life in heaven melt away, making her mortal mind a blank slate for new experiences.

The four principles chosen to be her companions were in awe. Blood, Weeping, Laughter, and Patience—they could not fathom why she had chosen them as companions. Each went to the diviners to have their future on earth divined. "New mysteries unfold," they said, "and each of you will play a role in their creation. Your purposes will only unfold as you make ebó, and iré will come when the child matures and you make ebó once more."

Odu was closed, and with its closure came the cries of the mother. So great were her pains that all in heaven heard the screaming. Blood quickly made his sacrifice as others were stunned by this sound; immediately, he found himself beside the mother. It was then that his mystery unfolded.

The mother bled from her womb as it contracted, blood heralding the emergence of new life. Some women who watched bled as well, but their wombs were dry, lifeless, for there was nothing therein. Others held their blood; their wombs filled with new life. All watched in awe as the first girl-child was born with the mystery of Blood. Olódumare saw these things and knew that they were good. He decreed that without blood, no mother would give birth. There was the blood of the menses, telling a woman her womb was barren but would soon be ready again for new life. There was the blood withheld to nourish the conceived infant. There was the blood that came with the pain before new life could come into the world. These blood mysteries were born with the first sacrifice in Obeyono,* and this blood is always watched for, always caught, and always measured. It is feared by men and prayed for by women. It is life, the giver of life, and the cleanser of life.

Weeping watched all these things unfolding on earth; once the girl-child began to emerge from the womb, Weeping remembered to make her sacrifice. It was then that she joined both mother and child on earth. The

---

*This is another name for the odu Unle Ogundá (8-3) in the diloggún.

mother no longer screamed dryly; she cried tears of pain as Weeping came to her side, helping the infant with her birth. Women began to cry in fear, for they knew not how to help with the mystery. Some cried because they knew that they, too, would suffer the travails of labor, while others who bled cried that their own wombs were barren. The baby was born, and she, too, cried in pain and fear while the mother wept in joy. Tears flowed freely that day. Olódumare saw these things and knew that they were good. He decreed that from that day forth, without tears, mortal offspring could not live.

With the second sacrifice in Obeyono was born the honor of weeping. Having arrived in the flow of blood, a child will cry and wail, and those in attendance will hear the cries ascending to heaven. They, too, will begin to weep in joy. The mother will cry tears of joy and pain with the arrival of her offspring. Devoid of tears, the infant will be spanked to make it weep; if it does not, all there cry tears of sadness, for there is no life. Thus were the predictions of odu fulfilled: Blood and Weeping followed the birth of children everywhere.

With the arrival of humanity's first child came a flood of new births as women everywhere had begun to conceive and ripen. Laughter and Patience watched in awe as each new child came with Blood and Weeping. So powerful were those mysteries that they could not bear to look away; they were overwhelmed. Once the first girl-child reached her fortieth day of life, Laughter, wanting the same blessings as Blood and Weeping, realized he had not yet made ebó. Quickly, he went to the diviners to make his offering, but he was told that because he took so long to come back, his ebó was doubled. Laughter did not care; he made ebó.

Immediately, Laughter found himself on earth.

Before him was the girl-child, the one who had requested that the principle of Laughter be her companion. When she saw him, a faint memory flickered in her mind but then was gone; still, she smiled. The smile grew into a short giggle. The sound was pleasing, and she laughed. Her parents were the first to hear this, and the sound was contagious. Soon, the entire household was caught up in laughter. Olódumare saw that this was good and gave her blessings to Laughter. As each child on earth came to the fortieth day, each was accompanied by laughter. The spirits of heaven looked down at this new mystery and saw that it was good. They gave their own ashé to the blessing. Soon, the entire world was caught within Laughter's grasp.

For nine months, Patience watched these blessings unfold throughout the earth and saw the goodness created by Blood, Weeping, and Laughter, for each had ashé and purpose in life. She wanted to be a part of these mysteries as well. Having been overwhelmed by what she saw, and having been the most patient of the four, she was slow in offering ebó. The diviners told her, "Patience, you waited far too long. Your ebó must be offered five times over." Wanting to go to earth, she made the sacrifices.

It was then that she saw the girl-child face-to-face for the first time.

When Patience arrived, the toddler looked at her and smiled. She then stood, reaching out for the principle. She fell. She tried again and fell again. Wanting to reach her new companion, she stood again. For a moment she had balance, and then she tried to take her first step. She fell. The child's mother saw these things, and sensing Patience in the room, she said, "Have patience, my child." With that principle as her guide, she learned to walk, to talk, to run, to skip, to jump. Laughter came with each new skill mastered, while Patience slowly helped her learn. Children everywhere learned new skills and grew into maturity with Laughter and Patience as their guides. Olódumare saw that these things were good and all the denizens of heaven increased his blessings.

Because the sacrifices of Laughter and Patience were larger, their blessings were greater, and when earth's first child matured into adulthood, they made the final ebós prescribed by Obeyono. Blood and Weeping became bitter over the years, for while they were the first mysteries to unfold, they were always less desired. Bitterness led to anger, and they refused to make ebó. The odu was sealed. Humans over the earth knew that they came to this world amidst blood and weeping, but they prayed for laughter and patience, looking for goodness and joy among the finer things in life. Their prayers were sincere, from the heart. Everyone on the earth prayed, "Let us not leave this world as we came to this world, through blood and weeping. Let us leave this world through laughter and with patience." Olódumare saw that this was good and gave her consent. So has it been ever since.

4

Osogbo, Orí, and Eleggua

Death held me and left me; sickness embraced me and fled; I have survived the evil plans of my enemies.

FROM THE OLODU UNLE

As noted earlier, there was a time when life was simpler: there was Iré, the spirit of blessings, and there was Osogbo, the spirit of misfortunes, and the two, who were twins, took turns ruling the earth. Neither was satisfied with such a simple arrangement, however, and a war began between brother and sister. So heated was the war that Olófin became involved, and in the end, Osogbo was named the greater of the two. Osogbo made ebó and gave birth to the spiritual principles known as the *osogbos*. Some of these wanted children themselves, and they made ebó. Soon creation was filled with multiple entities bringing various misfortunes to the world. Meanwhile, Iré, the spirit of blessings, became lazy. He preferred to rest and sleep, oblivious to his family's workings. Because Iré did nothing, failing to make ebó, Osogbo and her offspring became stronger.

A blessing is a simple creature, but misfortunes in the world are legion. Add to this the complication of humans. There are currently seven billion people on the earth, and each orí (head) has its own per-

76

ception of the world in which it lives and moves. Each of these seven billion heads has its own orí-inu, or inner head, in which every person's individual destiny is found.

The concept of destiny seems almost fatalistic to many; many believe that it denies free will and personal choice. This, however, is anathematic to Lucumí ontology and metaphysics. African scholar Oladele Abiodun Balogun writes:

> The debate on the philosophical nature of the beliefs in Orí and human destiny in traditional Yoruba thought has for some time now been controversial. Several metaphysical interpretations have been given by various African philosophers. . . . Some of these interpretations have been in tune with fatalism, predestinationism and hard determinism. Contrary to these philosophical accounts . . . the concepts of Orí and human destiny in traditional Yoruba thought fit very well into the framework of soft determinism. Such a metaphysical interpretation . . . can help in taking care of the inconsistencies and antimonies associated with the earlier metaphysical interpretations of the Yoruba concept of Orí; providing a philosophical justification for punishment and moral responsibility in traditional and contemporary Yoruba society."[1]

Balogun rejects the term *fatalism* and concludes that *soft determinism* is a better way to describe traditional Yoruba beliefs regarding destiny and predestination:

> Determinism is simply the thesis that every event, with respect to the past, present and future, has a cause. It is more of a scientific approach; through it, we can predict the outcome of an event if we know the necessary and sufficient causal conditions. In other words, determinism is the view that everything that occurs in the universe must be the effect of a cause, must be produced by, dependent on, and conditioned by what brought it into existence. Some determinists specify the character of the causes to events. Others leave open

the issue of what kinds and types of things could be the causes of events that must have a cause. However, there are two kinds of determinism: hard and soft determinism. Hard determinism does not allow for freedom, while soft determinism gives room for freedom.[2]

Balogun insists that while orí, specifically the orí-inu (the inner head or, in Jung's terminology, the *collective unconscious*), contains the blueprint of the destiny we agreed to before becoming flesh, the road we take to that destiny or how we achieve that destiny is a matter of free will and human choice. One way to illustrate this: choosing an orí-inu is the cause, and incarnation in the flesh is the effect, and incarnation itself then becomes a cause for us to live and seek out our destiny. And often, osogbo stands in our way.

Balogun defines *orí* as the spiritual head, not the physical head. It should be remembered that the orí is always in touch with one's iporí, our perfect spiritual double that exists in heaven, representing our true, higher self. He makes a surprising point regarding the orí and human achievement:

> Whatever orí does not sanction cannot be given to any person by the orisa (lesser gods) or even by Olódumare (God) himself. Orí is therefore an intermediary between each individual and the orisa (the lesser gods/divinities). The orisa (divinity) will not attend to any request that has not been sanctioned by a man's orí. No orisha (divinity) blesses a man without the consent of his orí.[3]

The interaction of iré and osogbo becomes more complex when seen in light of this statement. No orisha, not even Olódumare, can provide a blessing if one's orí does not agree to that blessing. Likewise, no orisha, not even Olódumare, can cause misfortune to exist in one's life if one's orí does not agree with that misfortune. During the course of a human being's life she will encounter successive misfortunes, events that will either propel her closer to her destiny (because osogbo is a principle that can assist human evolution) or move her further away from her destiny (because osogbo's goal is, ultimately, to crush the human spirit). The orí is integral to whether or not various misfortunes come into our lives; without agreement from the head, osogbo cannot afflict us. Despite this, how a human acts or reacts to osogbo is a matter of free will. If destiny was hardwired into the human experience, there would be no force under heaven that could move a person away from her destiny.

MISFORTUNE AS PART OF THE HUMAN JOURNEY

Living in the world, ayé, is enough to guarantee that at some point everyone must interact with osogbo. Life itself is the cause of blessings and misfortunes, and to live is to guarantee migration between the two extremes. Oba Miguel "Willie" Ramos writes eloquently on this subject: "Not all the blame lies with *ayé* [the physical world] and life," he says. "Human actions and inactions; human decisions, and the exercise of free will—Olódumare's greatest gift to the universe—often provoke the descent of *orún's osogbos*."[4] In short, being human is in itself enough to attract misfortune to one's life. The manner in which humans live call these forces down from heaven into the earthly realm.

Whenever life becomes harsh or when we seem to suffer one affliction after another, Lucumí adherents seek out a diviner to determine what is happening, looking to one of the many oracles we have at our disposal to learn what is going on spiritually, "behind the scenes," so to speak, that is making life so intolerable. Through our oracles—Ifá (accessed by the babalawo), diloggún (accessed by the olorisha), and obi (accessed by the aborisha, olorisha, or babalawo)— we consult with egun (ancestral spirits), the orishas, and Olódumare, asking for guidance on behalf of the person who is consulting. The use of divination brings into play iporí (our true self in heaven) and orí-inu (our inner head) to determine if we are on the path to attaining our destiny in life or if we are far off course. We learn the will of heaven as the oracles are opened and accessed. Controlling these oracles—indeed, controlling even the interaction of iré and osogbo in this world—is the orisha Eleggua.

Ramos writes:

As stressed by . . . Okana [one of the sixteen parent odu of the dilog-
gún], life and human existence are about harmony and balance.
The odu's most common proverbs affirm that for there to be good,
there must be bad. Like the Asian notions of yin and yang, Okana
upholds the basic philosophical and scientific principles that assert
that there is no positive without a negative; no action without a
reaction. These same notions are reflected in the Yoruba conception
of life in orún and ayé. Each plane brings harmony to the other.[5]

Ramos continues in this vein, stating that this world is a mirror,
almost a replica of the spiritual world. However, the mirror is murky
because the material forms are grosser manifestations of heaven's subtle
nature; heaven, in its purity, cannot be replicated throughout ayé, the
material world. He offers the image of a circle divided in half twice,
creating four quarters. Two of those quarters exist in heaven and two of
them are on earth. This results in orún reré, the good heaven in which
we find the orishas and ancestors residing with iré, and orún burukú,
the bad heaven where we find osogbo and other negative entities (including ancestors who lived with bad character while on the earth). In the
end it is all heaven; however, heaven has both a good side and a bad side,
a concept distinct and separate from Judeo-Christian theologies.[6]

Even though humans exist in ayé (the world), and the orishas and
ancestors in orún reré (the good heaven), and the osogbos in orún
burukú (the bad heaven), these realms interact regularly. Mortal creatures make offerings, ebós, to the orishas, and the energy of these offerings spans both realms. Those trying to lead selfless spiritual lives reach
out to orún reré regularly; our rituals of ordination call down the ashé
of heaven into the heads of our postulants, our iyawós. The orishas
cross the gate between heaven and earth on a regular basis. Whenever
a new orisha is washed for an aborisha or an olorisha, a spark of that
spirit comes down to take up residence in the otás and shells of the
newly created shrine. So do the orishas make the great trip from heaven
to occupy the body of their priests, and during a *tambour,* a drum party
dedicated to the orishas, one of our greatest miracles occurs: that of

trance possession. Egun, the spirits of our ancestors, make the same journeys. And the osogbos themselves are not limited to orún burukú. They can and do travel to our world and walk among us. They test us. They plague us. Sometimes they cross into orún reré and influence the orishas' actions, as can be seen from some of the more scandalous patakís told in the oral corpus of odu.

This testing and plaguing is not random; it is mandated by Olódumare and governed by the orisha Eleggúa, also known as Eshu. It is Eleggúa who controls the travel of the osogbos between the worlds. Of Eleggúa's participation in the actions and interactions of humans, orishas, and osogbos, Ramos writes, "Eshu's job [is] to signal out the possible weaknesses in the system [i.e., our world, ayé], which he often does by testing how the reactions on one side of the sphere affect the other side and its residents. Eshu, as agent provocateur, will continuously test all beings, celestial and mundane, to ensure that the weakest links in the system are corrected or eliminated. Undoubtedly, Elegbá [Eleggúa] is the most important orisha in the Yoruba-Lukumi pantheon."[7]

Note Ramos's phrase *to ensure that the weakest links in the system are corrected or eliminated.* This sentiment is echoed by Olófin when he commanded Iré and Osogbo to make ebó (in the olodu Ofún, 10 mouths) so he could determine which of them was the greater of the two. When Osogbo made ebó not once but three times over, Olófin had no choice but to acknowledge that the workings of misfortune would be the greater on earth. Still, he softened that decree by stating to Osogbo, "Although you think all you bring to the world is evil, with your misfortunes will come much good. For it is human nature to seek out blessings and to grow and evolve into something greater. Because of you, civilizations will grow and flourish as they try to banish you back into the shadows; great books will be written and art will be created. The weak will be destroyed, and the strong will become stronger. Each generation will grow into something greater and more powerful because tragedy encourages human nature to grow and persevere, while undeserved blessings make the heart grow weak and lazy. You will be both the catalyst and motivation for my creations to achieve great things."

Osogbo destroys—this is a central truth of its action in nature. However, it only destroys that which is weak. Whether we call osogbo into our lives by our actions, or whether Elegguá unleashes osogbo on us at his whim, it is both a test and a cleansing, and only that which is strong survives. Osogbo, then, becomes a cleansing force in nature. That which does not kill us makes us stronger, as one of Osogbo's functions is to improve and strengthen both the material world and the creatures living in it.

ELEGGUÁ'S ROLE AS ESHU AT THE CROSSROADS

When studying iré, osogbo, and their interactions among humans and orishas, it is important to understand that the gate between heaven and earth is not simply a gate; the gate is Elegguá himself. He is the orisha who creates the divide between heaven and earth. Likewise, Elegguá is the gate that stands between orún burukú and orún. It is he who allows the passage of osogbo into all realms at will. This is a power he obtained in the odu Unle Meji (8-8) in the diloggún:

Olódumare decided that it was time to bestow each orisha with ashé, ensuring their worship and adoration among the humans Obatalá was soon to create. One by one, he began calling the orishas to his throne in heaven.

It was Elegguá who was called first. He went to Olódumare's palace and was grieved when he saw his father, for the lord of all things was old, weary, and drained from the exhaustive work of creation, and now there was more work to do—giving ashé to the orishas. "Olódumare," said Elegguá as he prostrated himself before God, "you are weak. You cannot continue this work alone. Let me help you."

Wearily, Olódumare blessed Elegguá and raised him off the floor. Bending over to offer his blessing was difficult, and Olódumare knew Elegguá's words were true. "I am very tired, son," he agreed. "Creation was no easy task, and now that all things are complete, I still have to watch over the earth and finish what I began. I could use your help. So much remains to be done, and the work ahead is long and exhausting. You could be here for quite some time. Are you sure you wish to help me?"

Elegguá was old himself, not as old as Olódumare, but his once dark locks were tinged with gray and his body was slowly stooping and shrinking with age. "I owe everything to you, Father. I want to help you."

A weary yet grateful smile was Olódumare's answer to Elegguá, and with him at his side he continued to call all the orishas to heaven, one by one, to give them ashé. Elegguá watched everything God used and did, and by watching he grew in wisdom. As each orisha was called, each began the long journey to heaven, and after Olódumare gave ashé, each returned to earth, filled with all the power and grace Olódumare had to give. No one noticed how exhausted God was; no one except Elegguá offered to help.

The dissemination of ashé took sixteen years, and through it all Elegguá was there at God's side. As the last orishas approached Olódumare's throne, so wise had Elegguá become that it was he who administered the ashé while God watched proudly and thankfully. He was able to rest while Elegguá labored.

After the last orisha had come and gone, Olódumare looked at his son; he was exhausted from the work. "Elegguá, you have served me well and you have learned things no other orisha will ever know. Now, it is your turn to have ashé." God then ministered to the old man, and as ashé settled on his head, he became a young child. "You can be young or old as it pleases you, Elegguá." Refreshed, Elegguá embraced Olódumare with youthful vigor, and Olódumare returned the hug.

"I called you first," he said, "and you will always be first, and since you were the last to leave me, you shall also be the last in all things. And because you served me so well, I give you a special task in the world. The road between heaven and earth must be sealed. You will be that seal. Anyone who wishes their prayers to be heard by me must first go through you, and you have the right to demand payment from them before you let them pass. Those who bring gifts to you have my ear; those who come empty-handed you can block as you wish. You were my emissary and helper here, and you will be my helper and emissary on earth as well."

So Elegguá, after sixteen years of serving God, returned to the earth and settled at the crossroads separating heaven and earth.* Those who approached the gates to heaven had to first petition him, and Elegguá, at his whim, would either allow or deny access to heaven. He directs the flow between ayé and orún reré or orún burukú as it pleases him. No mortal dares approach without making ebó, and no orisha, no matter how powerful, can sway Elegguá without a gift. In time he learned that he could control the comings and goings of the osogbos between the worlds, and he let them pass or kept them locked up in orún burukú as it pleased him. This was the beginning of his great ashé in our religion, and how Elegguá amassed great wealth.

Elegguá's role as Eshu at the crossroads is that of an examiner; he creates interactions between humans and orishas, humans and iré, humans and osogbo, orishas and iré, and, finally, orishas and osogbo. There are times he lets the spiritual agents of orún burukú loose on the world, and there are instances when he allows the inhabitants of orún reré (including the blessed ancestors) interact with the material world. He does this so that Olódumare's work can be tested, tried, and refined. His work destroys that which is weak in the world, leaving behind only the strongest of material forms to continue the work of creation. Professor and Ifá priest Kola Abimbola explains:

> Es[h]u . . . is a neutral element . . . neither good nor bad. He is simply the mediator between all the entities and forces on both sides of the right and left divide [of heaven and earth]. To the Yoruba, Es[h]u has the ability to make sacrifices to Olódumare to be unacceptable. This suggests that Eshu can alter or work in favor of any man depending on the consideration given to him. . . . Whenever sacrifices are offered, the portion of Eshu must be set aside.[8]

---

*A special note to Lucumí diviners: the crossroads symbolism in this pataki is for deeper meditation. Please note that crossroads are born in the olodu Owani (11 mouths), and the crossroads is an Eshu-centric concept.

Humans are not the only ones who are subject to the machinations of osogbos; the orishas are plagued by them too. The odu of the diloggún are filled with patakís of the orishas' actions on earth (in mortal incarnations) and in heaven (as spirits), in which they behave in a less-than-stellar manner when under the influence of osogbo. Thus osogbo is more than a mortal affliction; it can be a heavenly one as well. And by studying the stories of an orisha's interaction with osogbos, we learn how to fight them in our own world and how to lessen their effects on our lives.

Although Elegguá is the one who keeps osogbo locked up or sets it free, his influence goes far beyond this. Ramos writes, "This often provocative and misjudged orisha serves as the major promoter of harmony. When the osogbo become restless and manage to break through Eshu's ever-watchful guard to afflict humanity and provoke chaos in the universe, he can remedy the situation. He brings matters into balance by providing the necessary guidance and suggesting the required ebós that are needed to appease the antagonist that has unleashed its onslaught."[9] Elegguá promotes and restores this balance, says Ramos:

When, for a variety of reasons and misbehaviors, human beings incur the wrath of the divine, including Eshu's, he is obliged to provide them with guidance and directions to make amends and atone for their misconduct through ebó or other means. Failure to follow his guidance will only incite his indifference toward the violator, something that could have dire consequences. If Elegbá's [Elegguá's] advice goes ignored, he will simply "step aside," in essence allowing the forces of osogbo, which may include disease and death, to disrupt the violator's life incessantly. Undoubtedly, Eshu-Elegbá keeps balance and harmony.[10]

And by what means does Elegguá keep this balance? This is done through the process of divination. This is why Elegguá's diloggún is most often used by diviners. Even when other orishas' cowries are put on the mat, Elegguá's influence and direction are paramount through the use of his ibó, auxiliary divination tools that involve the client's orí in the session as well.

As a force of nature, Elegguá is the orisha who divides the spiritual world from the material world and keeps humans from crossing that gate while in the flesh; he is also the orisha who allows the spiritual to filter out into the material world at his whim. Ultimately, it is Elegguá who decides when or if iré comes into each person's life, and it is Elegguá who allows the osogbos to travel to our world to test, strengthen, and destroy. Elegguá's influence is paramount, and to understand how Elegguá functions at this crossroads as Eshu, it is important to know the story from the olodu Owani titled "Eshu at the Crossroads."[11]

It was early morning, and Eshu was gulping rum and running through town between drinks, yelling to all who would listen, "There is danger afoot! Take care as you walk. There is danger afoot! Take care as you walk."

Men, women, and children were afraid, and everyone in town walked slowly and carefully. Many chose to stay home, for Eshu was a wise orisha, and when Eshu gave a warning, there was a reason. So slowly and so carefully did they move that nothing got done that morning, and by late afternoon everyone was angry that they had found no danger.

"We've been tricked!" they complained. "There is no danger today! And our day is half gone! That Eshu is nothing but a trickster!" Everyone went about their business, ignoring Eshu and his random warnings.

But there is danger, Eshu thought. Watch this! he told himself.

Thoroughly drunk, Eshu ran to the crossroads. From his small animal-skin bag he pulled out huge gallons of red palm oil, and like a child who spreads finger paint on paper for the sheer joy of making a mess, he smeared the oil on all four branches of both streets. He ran, he jumped, he slid through the oil wildly, all the while drinking more and more rum.

When Eshu was thoroughly sauced, a young man came to the intersection, and when he saw Eshu spinning frantically in the middle of both streets he yelled out to him, "Eshu! Can I cross?"

Eshu stopped mid-spin and looked curiously at the man. In his mind he thought, Is he crazy? The roads are slicked with oil, inches deep! *Instead, he stood there and said, "It is safe to pass, my friend."*

The man took but one step; he fell down and busted his head on the pavement. Covered in oil and blood, he looked at Eshu angrily and without a word crawled back the way he had come.

"I told you there was danger!" Eshu called out, skipping and skating wildly in the oil-slicked streets. He stopped as he saw an old woman walking with a cane. She hailed him: "Young man, I need to cross here, but the road looks dangerous. Will you help an old woman cross the street? Please?"

Eshu smiled warmly at the lady and offered his arm. She held him tightly, and together they crossed the street safely. "Oh, thank you, young man!" she said, holding his hands warmly before walking away.

Eshu stood there and cried. "They told me there was no danger. They were right. I was wrong."

By now, so drunk was Eshu that he saw himself standing in front of himself, and he asked his doppelganger, "Eshu, I heard there was danger in the streets, and the crossroads looks unsafe. May I cross the road safely?"

Eshu said, "I was told that there is no danger today. If there is no danger, it must be safe. Of course you can cross safely!"

Trusting himself, Eshu took a few careful, faltering steps, but the oil was thick and slick, and he fell down, hard. His leg snapped in two, twisting at an unnatural angle.

"That trickster, he lied to me!" Eshu screamed in agonizing pain.

But his anger did not last long. On his broken leg, Eshu danced, and he laughed at Eshu's folly and pain. "The next time I tell you there is danger," he told himself, "I bet you will listen!"

Even though Elegguá, as Eshu, is a trickster and the guardian of the crossroads that separates orún and ayé, heaven and earth, and divides those two realms again into the concepts of reré (decency) and burukú (depravity), he is also the orisha who guides and controls the evolution of humanity. Remember, osogbo is more than misfortune; it is the driving force of evolution in nature, and humans, trying to overcome osogbo, seek to unravel the secrets of life itself.

In our world we simply assume that better technology, more

medicine, and more knowledge can keep life's misfortunes at bay, and we forget that if we do not develop *iwa pele,* good character, no amount of knowledge, learning, or scientific achievement will keep us on the side of iré, blessings. Because we have eledá, a spark of Olódumare buried in the atarí of orí, we know intuitively that for everything we learn about nature and the material world there is more hidden beneath surface appearances. Science, mathematics, physics, astronomy—as we dig deeper into the physical reality of each academic discipline there is always more beyond what we can learn, and the eternal quest for knowledge is itself a spiritual experience. As humans, we want to know, intimately, the deeper workings of Olódumare in the universe.

Unlike many other religions, Lucumí ontology does not include a punitive aspect in the nature of God; instead, God is seen as benevolent, beyond the forces of iré and osogbo, existing in a continual state of grace. While Olódumare seems remote and distant, in truth Olódumare is at the core of everything. If mortal beings learned to access that core, especially now, at a time when our technology outstrips our humanity, chaos and total destruction would be the result. Eshu is also the block between us and perfect attainment, a concept found in the olodu Merindilogún (16 mouths). In that odu we find a patakí about a man who not only wanted to know Olódumare but also wanted to know the essence of his power.

There was once man who wanted to know not only Olódumare but the essence of his ashé and the secret to life itself. He devoted his life to both the study of science and the nature of God. The day came that he found his way to Olódumare himself—he discovered that God existed in him, and with him, and while still in the flesh his emi, his breath, fled his body and found its way to Olódumare's feet. In awe, he put his head to the floor in obeisance, and when Olódumare's hands touched his shoulders, for a moment he knew everything. God embraced the man and held him at arm's length before gently letting him go, and just at that moment all the knowledge he had known in those fleeting moments slipped away like water off a glass pane. A smile—God's smile was so kind and loving that it froze him, and the Great One had but a single question: "Your entire life you've sought me. And now you've found me. Why, my son? Why have you spent your entire life looking for me when the day would come that, in death, you would see me face-to-face?"

"I want to know," the man said, his voice barely a whisper. "I want to know how you did it. How you created me. How you created life."

"That is such a simple thing, barely a mystery at all," said Olódumare. His voice was musical; his laughter filled space. "Bring me back some mud from the earth and I will share the secret with you." For Olódumare denies us nothing when we stand before him, and if all the man wanted was to witness such a simple mystery, God was more than happy to share. It is God's nature to share.

Eshu, however, was not so happy. Eshu watched humans as they grew over the earth; he saw the simplest mysteries create the deepest sorrows, for although humans were intrinsically good, a spark of wickedness existed in each heart, and the osogbos, especially Arayé, were quick to latch onto this in their quest to destroy life. Give a man the secrets of life itself, thought Eshu, and there's no end to what Osogbo can make them do with it.

When the man returned to Olódumare with the mud, God sculpted a human form; it was male, and it was the most perfect sculpture the man had ever seen. "You are surprised?" asked Olódumare. "I am the source of everything in this world. I am the fountain of ashé for even the orishas. It was I who taught Obatalá how to sculpt. It was I who taught Ajala the secrets for carving human heads and destiny. Anything the orishas do I can do, and I can do it with more skill because their ashé comes from mine. But now we must wait. The mud must dry and harden. Once it is done, I will show you how I give life."

Patiently the man waited for the sculpture to dry; he watched as the dark mud lightened in color as the moisture evaporated. The statue shrank, but just a bit, its features becoming stronger and more pronounced as the edges hardened and deepened. Olódumare left to do other things. Unknown to either the human or God, Eshu stood in shadows, watching, waiting for his chance to intercede. When Olódumare was gone Eshu walked in the room and said, "It is time."

"It is time for what?" asked the man. He looked sharply at Eshu. "And who are you?"

"I am Olódumare's helper. I am Eshu. I was the first one created when Olódumare awakened to himself, and I alone saw everything woven in this world by his hands. I am going to help you learn the lesson you seek." Gently, Eshu picked up the statue; it was something sacred, something special, something made by God's own hands. He treated it with the reverence it deserved. "Follow me," he said, walking to the crossroads separating heaven from earth.

When the man awakened in his own body, he saw that Eshu was still with him, the male statue standing beside him. "It is almost dry," said Eshu. "There is a great lesson here for you to learn. I want you to guard this statue; guard it with your life. When it is dry you will understand."

Then Eshu vanished.

The man sat. He waited.

When Olódumare returned to his chamber, he saw only Eshu where once the human and statue had stood. "Eshu?" he asked. "Why are you here? Where is the human? Where is my sculpture?"

"Father," said Eshu, putting his head to the floor in obeisance to Olódumare, "do you not understand the danger of even a single human knowing the secret to creating life?"

"Humans are good," Olódumare said. "With each generation they grow on the earth. They evolve, and they do great things."

"Father," said Eshu as Olódumare lifted him, "humans are good, I'll give you that. But they embody within them all the mysteries of the universe. They seek iré but are touched and tainted by osogbo. Still, you need to remember that their world, ayé, is a foreign land and heaven is their true home. There are secrets that should never be put in that world. The secret to creating life—they're not ready for it. They're not ready for it until they are here, with you, resting eternally at your feet. Remember, there is a reason they forget everything when they leave orún and are reborn through a mother's womb."

As always, Olódumare understood the wisdom in Eshu's words.

They embraced, and Olódumare realized that because of his most trusted helper, things remained as they should be.

Back on earth, the man waited; the statue dried, but it did not move. The man touched it, and it was cold, cold like death; it had no pulse; it had no breath. For a moment he was sad, but the sadness lifted when he realized he had, indeed, discovered a great mystery. By crossing the great divide between heaven and earth in spirit, he learned that heaven really was not that far away. He learned that heaven exists within us and that Olódumare, God, was there as well, at our core. He learned that Olódumare was a kind God, a giving God, a God who wants humans to grow and learn and evolve as they seek the mysteries of the universe. And he realized that Eshu, Olódumare's helper, was a trickster, but because he was a wise man he realized that Eshu did not trick without reason. He knew in his heart that Eshu was the balance of nature, the one orisha who keeps humanity's quest for knowledge in check. Eshu, *the man thought,* intervened when I asked the ultimate question: What is the secret of life? Eshu made sure that I saw part of the answer, but not the entire answer. Perhaps it is not time for me to know the ultimate answers about Olódumare and the nature of life; perhaps evolution is meant to happen slowly and in its own time. *In silence he gazed at the perfectly sculpted form and sighed; it simply was not time for humanity to know the ultimate secrets.*

MISERY AND NECESSITY

Elegguá/Eshu is the orisha to whom we turn when osogbo runs rampant, making life unbearable or, even worse, unlivable. He is the orisha who offers guidance on proper action, ethical behavior, and ebó. Being the mediator at the crossroads between heaven and earth, between orún reré and orún burukú, and between iré and osogbo, Elegguá gives us both freedom and restriction. Consulting him is necessary but tricky, for as Ramos notes, if we seek the orisha's advice but do not put it into action, he steps aside, allowing osogbo to do its work in our lives.[12] Ultimately he is the owner of all the oracles used in Lucumí religion:

Ifá, diloggún, and obi. It is because of this that Elegguá controls everything on the earth and knows everything in heaven. Balogun explains
why: "In the Yoruba cosmological account of creation, Esu is known to
be one of the . . . divinities which had always coexisted with Olódumare
. . . as a minister in the theocratic governance of the universe."[13] Being
the first in creation, he awakened when Olódumare began the task of
creation, and he knows everything. Elegguá knows what is good and
proper for us; Elegguá knows what is bad and inappropriate for us.
Elegguá, as an orisha, is beyond the concepts of iré and osogbo and is
an entity controlling them all. Joseph Omosade Awolalu, a Nigerian
scholar, educator, and writer, says "What is intriguing about Esu is that
he does not discriminate in carrying out errands. . . . He can be used as
an instrument of retaliation, he can create enmity between father and
children or between husband and wife, as he can do between two good
friends. At the same time, he can provide children for the barren or
good bargaining power for market women."[14] Eshu is the balance giving
us goodness; he also creates what Western society knows as evil, but
what we know simply as imbalance. He does all this because he controls
the comings and goings of iré and osogbo in our world.

    If one learns nothing else from this book and these patakís, know
this: Lucumí ontology does not promote a belief in misfortune as retaliation from a punitive God or angry orishas. Instead, as an indigenous
faith, it is based on an ancient but holistic view of nature and natural
law, to wit: Poison the earth, and the poison seeps into the river and
flows to the sea. It finds its way into the food we eat and the water we
drink. Our health crumbles bit by bit, and we accumulate and trans-
mit those poisons to our offspring. We might say that Orishaokó and
Babaluaiye, orishas of the fertile earth, are angry with us and afflicting
us with illness, but in truth we ourselves are the ones who opened the
channels for the sisters Ano and Aro to infiltrate our bodies, and if they
don't kill us, the diseases they bring might make us wish Ikú would come
for us. When we cut down the trees and destroy the plants, the realm of
Osain and Aroni (orishas of the forest who know all the secrets of herbs
and herbal medicine) grows smaller; our divine physician Érínlè loses the

ashé to cure us, and the very plants that Olódumare, in his benevolence, created for us to maintain and restore our health go extinct. Weather patterns change; drought comes; hunger, thirst, and poverty spread in places that were once blessed and had wealth. We say that the orishas are angry and instead of giving us their blessings, iré, they rain down osogbo on our heads. But if we destroy their natural environments, their bodies on earth, how, then, can they come to earth and bless us? Bit by bit we are locking ourselves in a world of tragedy, Eyo, and we give the divine fewer resources with which to restore our world to its former glory. In many ways, each of us is *onise ibi,* a "worker of osogbo" in our world. We create our own misfortunes, even though Olódumare and his emissaries, the orishas, want us to live in a world filled with blessings.

But are we truly lost? Thankfully, in the process of evolution and the creation of iré in our lives we have one orisha who is always on our side, always willing to forgive us for the messes we ourselves create *if we are willing to do our work*—if we are willing to grow, evolve, and work to clean up the osogbos we have set loose (under Eshu's every-watchful eyes) in our world. That orisha is Obatalá, and the secret to our salvation lies, I believe, in the odu Oché Ejioko (5-2) of the diloggún. It is there that the qualities of misery and necessity were born, and even Ikú, the mother of death, helped give us the keys to save ourselves. For if humans ever become extinct, even the osogbos will suffer; they will have no purpose if this world ends. They see their purpose as human affliction and suffering, but Olófin decreed that their true purpose in life is to help us evolve into something greater. Osogbo might be undesirable—no one prays for sickness or death or tragedy to come—but it is through osogbo that we become stronger and greater. It is through osogbo that we realize we have needs, and then we work to fulfill those needs. For in Oché Ejioko the qualities of misery and necessity are born, and it is in the story "Where Misery and Necessity Were Born" that we learn that human suffering at the hands of Osogbo causes us to reach out to the orishas and bring goodness back into our lives.

In the land of Boroboché, the land of excess, there lived a creature named Misery, and he lived in a state of suffering. No one wanted Misery in their lives, and the people of Boroboché rose up against him like an angry mob. Late one night, when Misery was sleeping the tortured sleep of the miserable, they came to his home with their torches and their pitchforks and their machetes. They set fire to his home, and when he tried to flee they followed him to the gates of town, poking him and cutting him down if his step slowed. Misery begged to stay; they forced him to flee. Guards were set up at the village entrance to make sure Misery never returned, for in the land of excess there was no place for unhappiness. Misery's misery doubled that night; he wandered from his home in hunger and despair.

As the sun rose, exhaustion overcame him and he collapsed on the earth; in the dirt and the mud he lay down to rest and think. Through the heat of the day he slept, and when night came he was hungry, thirsty, and sunburned. His misery was doubled yet again, as he had awakened to more discomfort and pain. From the deep shadows of the forest, as if someone had been waiting for him to awaken, there came a voice; it was soft, sweet, and almost seductive. The voice knew his name and said, "Misery, I know the sufferings you felt in the land of Boroboché, the land of excess. Everyone there had more than enough to satisfy their needs, and in that place of indulgence and excess no one shared their prosperity with you. It has been like this all your life. Since you were a child, you have been forced to wander the world from place to place. It does not seem fair."

Misery sat up; he was covered in dried mud. Tears slipped down his face. It was Ikú, the mother of death, who had emerged from the shadows of the forest. Under the light of a full moon, Misery saw her clearly; he recognized her by the scythe she carried. Although he was afraid of Ikú, in his fear he also felt relief. "Is it my time?" he asked. "Is it time for me to die? I welcome you, Ikú, for I cannot bear to suffer another day on this earth."

"I am not here to take you, Misery. I am here to help you." She extended her free hand to him. "Let me help you."

Misery took Ikú's hand; it was cold like ice and yet warm like a mother's embrace. He shivered. Her ashé flowed into him, and for a moment he felt as if his breath was leaving his body. Ikú pulled; her arm was strong, and soon Misery stood on his feet. Hunger made him weak, but strength flowed from Ikú's hand into his body. Never had Misery felt so confused. "Don't worry, my ashé can make you feel weak but it can also make you strong. There is strength in me, strength in death. Now follow me."

Misery wanted to run, but as Ikú walked away, so did the strength she gave him. So instead he followed her, but at what he thought was a safe distance. Just before dawn they arrived at a town known as Maloní Malonún, and when the sun was just breaking the horizon Ikú knocked softly on the door of a hut. It was a humble home that had little more than a bed and a chair inside; this was the home of Necessity, and Ikú made a formal introduction.

"Misery, I would like you to meet my friend, Necessity. And Necessity, this is the man about whom I have spoken many times, Misery. I think the two of you have much in common."

As Ikú stood in the hut's darkest place, Misery and Necessity began to chat. They were guarded at first but soon realized they had more in common than either had known, for in the world, no matter where they went, they were each considered undesirable. For years Necessity had wandered the world, and in each place he went he was eventually driven out. When Misery told Necessity his own story, both men cried, and soon their cries became shrieks and wails. Each man had ashé; alone, their ashé was weak, but when the sorrows of Misery and Necessity fed each other, the ashé became powerful, unbearable.

"Now, cry out for the orisha Obatalá," said Ikú. "Your voices will reach heaven; your ashé is that great. Cry out for Obatalá and plead for him to come."

Their sorrow was so deep that the ashé of their cries shook the very earth on which Maloní Malonún was built. And as the earth rumbled, everyone in town cried out in fear. Darkness descended over Necessity's humble home; fear became terror, and so great was its ashé that Obatalá felt it in heaven. He crossed realms to find out what was happening in the land of Maloní Malonún. When he saw Misery and Necessity embracing each other in sorrow, his heart broke.

Ikú emerged from the shadows. "While you enjoy all that heaven offers and live a blessed life, Obatalá, this is how these mortal creatures must live: in sorrow, in need, in despair so great that their cries cause the very foundation of the earth to shake. How can you live with yourself, Obatalá, when there is so much suffering on the earth? These two men represent everything that is wrong in this world. These two men represent all the shortcomings of your own kind, the orishas. You should be ashamed to have Misery and Necessity alive and walking the earth."

Obatalá wanted to chastise Ikú for her words, but when he opened his mouth he found nothing to say, for she was right. Great sorrow existed in the world, and all of it bore down on these two mortal creatures. He ordered Ikú back into the shadows with a flick of his wrist, and tenderly Obatalá cared for Misery and Necessity. He fed them with the meat of white pigeons and the root of the ñame, and once they were fed he bathed them and dressed them. He did all this in silence, thinking about how to make use of their ashé in the world. And then he spoke:

"The problem here is that you were both born with ashé, but you have lived in the world with no purpose. Now I am going to ease your misery and tend to your needs forever. I am going to give you both a purpose in life. The two of you are to walk through the world together. Necessity, everywhere you go people will realize that they need certain things in life to live, and they will realize that they lack some or all of what they need to live and live well. Misery, you will walk with Necessity, but behind him, and when people realize they do not have all that they need to live and live well, they will be miserable. And then they will go to the diviners to make ebó to obtain what they need and lift misery from their lives. They will turn to us, the orishas, and our worship and wisdom will spread over the earth. People will no longer fight against you and throw you out of each town you go to. Instead, you will make people realize what they need in their lives, and their misery over this will draw people to us. Necessity and Misery—you will be two of the many forces in the world that will help humans evolve spiritually."

And since that day, Necessity and Misery have walked together in the world, and those who are wise do not hate them or fight them; instead, they see them as reasons to go to the diviners and to the orishas. That is why necessity and misery are two of the most important qualities that force us to evolve in the world.

5

Ikú, the Spirit of Death

Death told Life, "I do not care if you die, because it will only make me stronger." To this, Life replied, "While I live, I transcend over you and the necessary heartbreak you bring the world; but for the world to be a world, our dual existence is necessary." For there can be no life without death, and there can be no death without life.

FROM THE OLODU OFÚN (10 MOUTHS)

In each class I teach, and with each olorisha to whom I speak, and even with my own editor for this book, I find that everyone falls in love with the stories about the osogbos, despite their negative characteristics. I think my editor, Laura, summed it up best when she wrote to me that "one of the things that I love about these stories is the inherent contradictory nature of the characters. Osogbo are by nature negative creatures, but they're necessary, too, for motivating us to get our act together and do better next time; and, also, especially in the case of Ikú, for maintaining the balance of nature and releasing us from eternal misery." Everyone notes their deep flaws, the character foibles that make them desperate and dark; yet those who truly read into the stories understand that behind their darkness is a purpose: to help the human

97

race evolve. So it is with Ikú, death. We fear death; we see it as the enemy, and indeed to die an early death, to die before one's time, is a misfortune from which no one recovers. When a mother buries her daughter or a father lays his son to rest, we understand that sometimes life just gets away from us; it hurtles ahead of us, out of control. Yet when things are in balance—when a child buries a parent, because in the normal scheme of things parents are meant to die before their children—we realize that Ikú herself looms ahead somewhere in *our* future; we feel our mortality, the cold chill of the grave, and we do all we can to push death back into the shadows. Perhaps that is why we have come to be a culture that values youth over old age. But that is a philosophical discussion for another book . . .

There are dozens of stories about Ikú, the spirit and the mother of death, but for this volume I had to be selective, picking those that would make my points easily. Of course the "birth" of Ikú into this world is a story that had to be told; we find it buried in the corpus of Ejioko and discover that death exists simply because there is life. The marriage between Ikú and the odu Ejioko is an important one to know as well, for we see that while Ikú is a selfish creature, she is capable of love as well as hate. She, like us, has emotions—flawed though they may be. "Oyá Brings Death to the World" seems to conflict with the initial story of Ikú's birth, but many patakís in the odu contradict one another. Osogbo itself is a contradiction, a paradox in a design that was meant to be perfect and *is* perfect, although from our mortal vantage point its beauty and purpose might not be so easily seen. "How Ikú Overcame the Flies that Plagued Her" shows us her creativity; "Ikú and the Serpent that Was No More" shows how the human spirit, when humans choose to do the right thing, can overcome any adversity.

Of all the stories in this chapter, however, it is "The Death of His Love" that is my favorite, for it shows that Ikú is not all anger and rage; Ikú, as a woman, once knew love and still values love. It shows a softer side to her, one rarely seen in the patakís we know and remember. And it brings out Ikú's greatest character contradiction: that depite the dark work Olódumare gave her to do, she doesn't do it with a cold, evil heart; she does it, simply, because it must be done.

Forever fatal, forever flawed, Iků is both our worst enemy and our best friend.

THE BIRTH OF IKÚ
From the Olodu Ejioko (2)[1]

Evening shadows lengthened as the sun set on the first day; they stretched over the earth beneath a rich black velvet cloth that unrolled from the eastern sky. Soon everything was dark, and animals, heavy-eyed and fatigued, lay down to rest. They slept, lost in dreams.

When the last creeping thing closed its eyes, something else on the earth awakened. As shadows deepened, something umbrous and sinister slipped through; it congealed slowly, rising and taking form: Iků.

At first she was nothing more than a shadow, a whisper in the night air, insignificant and intangible. But the darkness continued to gather itself, becoming solid. It created a body. She looked down at herself and felt her new form with eager hands. Iků was pleased. It was soft but firm; her flesh was smooth and seductive. Wide hips swayed sensually as she relished in her existence. Chills coursed through her body as she felt her full breasts meant for suckling children and tempting men. The color of her skin was darker than the night; she held her hands up to the starlit skies and saw that her own blackness was deeper than the velvet of space. Though she reeked of danger, she was every woman's dream and every man's desire.

She closed her eyes, breathing in deeply, and called more of the darkness to herself; it became solid, whipping and folding over her form until she was wrapped in whole cloth made from the cold night air.

Iků studied the night. Though she could not see far, she knew there was something vast hidden in it. She wanted something that was out there, although she didn't know what that something was, and while she thought about that, her belly rumbled. She craved . . . she didn't know. So for countless hours Iků just stood there and waited to see what would come after the darkness.

Sunrise came, and as Ikú watched the mottled light erupt in a cacophony of colors on the horizon, she knew birth. *This is how all things begin,* she thought. *Like the sunrise. It all begins with birth. Everything comes from darkness, as did I, and erupts fresh and new in the world. But how do all things end?*

Ikú walked through the world, losing herself in its beauty, and after she walked for some time and had crossed over a hill, she spied a herd of animals grazing, feeding off the fresh young grasses. She felt again the emptiness in her stomach, the rumbling that insisted she do something, and there, she realized what she must do: *I must eat.* As the animals themselves were doing, Ikú bent down to graze on the earth; the sweet grasses filled her, but they did not sate her. While she pondered this, she saw other animals in the trees, biting at the colorful fruits in their branches.

This is what I must eat, she thought, *to feel full.* So Ikú walked up to the trees, annoyed when all the animals fled her presence; she reached up into a tree and grabbed some of the brightly colored fruits that hung there. As she bit into them, she was pleased. Sweet juices flooded her mouth, and once again what she ate filled her stomach but did not sate her. Again, she stood there and pondered that mystery.

Ikú could take the emptiness she felt in her stomach no more. Anger flared up within her, and she went on a rampage, eating and gorging herself on every grass, vine, and fruit she could find. The more food she ate, the hungrier she became, and as her hunger grew, so did her anger. It swirled about her like an icy wind, and soon she noticed that everything she touched turned black and withered; it died right there with her touch. Anger left her; sadness came. *This is how all things end,* she realized. *They end with me, in death.*

From deep in the forest she heard a primal, hungry growl, and a painful scream that was cut short; she forgot what she was thinking and ran toward it. She saw a leopard and another fallen animal that she could not recognize, so torn beyond recognition was it, and she watched, amazed, as the leopard's blood-soaked lips and teeth tore again and again into the animal's flesh. Hungry growls turned to purrs of satisfaction, and Ikú thought, *That is what I must eat to feel full.* Ikú felt the cessation of life deep within her being and knew, *This is what I am. I am the bringer of death.* Without a sound, she descended on the leopard; with her hungry touch, it fell dead, and she gorged herself on its flesh, fat, and blood. For the first time her hunger was gone, but still, she wanted more.

Ikú went on a rampage over the earth, gorging herself on its animals until she could hold no more. But nothing sated her hunger, which angered her more. And one by one, she set out to eat every animal that lived, crept, or crawled on the earth, never noticing that for each animal she ate, yet another sprang up somewhere to take its place. All Ikú knew was that the world was her personal buffet; her greed continued to grow, and she continued to eat. But while she gorged herself, Ikú could never really feel full.

So intent had Ikú become on filling herself that she missed the creation of humans. For centuries their race had grown, never knowing disease or death. In the beginning, humans grazed only on the grasses, grains, and fruits given freely by the earth. Ikú felt the death of each of these but paid it no mind; it was no different than the death brought to these things by the animals on which she herself fed. But in time humans learned, as had Death, that the animals were good for food as well. As the first band of hunters killed their first prey, Ikú felt that death, although she had not brought it about. She followed the scent of blood and saw these new two-legged animals feeding on another with four, and wondered who had such power equal to her own.

For years Ikú watched humans evolve, and in time the first of their kind grew weak and died of old age. Death felt this passing, as she had that of the first blade of grass and the first animal formed on earth, and as she tasted the death of the first human she realized that for the first time she was full. Her hunger had finally abated. The meat was sweet and fulfilling, but in time the hunger returned, and Ikú set out to eat her next human.

She fed freely, and great cries were heard over the earth and in heaven. People who had never known death now faced it every day, and Ikú, in greed, slaughtered humans in the prime of their life. She found that the younger humans were the sweetest, their meat the softest and tastiest, and the life of a child was rapturous. Powerless, humans resigned themselves to a fate of continual death and watched as Ikú picked them off one by one.

It was during this time that Ejioko* incarnated among mortals. At first Ejioko saw the wisdom in death, for not even humans could be allowed to propagate and live forever, as they would destroy the earth in a matter of centuries. Yet Ikú was intoxicated by the scent of human flesh and, if allowed, would one day wipe out the whole world. The orishas, as well, were concerned, for all the hard work they had put into the world was being swallowed up by this one being. Ejioko divined and came up with a solution. He marked an ebó of one goat, sacrificed to Eshu (a manifestation of Elegguá), its meat cooked with a thousand small pebbles, and also a rooster for Elegguá, to be sacrificed the following day.

That day, they gathered and sacrificed, and as night fell over the earth, they sat around a fire and cooked the goat's meat with the pebbles. They feasted silently, eating around the stones. The air was thick with their fear as they watched the darkness for any sign of Ikú. Sleep, however, overcame them, and as they sat ringing the fire, one by one they slumbered. Finally, the last human closed his eyes. Ejioko tied Elegguá's rooster close to the fire so it would not escape and would stay warm during the cold night, and then he settled in and waited for the enemy to arrive. But despite wanting to stay awake, he, too, fell into a deep sleep. In the last hours before sunrise, Ikú came; quietly, like a leopard stalking its prey, she crept into the camp, cloaked by darkness. The fire was but a collection of embers, yet it was still hot, and she knelt beside it to warm herself. She took in a deep breath, enjoying the scent of so many sleeping humans crammed into one space.

But something smelled different.

Ikú followed the strange scents; sniffing at the air in short, rapid bursts, she came to Ejioko's side. He looked human, delicious in his

---

*One of the sixteen olodu in the diloggún; it consists of 2 open mouths on the mat.

slumber, but there was something different about his odor. Carefully she touched his face, almost a loving caress, and then she knew. *It's the soul of an immortal trapped in human flesh!* She licked her lips hungrily. *This one will sate my hunger for a long, long time.*

Then Ikú traced the other scent back to the fire. Sitting off to the side was a large pot of stewed goat's meat, still warm and steaming. She looked around at the sleeping humans and saw that each had a gourd of the meat sitting at their side. *So this is what humans eat,* she thought. *They love the goat's flesh, as do I.*

Knowing that Ejioko would fill her so she could eat no more, she decided to feast on the stew first. She took her first bite, and as she bit down something hard in the meat shattered her teeth. She cried out in pain.

What are these animals? she gasped, spitting out a mouthful of tooth fragments and stones into her hands. *They can eat rocks? They are getting stronger! What has this immortal taught them?* It was then that the rooster tied to Elegguá's shrine awoke and felt Ikú's presence, and it crowed in fear. Everyone around the campfire awoke, grabbing their weapons and letting out their own fearful cries. Ikú ran away from the humans that day, afraid of the race that had evolved to eat stones with their own teeth. So afraid was she that she never again lifted her own hands against those who could eat such hard food.

Since that time when Ejioko taught humans how to fight death by making ebó, Ikú has been afraid to feast freely on humans. She can eat only by the graces of the orishas, who say who, when, and where their children on earth may be taken. And those who live by the orishas' will do not suffer untimely death; they see to it that those who make ebó live the full lives granted by Olódumare.

THE MARRIAGE OF IKÚ AND EJIOKO
From the Olodu Ejioko (2)[2]

Ejioko was alone in the forest. It was night, and he warmed himself by the fire he had built. Over the pit roasted the meat from his day's kill;

its juices snapped and sizzled as tongues of flame licked at it. Pleading for food, his stomach rumbled, and in response Ejioko poked at the meat. It was still rare. *Soon,* he thought, eyeing it hungrily.

Later, when his belly was full, Ejioko spread his animal skins on the cool earth and curled up beside the fire. Sleep came quickly.

It was then that Ikú slipped from the shadows and stood silently over Ejioko's sleeping body. For a moment he stirred and it seemed he would awaken. Ikú put her index finger over pursed lips and whispered, "Shhh . . ." Ejioko fell back into a deep, dreamless sleep. This was but one of Ikú's powers, for sleep is but a form of light death, the soul slipping into the world between heaven and earth.

What a beautiful man, she thought, eyeing the thick chest, slim waist, and muscled legs. His arms were toned, defined, and venous from handling the bow and arrow every day. She trembled with desire. *And we are both hunters, he and I,* for Ejioko spent all his days in the thick jungles, tracking game, and she was a huntress whose jungle was all of creation. There was only one animal Ejioko could not hunt: humans. They were her prey exclusively.

"And what a clever man he is," she whispered into the night. For hunt him she had, but Ejioko had the wisdom to make ebó and had thwarted her each time. *Still,* she thought, *if I cannot eat him . . . I can have him another way.* A lustful fire burned in her loins. *One way or another, I will have him inside me.* She smiled a wicked smile and retreated into the shadows.

Ikú thought she was clever each day that she followed Ejioko, but he, ever the hunter, knew he was being hunted. Time and time again he tried to focus his preternatural senses on the thing at his heels, and each time it melted into the forest so quickly he lost track of it. *It's not an animal,* he thought, breathing deeply and trying to take in its scent. *It's not a human either,* he realized, when the air was filled with everything but the smell of humans.

In that moment, Ejioko knew fear.

Slowly, quietly, he lifted an arrow from his quiver and loaded his crossbow. He lifted it to the sky and cried out, "Let this arrow pierce the heart of the evil that follows me!" His muscles tensed and then relaxed as the arrow sailed into the sky.

He ran as fast as he could, following the arrow as it arced and came sailing back down, and at the projectile's end he saw a dark form, waiting. He watched in awe as its hand came in front of its own chest and caught the arrow, just mere inches before it would have sliced through. It was then that he realized he was being followed by Ikú, the one who had tried to kill him. And by daylight he found her most beautiful.

"No one has ever come so close to killing me," she said as Ejioko walked toward her.

"And no one has ever been able to track me so well," he answered.

"We are very much alike. We are hunters, you and I."

"Yes," agreed Ejioko. "We are." Desire flooded him, and he embraced her. They were wed that night.

Ikú and Ejioko spent many years together, in bliss, in love, and making love. But as centuries passed, it became painfully obvious to both of them that they would never have children, for Ikú was the mother of death, not life, and her womb was like that of a dead thing. Despite their love, this was the one thing that, in time, caused Ejioko to seek out the embrace of other women.

Ikú never knew he was cheating on her; Ikú never knew of the children he fathered with his mistresses.

After many years and many affairs, Ejioko found himself in the arms of Nanumé. Of all the women he had known, none made love better than she. When he was with her, the world was timeless, and each night he spent more and more time away from Ikú, and more and more time in Nanumé's arms.

One morning, things went too far. Ejioko awoke, confused, and was shocked when he discovered it was morning. Sunlight had slipped through cracks in the bedroom curtain. *Have I been here all night?* he thought.

He looked at Nanumé and sighed. Her body was youthful, supple, with ample breasts that rose and fell with each breath. He pulled the sheets down just a bit, exposing the narrow curve of her waist.

Below that . . . *I could spend the night in worse places,* Ejioko thought.

Nanumé stirred and woke under Ejioko's lustful eyes. As she moved, a ray of sunlight caught her black skin. In the light, it dazzled like polished onyx. "You're still here," she whispered, her voice tangled in sleep and dreams.

"I couldn't leave if I tried." Ejioko kissed her neck in the soft spot between the collarbones and nibbled at her throat for just a moment. His tongue tasted something rough and sour. He drew back, surprised, and saw a hard, crusty pustule where before he had seen only silky smoothness. "What is this?"

Nanumé brushed her fingertips lightly against her throat, and when she touched the tiny pustule, she drew in a deep breath. "Something must have bit me. A bug, perhaps." She sat up, pulling the sheets to her chin. She inhaled deeply, arching her back and shrugging her shoulders. "I love you so much," she whispered, leaning over to kiss him. Ejioko forgot about the small pustule rising like a grain on Nanumé's skin; Nanumé, however, was worried. *Not again,* she thought. *How many more times must I suffer the family curse?*

Ikú was furious with Ejioko when he came home that morning. "I was lost in the forest," he said. "It was dark, and I was confused."

"Don't lie to me," she wailed like a banshee. "No one in the world knows the forest better than you. You do not get lost."

Ejioko hung his head in shame. "Forgive me," he said. "But I was. I was lost, and all I could think about was getting home to you." His face was sincere, for truly, he was lost—lost in the arms of Nanumé, lost in her embrace. Ikú believed him when she saw the sincerity on his face. Forcefully, he took her into his arms and kissed her. Desire rose in her loins, and for the moment Ikú forgave him. She forgave him all day and all night.

So intense was their lovemaking that Ejioko forgot all about Nanumé. It was as if he knew Ikú for the first time.

It took only a few days before the sores broke out on Ejioko's skin. Soon, Ikú's skin erupted. "Smallpox!" Ikú cried. "We have smallpox." Ejioko healed quickly, with only a few scars hidden in places that most would never see; perhaps it was because Nanumé's love was like a healing ashé and had spared him the full scourge. He never knew.

Ikú's skin became ugly and deformed, and Ejioko never forgave Nanumé for infecting him and, in turn, his wife. He never, ever went back to see her. Nor could he bear to look at the deformed face of Ikú; disease had marred her beauty and turned her into an evil-looking creature.

Nanumé could not forget Ejioko. She was with child—his child. As sores erupted over her body, her belly grew, and her agony was great. So disfigured was she that she did not go out into the world to look for Ejioko; she hid in darkness and waited for the contagion to pass.

He never came. He never knew that she was pregnant with his child.

Nobody came to help Nanumé with the baby's birth: not Ejioko, not the doctors, not the midwives, not even the other orishas. For nine months her flesh ripened with life and was ripped with foul, pus-filled pustules that filled the room with an acrid odor. Her beauty was still there but marred by disease; her womb, full, was stretched and painful as her belly tore around the sores with the added pressure. A contraction came, sharp and earnest; she cried out as wetness poured from between her legs. She screamed, and only the echo of her own voice answered her. There, exhausted, lying on the floor, with consciousness fleeing her like a shadow, she gave one final cry and heard another faint one, not unlike her own. Her child was born out of her misery.

Eventually, the sores on Nanumé's body healed, and as was her ashé, when the sickness had passed she was again young and beautiful. The child born that painful night grew quickly into a toddler, and to ease the loneliness in her heart, the longing for Ejioko, she spent all her days in the fields playing with her. She was walking, and until now had shown none of the family's curse, the scourge of smallpox. Nanumé smiled. *Maybe,* she thought, *it all ends with her . . .*

Unbeknownst to Nanumé, Ikú had been stalking her. Since Ejioko had brought home the rotting disease, she had been an outcast, forced to wander at night and stay in the shadows. Unlike Nanumé, smallpox was not her ashé, and her form remained blighted. Rumors spread in the world, and eventually she knew that Ejioko had slept with Nanumé. She left him and set out to exact revenge on the woman who had dishonored and disfigured her.

Ikú found her in the forest; Ikú watched as she played with her child, her husband's child, and she realized, *This is her source of happiness now that my husband has left her.* Ikú drew herself up to her full height; she blocked out the sun, and a great shadow fell over the girl. Nanumé looked up at the sky; horror melted her beautiful face as she saw Ikú, menacing, so strong that not even the sun dared shine on her. She rose from beneath her tree and ran toward her daughter to protect her. Instinctively she knew that Ikú was about to exact revenge on both her and Ejioko for their adultery. But before she could reach her, the child's step faltered; her body went limp, and the breath left her as she crumpled on the earth, dead. Nanumé collapsed over the child's lifeless body and wept. For years, she wept over the corpse of her child. The pain seemed eternal.

After that, Ikú banished herself from the light of day and crept in the shadows, a horrible figure that brought fear and despair to those who saw her. In anger, her three sisters, Arayé, Ano, and Aro, rose up and swore to destroy Ejioko and all his children on earth. Their sole purpose became vengeance, and they sought to destroy any good that Ejioko brought to the world.

But before they could do that, they had to destroy his iré.

OYÁ BRINGS DEATH TO THE WORLD
From the Olodu Osá (9)

There was no death in the world, and because of this everyone suffered.

Great cries rose to heaven from the mouths of the elderly who lay weak and untended in their beds. The voices of those younger rose to heaven as well, their own bellies swollen and bursting from hunger. Mothers suckled their emaciated children with dry, hanging breasts, and toddlers no longer toddled, insead lying exhausted under the shade of trees. Silence hung over village streets once filled with the playful screams of children and the sounds of merchants hawking their wares. Priests and priestesses no longer made ebó to the orishas; instead, they offered only prayers and incense, and soon even the orishas in heaven felt hunger pangs. It was Oyá who first felt the world's need; her priesthood was small on earth and she was the first to feel hunger. With pain in her belly, she went to complain to Olófin. Her stomach hurt all the way to his home.

Once Olófin's guards let her inside the front doors, she weakly walked to his chambers and found him sitting on his great throne, thinking. She took a deep breath and made a sigh; he looked up and she walked to him. "Father," she said, putting her head to the floor in obeisance, "the world suffers. Humans outnumber the world's ability to feed them, yet more babies are born into it every day. The oldest of all the people lie weak and helpless in their beds, and no one has the strength to help them. We ourselves are suffering, for our priests and priestesses no longer offer us ebó. What can we do?"

Olófin looked down on Oyá as she spoke; she lay on her right side, one fist tucked against her head while the other arm was perched on her left waist. He saw that she looked frail from hunger. Gently he bent over to touch her shoulders, blessing her as he bid her to rise.

"I've known this day would come," said Olófin. "For when the world was born, it was not meant to be like this."

"Like what?" Oyá asked. "How was the world supposed to be?"

Olófin sat back in his great chair, and Oyá, gently, sat before him on the floor, her legs tucked beside her gracefully. *Even in her suffering,* thought Olófin, *my daughter looks like a queen.* "When the world began, Oyá, it was not meant to hold an infinite number of people. Oh no, it was meant to hold only a limited number of people. And when their time was up they were to cross back into heaven while a new group of humans came down to take their place."

"I remember how the world once was," said Oyá, her voice soft as she remembered. "There was a gate that humans could cross at will. They were perfect then, spiritual beings born in heaven before traveling to earth."

"Yes," said Olófin. "But the day came that one couple noticed the animals copulating. It was the olodu Odí who taught them that trick. But the animals were supposed to multiply. On earth, material beings had material appetites. They needed to eat meat, roots, vegetables, and fruits to survive, at least while down there. It is how their bodies obtain their energy, the ashé to live. But up here ashé is exchanged freely among everyone and there is no need to eat. So animals were given the power of procreation to make sure that not only could they eat, but that humans could eat as well."

Her eyes narrowed. "And this couple changed things, I assume?"

"Oh yes, they did. There was a time when the gates between the worlds were open wide and we crossed as easily as passing from room to room in our own homes. When the earth was new and the first generation walked on her face, no great chasm divided heaven and earth. The first creations lived in both worlds freely, and the path between the two was unguarded. Heaven was home and the earth was the marketplace, and those with time to travel could walk between the two freely."

"But," continued Olófin, "this young couple, they thought, *How powerful are the plants and animals—they can create life from their bodies and we cannot.* They wanted to be powerful like the animals, so they came and petitioned me for this ashé."

"And of course you refused it?"

"On the contrary—I accepted it. I allowed them the power to conceive and have one child on the earth. I told them this child would be born weak and illiterate, and as it grew, it would need to learn things, including its culture and religion. The parents agreed to be its teacher, for there were no teachers in those days. Everyone knew everything. There was one catch to it all, and to this they agreed: since it was a child of flesh born from flesh in the material world, I told them it was not perfect as were they. This one child would not have the ashé to cross the gate and walk into heaven of his own free will. He would be forever bound in flesh and bound to the material world."

Olófin was silent. Oyá stared at him, her eyes narrowed. "And they agreed?" He only nodded his head yes. noddedAnd you trusted them? They were humans!"

"But they, because of how they were made, were perfect humans. I had no reason to not trust them. And conceive a child they did. A child who grew into a man that disbelieved in the orishas and heaven but was open to the possibility of their existence. He set out to find this gate on his own. And it wasn't hard, since he grew up with all the old tales, as he called them. For truly he thought they were tales and not truths. It took many days and many nights, but finally he did find the gate to heaven. And he took a single, fleeting step on the path."

"No!" Her voice rumbled through heaven like thunder. "Tell me he did not!"

"But he did." Olófin's hands hung loosely at his sides. His face was forlorn.

"And . . . how did you fix this, Olófin?"

"There was no fixing it. The natural laws had been broken, and the gate slammed shut. There was no way for humans to descend into the world, nor was there a way for them to leave the world. Trapped there, alone, Odí taught all the humans the mysteries of sex, pleasure, and conception. Soon everyone was doing it."

"And having babies." Oyá shook. "And now look at the mess they've created. We all suffer because of their lack of foresight. This must be fixed." Again, lightning flashed in her eyes and thunder rumbled through the palace. "What must I do to help make this right, Olófin?"

"There is a solution, Oyá. You must take Iků into the world with you, for life cannot continue unchecked. One human at a time, Iků will sweep the land, taking the oldest, the weakest, those among them who are suffering the most. Those who are left will be able to recover and rebuild, and with death in the world it will be all but impossible for them to overpopulate again."

"Me? Take Iků into the world? Bring death on all the innocents on the earth, even the first race that walked its face? I cannot! They will abhor me! They will see me as something vile! They will turn away from my worship."

"They will do no such thing," said Olófin. "In the end, they will still love you, for the balance will be restored."

"I cannot." She hung her head low. "I cannot do what you ask." With her face in her hands, Oyá ran from Olófin's sight.

Silence—there was only silence as Oyá's sobs became softer, receding as she put distance between herself and Olófin. He breathed softly, the rising and falling of his chest exaggerated with his pain. *There is,* he thought, *no other way. Unless the earth is destroyed, there must be death in the world.* Olófin bit his lip with resolve. "Babaluaiye!" he called out. "Babaluaiye, are you still here?"

From a side room the old man hobbled in on a crutch. He tried to put his head to the floor in obeisance to Olófin, but Olófin stopped him from going down by reaching out and embracing him instead. "I am at your service, Father," was all he said.

"It is time," said Olófin. "It is time for you to take Aro into the world with you."

"But Aro is constant torment," said the old man, wavering on his crutch. "There will be no escape for those on the earth. It is cut off from us. They cannot cross; they cannot come home to be healed, to receive new bodies. Without Ikú in the world, those whom Aro touches will be in eternal torment. Is not the earth burdened enough?"

"There is more to my plan, Babaluaiye. There is more to the design of Olódumare than a world of torment. Have faith, at least in him."

By nightfall, Babaluaiye had begun the descent to earth with Aro as his companion. For seven days and seven nights they made their way through the bush that separated the two worlds. When Aro was let loose on the world, she was a hungry, greedy specter; she found the weakest of the humans first, the elderly who already lay in bed unable to stand. Even greater cries rose up from the earth.

From where she hid, Oyá cried. The misery of her people doubled by the day.

Oyá could not bear their cries, the misery of the humans afflicted by Aro. Her constant torment made them wish for death, call for death, pray for death, but Ikú was not yet in the world. She was locked up in heaven with no way to cross. For days Oyá hid, listening to their pleas, and when she could take it no more she walked, cloaked, through the villages and towns that humans had created for themselves. The stench of sickness and decay was everywhere. Even the young wished that the oldest and sickest of their people would die. Finally, when she could no longer bear their pain, Oyá screamed to heaven in a great voice that split the sky with fire and thunder, "I will do as you ask, Olófin! I will bring Ikú down into the world! These people suffer, and I can bear their suffering no more!"

She heard Olófin's voice inside her head, a gentle whisper: "There is wisdom in this, Oyá. With Ikú, they will cross back into heaven, but because they know the mysteries of conception and birth, the human womb will be the new gate through which these ancient souls will return. There will again be balance in the world. Things will become what they should have been."

Oyá cried; her tears fell on the earth like rain as a great storm swept the land. Darkness came, and Ikú came with that darkness, the darkness created by Oyá's own sorrow. For days the storm lashed the earth, and thousands of souls were ripped away by Ikú's strength. As the storm weakened and turned to gentle rain, the number of deaths declined. In time, death was balanced by birth, and birth was balanced by death, and everyone saw the wisdom in this.

Oyá became the queen who controlled the gate between life and death for material beings. And instead of being feared or hated, she became revered and worshipped as such. Never again did she question Olófin's wisdom or Olódumare's design for the world.

HOW IKÚ OVERCAME THE FLIES THAT PLAGUED HER

From the Odu Oché Ejioko (5-2)

A plague of flies surrounded Ikú. There was nothing she could do to get rid of them.

She stalked the forest in search of prey—an animal here, a bird there—and when the creature succumbed to her fatal touch, the flies descended in a swarm, a buzzing mass that devoured the corpse. They were no fools, the flies; they learned that if they followed Ikú everywhere she walked, soon she would kill another creature and they would feed well again.

Ikú had no peace; Ikú was not happy.

One day she passed the foothills of a mountain where there were thousands of spiders living, spiders who spun webs in the branches of the trees. She saw the dried bodies of bugs and flies caught in their sticky webs, and Ikú, being no fool, had an idea. She waited until nightfall, when the buzzing flies went to sleep in the grasses, and then, quietly, she approached the spiders.

They were afraid when they saw her, but before they could hide she called out, "I bear you no ill will. I want to make a pact with you."

"And what might that pact be?" asked the bravest of the spiders. Ikú, as mortal beings had learned, was not to be trusted.

"The flies have learned that wherever I walk, soon there will be death. And the corpse of the dead feeds them well. So they follow me. They plague me with their constant buzzing. I am tormented and cannot escape them. Thousands of flies buzz around my head each day waiting for a meal. But if I were to kill most of my prey here, where you live, and if you were to spin your webs over and near their bodies, soon the flies would be dead themselves, and you, my sweet spider, would feed well yourself. All of your family would."

"But then you would have us following you in your travels as well," said the spider.

"I would rather be followed by a thousand silent spiders than a single buzzing fly," said Ikú.

All the spiders listened to Ikú's words. One by one they came out of hiding, and soon they spoke among themselves about her offer. Finally, the bravest of the spiders spoke up again. "We accept your pact. As you feed in our foothills, we will spin webs over the dead bodies of your prey. We will help you rid yourself of the flies that plague you."

The next morning the flies awoke, and as always, they began to follow and buzz around Ikú. And Ikú, as was her nature, began to kill the birds and animals of the forest. And the spiders, as agreed, began to spin their webs near the carcasses of the animals. Soon the flies learned that to follow Death was to find death themselves, and they began to leave Ikú alone.

And that is how Ikú rid herself of the flies that plagued her.

IKÚ AND THE SERPENT THAT WAS NO MORE
From the Odu Ofún Meji (10-10)

It ends now, thought the king of Ayashenilu.

He was alone in his chambers, dark drapes pulled tightly so no light entered. Pacing the floor, his feet kicking up dust, he held his head in his hands as he walked; his breathing was fast and shallow and he shook. "It was all so simple in my father's day," he whispered to the dust that floated in the razor-sharp slice of light that had forced its way between the drapes. "Each month, he offered one child to Ikú to spare our village from disease and death. Everything was so simple then."

Now things weren't as simple anymore. His father was dead, and after the funeral he had been installed as king, the monarch's only heir. *How can we live with such superstition?* he asked himself. And then he answered: *We can't.* His father's morals were outworn and outdated.

That night, the full moon would rise over the hills, casting its pale glow over the village. That night, Ikú would slip through the shadows of the village looking for her sacrifice. "She won't find it, not from my hands," he said. His voice was strong, unshaken. "No child will I offer under my reign."

When word went out, the town issued a collective sigh of relief. Still, they were afraid. Wasn't it better to send one so young and unwilling to his death instead of watching untold numbers die?

No one knew the answer. No one dared defy the king.

That night, a great bonfire was lit in the village square to fend off the darkness—lit in the same place where each month for untold years a single child was tied to a pole. It was as much a statement as a warning from the town—there would be no more lives offered willingly to Ikú, the spirit of death. No more innocence offered or taken randomly, no more feeding a spirit whose only reward was to let everyone else live out their natural lives. So tonight, there was no child tied to the stake. Instead there was only fire, its yellow flames licking the night hungrily as shadows danced beyond its reach.

Ikú came. She came while everyone slept; they were confident that the fire would scare her away.

She slipped through the village, umbrous and sinister, sniffing the brisk night air. She slipped to the center of town where, with each full moon, one child lay sleeping under the full moon's light, tied securely to a pole by its feet. She never understood why the children slept, why they never understood the danger they were in. Innocence—it consumed her with its possibilities. Each time she came, she would stand over the child, feeling the life that lay before her, the unrealized potential youth held, and then she would lie next to it, embrace it, and take it into herself. Thousands of children had she taken like this, the life of each one settling in her belly before it was snuffed out, the soul having fled beyond her reach.

For just a moment, she felt that life move within her, reaching and stretching her belly, and her hands would flutter down and feel that movement. A child—all she wanted was a child of her own, but death could not give life. When the soul fled each time, she felt emptier than before.

A child. All she wanted was a child of her own.

Tonight, there was no child. There was only fire, and Ikú screamed. Everyone in town woke up, and for the first time everyone was afraid.

Ikú declared war on the town of Ayashenilu.

It began with the dark of the moon. At the edge of the village, Ikú reached up to the sky and stretched, her body elongating and her limbs fusing into one long tube. She grew and stretched, grew and stretched, grew and stretched. And then she fell back on herself in coils. Slowly, silently, she slithered through the town, a serpent of mythic proportions. With darkness as her cover, she worked her way through one house after another, sucking down entire families with her great jaws before she was sated.

She would do this each night until the first pale crescent moon rose, its waning silver light dissolving her disguise like smoke. One night, she was sucking in a palace guard when the moon rose, and he screamed in pain until her smoky jaws could no longer hold him. He lay on the ground in terror.

Word spread: Iků was angry, and her anger took the form of a *pitón,* an evil serpent.

Even the king felt fear.

One morning, the king's advisors gathered around him. "This plan is no good!" said one of the youngest in his court. "We sacrifice one life a month to save dozens, perhaps a hundred. If Iků returns each moonless night to have her revenge, within months none of us will be left alive!"

The king paced. It seemed that all he did lately was pace, his feet pushing his mind forward to think, to plan. "We are not in the dark ages!" he said, turning to face his advisors. "We should not make offerings to the osogbos to placate them; we make offerings to the orishas to overcome the osogbos. Since when did everyone in our kingdom decide that sacrifice to Iků was wise?" Everyone went silent. "This," he said, striking his left hand with his right fist, "this is why we are so far removed from the other kingdoms—for our barbaric ways. We should not send children to their death. We should not sacrifice innocence so that the old among us can live a few more years."

"What else can we do?" the young man asked.

There was a soft voice from the back of the room, almost a whisper, so shrouded in age was it. "We should consult the orishas and make ebó, a real ebó," it said. The crowd in the king's chamber parted, and, shaking, an old man walked to the front. "We should cast the diloggún on the mat and see what the orishas can do to save us."

"And who are you, ancient father?" asked the king.

"I am Ofún," he whispered. "I was there when your father seceded from the kingdom. I was there, and I warned him of the evil he was about to bring to us. And I was there when he tied his first child, your brother, to the great beam that was pounded in the earth at the center of town. I was there, and I begged him not to do it."

"I have a brother?" The king's mouth fell open. The room was silent.

"You *had* a brother," Ofún corrected. "Ikú took him when he was quite young."

A quick flick of his hand in the air, "Leave us!" the king commanded the rest of the advisors.

The room was empty save Ofún and the young ruler.

Ofún spread his mat on the floor and sat with his back to the wall. He invited the young king to do the same. "What is this?" the king asked the old man.

"Divination," said Ofún. "An art all but lost here it seems."

"What happened here? In this town?" he asked.

"I was young when it all began," said Ofún. "Young, about your age, I was. I was here when your father and his wife had their first child. And then the plagues came." Ofún sighed, holding sixteen of the twenty-one cowries in his left hand. "Your brother was barely a toddler, still holding on to chairs and tables when he stood, his milk teeth barely cut, and your mother was heavy again with child. With you. When the first people got sick no one paid much mind. But when they started to die, one by one, and the sickness continued to spread, that's when everyone took notice. And everyone came to your father looking for answers."

"What did he do?" the king asked.

"There wasn't much he could do. He sent me out to tend the sick and the dying. I was able to save a few. But I'm only one man, and one doctor among the hundreds who were slowly falling ill? Well, it was a losing battle," Ofún sighed. "I wanted to divine. I wanted to make ebó. But your father, he had little faith in anything outside of himself. And when his wife, your mother, caught the plague and died, he was beside himself with grief. To lose the love of your life is a tragedy, but to lose the love of your life and your unborn child—that was worse."

"So your father was sitting by your mother's bedside, and I was trying, in vain, to heal her. I had the ashé to fight death, to save people, but I saw the candle burning at her feet and I knew there was nothing I could do. It was late when Ikú came to collect her soul, and the soul of her unborn child, you. Until that day no one could see her but me, but somehow your father saw her. Maybe it was because I was there and Ikú herself was my godmother. Maybe it was his grief and his love. But Ikú was moved by it, and she offered your father a deal."

"A deal?"

"Your brother's life in exchange for your mother's and that of her unborn son, you. I warned your father not to take it. I told him, 'Sir, it is her time.' But he wouldn't listen. And your father was a man of duty. Hundreds of villagers were ill, many of them dying, and being a smart man, although misguided at times, he asked Ikú, 'What of the others in the village? How can I save them?'

"'A pact,' Ikú had said. 'You would need to make a pact with me.'

"'And what would that pact be?' asked your father.

"'One young child every month with the rising of the full moon. Twelve children a year to save the lives of hundreds in your village.'

"Your father grew silent and buried his head in your mother's breast, holding her hands tight with his. 'Time grows scarce,' Ikú had said. 'Soon, with or without me, your wife will die. Make your choice.' And while I protested, your father made his choice. He offered your brother in exchange for you and your mother. And he agreed to send one child to its death in the middle of the town square every month for the rest of his reign as long as the lives of his villagers were spared. Your brother died that night. The plague lifted from the village. You were born, and no one died an early death. As long as your father was in power and kept the pact, people here have lived to an old age and have died peacefully, in their sleep. But you, my king, you have changed all that by your refusal to honor the pact. And now we must look for another way."

Ofún rolled the cowries out on the mat. "This is what we are going to do. We are going to make ebó. You will need a sturdy cane and a pigeon. You will need to feed Elegguá a rooster, smoked fish, jutía, and red palm oil."

"What do I do with the pigeon?" the king asked.

"Tonight, tie it to the pole and wait in the shadows with the cane in your hands. You will be safe from Ikú, and once she arrives you will have your chance and will know what to do."

The king did as he was told. Again, at night, Ikú arrived as a great serpent. The king was resting with his eyes closed in the shadows when the pigeon, tied to the pole, woke up to warn him. Ikú, not wanting the young monarch to wake up, rose up against the pigeon and tried to swallow it, but the great pole was caught in her mouth and she could neither swallow nor vomit it out.

And then the king rose up with his cane. He began to beat Ikú on the head until the form of the pitón fell down, dead itself, and Ikú flew out into the night, no more than a specter, a shadow.

She could no longer take the form of the pitón, and Elegguá made sure that she would never be able to return to that town again unless Olódumare decided that it was, indeed, someone's time to die.

The king of Ayashenilu returned to the way of the orishas, and in his kingdom no one ever again made pacts with the osogbos.

WHY THE IDÉ OF ORÚNMILA WARDS OFF DEATH

From the Odu Unle Owani (8-11)

Ikú had a voracious appetite.

Nothing sated her hunger, and every five days she went through the world gorging herself on whatever was in her path. Fathers wailed, mothers cried, children ran, and elders sighed. Everyone resigned themselves to a life of being little more than food for the greedy spirit of death.

Orúnmila was angry and he divined. He marked ebó with kola nuts and strong liquor, and he gave Eshu a wide array of meats and fruits. He put everything outside his front door and went to bed, assured that Ikú's defeat was imminent.

That morning, he found Eshu outside his front door, eating greedily. "Eshu," Orúnmila said, "I made ebó to you for help. Ikú has gone wild and eats everyone she can find. I am afraid that if she is not stopped she will destroy every human being until they are all gone."

"Even worse," said Elegguá, "you yourself are human now. She will feast on you if you are not careful."

Orúnmila shuddered. He had no intention of being food, at least not yet. "Can you help me?"

"Of course I can help you. I can do anything. But you need to cook more food, Orúnmila. And do it quickly, and bring it here to me. Because today I am afraid that Ikú will come for you and all your babalawos."

Orúnmila spent his morning slaving over a stove. He seasoned and cooked every type of meat he had, putting it in a jícara before serving it to Eshu. He called to his babalawos to bring more meats, and they did as he asked. Eshu tasted everything Orúnmila cooked and set the rest on the road leading to Orúnmila's front door. When the sun hung high in the afternoon sky and the last bit of food Orúnmila had in his home had been cooked, Elegguá told him, "Go back inside and hide. Let me do the rest."

No sooner was Orúnmila safely tucked away with his babalawos than Ikú came down the road leading to Orúnmila's house; she walked toward the front door, sniffing the air. Hungrily, she emptied the contents of each jícara into her mouth and howled in anger when its contents only teased her appetite. Nothing sated her.

"Ikú," said Elegguá, "what is wrong with you?"

"I am hungry," she screamed, pulling at her hair in anger. "Nothing I eat fills me. The more I eat, the more I want. I will eat this entire world if need be to feel full."

"Sit here with me and eat," said Eshu. "I have plenty of food left."

"No, Eshu, I have eaten everything laid out on this path. Nothing filled me. I am going to eat Orúnmila, and when I am done with him I am going to eat all his babalawos. Then, maybe, I will be full."

"You ate everything in the jícaras and still you are not full?"

"I am hungry," she roared.

"All that food you ate and still you want to eat Orúnmila and his children?"

"Yes!" she cried.

"What an evil creature you are," said Elegguá, "to want to do that."

"Evil?" she hissed. "I only do what Olódumare has charged me to do."

"Yes, but Orúnmila himself prepared all those tasty dishes from the meats of all the sacrifices his babalawos offered him, and even after such kindness you want to eat them all? Olódumare might have something to say to you about that!"

Ikú froze, her face twisted in anger and surprise.

"You cannot eat someone who served you," Eshu said. "I will go immediately to Olódumare and tell him how evil you have become. I'd be very afraid if I were you, for although you are immortal, Olódumare's powers far outweigh your own. God might not be able to remove and destroy death in the mortal world, but he can make you wish you were dead."

"That man Orúnmila tricked me!" she screamed.

"No, he didn't trick you. He divined. He made ebó. And now that you accepted his kindness, you can feast neither on him nor on his children, at least not until Olódumare himself says it is their time to die."

In anger, Ikú turned and started to flee. "By the way, Ikú," Elegguá called out, "people wearing green and yellow bracelets on their left wrists are Orúnmila's children. Those are the ones you cannot eat."

That same day, humans all over the world put on the idé (bracelet) of Orúnmila, and Ikú's gluttonous hunger remained unsated. She was a miserable creature, crying in despair.

Since that day, Orúnmila's children and his babalawos have worn the green and yellow idé on their left wrists, and when Ikú seeks to feed on those, she checks with Olódumare to see if it is their time. Only if Olódumare gives his consent can she take one who wears his bracelet.

And Ikú remains hungry.

THE DEATH OF HIS LOVE
From the Olodu Osá (9)[3]

Death took her one day, without warning. She was young and beautiful when she died.

The man sat on his bed, mourning. He was dirty, unwashed, as were his clothes and his sheets. His hair was knotted, his beard uneven, and his eyes reddened. He tried to cry, but the tears wouldn't come; his orbs felt dry and gritty in their sockets.

"She was the only woman I've ever loved," he whispered. No one answered.

"She was the only woman I've ever loved!" he screamed, pounding his chest with his fists.

There was only silence.

He sat there hugging himself, unmoving, until he admitted, "She never knew how much I loved her." His lips trembled and his body shook violently. "Now, she'll never know I loved her at all."

That was the truth.

For the man loved this one woman with all his heart, but he never told her how he felt. They were neighbors, having lived in the same neighborhood all their lives. When they were young, they had played together, but time had soured their childhood ties and they grew up as strangers. She was his longing, his heart's desire; to her he was just an anonymous face on the street.

Still, he had always loved her.

That day was her funeral, and the man cleaned himself up as best he could. He shaded his reddened eyes with dark glasses and hung at the back of the crowd during her service. After the ceremony was over, after the pallbearers had lowered her casket into the ground, and after everyone had peered into the hole for one final good-bye, he stayed behind, watching the gravediggers shovel the dirt back into the hole.

He stayed behind and kept vigil that day and all night. When the moon slipped below the horizon, leaving only the useless light of stars, he sat by her grave and cried. Nobody heard him.

Ikú, however, heard him.

Ikú came to him.

He froze as she appeared. At first, she was nothing more than a deeper blackness within the darkness, a curious splotch in the night that could have been nothing more than his eyes blurring with tears. But the wind shifted, the leaves rustled, and something took shape in the air. A solid form, not a dream, Ikú towered above him, a nightmarish statue. In one hand was her scythe, and the other reached out to touch him as he knelt, trembling beside his beloved's grave. Her thin hand rested on his shoulder.

He found her touch curiously soothing, like warm soup on a cold, rainy day. He lifted his shoulder and rubbed the side of his head on the back of her hand for comfort. "So this is how it ends?" he asked, not expecting an answer.

"No, this is not how it ends." She cupped his chin with her cool palm, lifting his face to look at him. Where her face should have been, he saw only emptiness in her hood. "I have not come to take you. It is not your time."

He looked at her with narrowed eyes. "Have you come to punish me for intruding on your land?" He shuddered. He knew it was taboo to be in a graveyard after dark.

"No. I have not come to punish you." She rubbed his lower eyelid with her thumb gently and caught a tear spilling from its edge. She looked at it on her black skin as though it was a brilliant diamond and gazed at it for quite some time.

After a strained silence, he asked, "Then why have you come?" There was no more fear, only sadness and curiosity.

"Your tears for this woman have moved me. Your sadness is deep, and your love pure. It has been an eternity since I have felt sorrow and pining this intense."

"She never knew that I loved her." Finally, the tears came freely.

"Oh, but she does. She hears you as I hear you. The dead are always around us. Even if we can't see them, they are there." Ikú looked up at the stars, and the man followed her gaze with his own eyes. *Such beauty,* he thought, *and totally useless,* he felt in his despair.

Ikú shook her head in disagreement as if she heard his thoughts. "No. Beauty is never useless. Futile and fleeting, yes, but it is never useless. Did you know there is a star for every soul that has ever lived on the earth?" she asked. "And just as they burn with a cold, lonely light, every soul that has ever lived has felt loneliness at some time. I, however, feel alone every day that I exist."

The stars didn't seem so useless to the man anymore.

"I want you to go home. What happens in a graveyard is not for mortal eyes. But tomorrow night, at midnight, I want you to come back. I will thin the veil just a bit and let you see your beloved one last time, so you may have closure."

The man fell at Ikú's feet. He meant to kiss them and thank her, but she melted into the night like so much black smoke. She was gone, and as she had told him, he went home.

He came back the next night. Just before midnight, he was there at her graveside, only instead of hiding in darkness he was surrounded by dozens of lit candles. In his arms he held a simple bouquet of roses, and he waited, standing, for his beloved to appear.

"Why are you here?" a voice asked, almost a whisper. A chilly wind blew through the graveyard, and all the candles went out. There was moonlight, and it illuminated the cemetery just enough for the man to see a faint figure standing before him. "I am happy among the dead. Are you not happy among the living?" Her form became stronger, and he saw that it was his one true love.

"I love you!" was all he could say, his heart beating wildly in his chest. He held out the roses to her, trembling with fear and desire, and although she lifted her arms to take them, they fell through her ghostly grip and rested on her grave.

She smiled, but faintly. "The flowers are beautiful, and I thank you for them, but . . . I do not love you." His wildly beating heart stopped so quickly that the man thought that he, too, was dead. They stood in silence for what seemed an eternity. When he continued to say nothing, the woman spoke again. "I did not love you when I was alive, and now that I am dead with no relatives to remember my name, all I want is rest and peace. But your devotion to me is so pure and gives me such light in the next world that I want to thank you for the love you offer."

She paused for just a moment, and still the man said nothing. He looked at the ground, crushed. With narrowed eyes and pursed lips, she told him, "My father was a very wealthy man. He didn't trust banks or vaults, and he worried that if we stored our wealth in our house, thieves would murder us in our sleep and steal what they could carry away in the night. So he hid everything far away from our home. In the ground he buried many treasures worth more than the richest king's coffers. Before he died he told me where our family's treasures rested, and from time to time I raided those to provide for my needs. But since my needs were simple, and because I died so young, I never took much. And in death, I have no need of treasure. I give these to you, if you will live your life and leave me to my death."

His heart was broken, but he listened carefully as the spirit told him where the treasure was hidden. With all her secrets revealed and no more to say, her form dissolved. She was gone.

And what happened to the man?

Time heals all wounds, at least those that don't kill us, and one by one he unearthed all the contents of the treasure the woman's spirit had left to him. No one knows if he ever found love, but everyone can assume he lived as a very wealthy man. If he had nothing else, he had that.

6

Arayé, the Spirit of Wickedness

When one sees a wicked man and mistakes him for a good man, it is then that one talks into a leaking basket.

FROM THE OLODU OWANI (11 MOUTHS)

"Arayé is a bitch," I tell my students, and they recoil when I refer to her as such, but what more can be said about an osogbo that not only embodies all the wickedness in the world but also infects the human heart, pushing us to enact both catastrophic crimes against humanity and simple unkindnesses on our fellow humans? As with Ikú, there are dozens of stories I could have published about this complex creature, the senior of all the osogbos, but I chose ones that brought out the magnitude of misfortune she brings.

"The War of Arayé and the Osogbos" sets the tone for this collection. It shows not only her hatred of humanity, but how one simple child of Ano, Lunacy, infected her and caused great destruction among her own kind. In the end, Arayé became the enemy not only of humans, but also of her brothers and sisters, and even now, the other osogbos would kill her if they could. "How Elegguá Saved Wisdom from Arayé" shows that even though she is the senior and the most powerful of all the misfortunes, in the end she can be outwitted and foiled; it is with faith and the help of the orishas (especially Elegguá, who controls the comings and goings of osogbo in the world) that this is accomplished. "Osía's Affliction" was an important story to share because wickedness cares not about innocence; she seeks only to corrupt. Our last two stories, "The Dance of Araýe" (almost Poe-like in its theme) and "Obatalá's Insanity: How Araýe Destroyed Him," show us that no one is safe; wickedness is in the world and is a major player in our lives, and sometimes neither the orishas nor the odu can withstand her weight.

THE WAR OF ARAYÉ AND THE OSOGBOS
From the Odu Oché Ogundá (5-3)*

Lunacy was Ano's child, but she was powerful on the earth and growing stronger all the time. Of all the afflictions, she was the strangest, always beginning as a small seed of confusion in the mind, or even the soul, then slowly taking root, growing and squeezing rational thought until perversity was all that remained. For centuries Araýe had been going mad, falling under Lunacy's spell, although Araýe knew it not, and in her madness she hated the world of humans growing over the earth like a cancer. Her hatred rooted deep in her core, squeezing out the little bits of humanity she might have had hiding in her heinous heart. And like a pumpkin's vine races over the plowed soil, once the roots were strong, Lunacy grew. Her influence held Araýe firm in its tendrils and crushed her with its vines, and something inside her head snapped. Araýe went insane. Finally, Lunacy had the power she craved—she had Araýe in her grasp.

It was late the night her mind snapped, and the full moon's silvery light found Araýe pacing her halls. Her nightgown clung to her dark body; it was damp, wet with sweat, her sweat. For hours she had lain beneath her sheets, feverish, dreaming of a world free of the humans

---

*Thanks to Joseph Pagan, who translated one fragmented version of this story from the original Spanish text.

she so hated. Her hatred consumed her; it flushed her skin like a hot summer's night, thick and sticky. For centuries Arayé had tried her best to rid the world of humans, to plague them and make them suffer. In her slow-growing madness she dreamed of a world in which no human lived; she fantasized about their misery and their slow, painful demise. She tried to destroy them one by one, and some gave up the ghost under her crushing weight, while others only crumbled in misery. But no matter how strong she was, there were always those who were stronger than she was. *We need to work together,* she thought, *all of us together—if we united, we would have strength.* The *we,* of course, were her brothers and sisters, the osogbos.

Her fever rose; it was fed by her anger, and so hot was her head that her temper flared. Centuries of trying to destroy humans while watching them grow despite her efforts, and grow stronger—it was all too much for her. Arayé, a creature who was all the wickedness in the world wrapped in one beautiful, seductive body, screamed; her house shook. She flew out into the night, a frightful specter, and she sought out her kin: Ikú, Ano, Ofo, and Iñá. She found them gathered in the forest, hiding in the shadows as the full moon slipped under the horizon.

"Sister," said Ikú as Arayé walked into their midst, her gown clinging to her form, "what brings you to us?"

Had there been more than the ghostly glow of the Milky Way overhead, perhaps Ikú would have seen the madness in Arayé's eyes, but instead she felt only her hot, damp cheek as she kissed her lightly. As Arayé's dry lips grazed her own, maybe she would have seen the flush of her cheeks or the evil grin she cracked as she stood back and held Ikú at arm's length. Instead, she stood still waiting for Arayé to speak.

"The humans—they plague me. They plague us." Ikú heard the hollowness in Arayé's voice. "I want to destroy them. I want to destroy all of them."

Her voice echoed among the trees. Ikú froze in Arayé's grip. *Something is not right with our sister,* thought Ikú. *She reeks of . . . danger.*

"We all want that," said Ano, standing at Ikú's side. "And that is what we do. I make them ill and the weakest die as easily as falling asleep."

"And I create wars that kill humans by the thousands," boasted Iñá, "and I laugh as Ikú carries them away to the next world."

"And I," said Ofo, "I bring loss to their lives, losses so deep that the human soul never recovers from its misery. We all work to destroy them."

"One by one, that is what we do," said Arayé. "And one by one, we fail. Sometimes we fail because the human spirit is too strong to conquer, and other times we fail because they go to the diviners and make ebó. But if all of us were to work together, to come down on the human race like a great, angry storm, we could win. We could destroy them all. And then . . . and then this world would be ours."

Ikú shrugged off Arayé's hands and stood closer to her sister, so close that she could feel her hot breath on her face. She saw, even in darkness, the wavering of Arayé's body; she trembled and shivered as if she were cold. "The night is warm and yet you shake. Are you well?" Ikú was the mother of death, it was true, but when it came to her family, the osogbos, she was almost tender, almost concerned.

Arayé ignored her. Ikú felt something slipping through the night, something that brushed her skin so lightly it was almost not there. Arayé's madness grew in the night around them; its ethereal vines reached out, spreading, elongating, and waiting to catch them all in its embrace. Ikú could not see it but she felt it, and then the feeling was gone. Lunacy, Ano's child, was the sneakiest of all the creatures on earth. Now that she had Arayé in her grasp, she reached out to infect the other osogbos as well.

"If we come together as one and bear down on the human race like a great, angry beast, we can destroy them. They won't have time to run to their diviners. They won't have time to make ebó. No human spirit is strong enough to stand against us. They will crumble under our weight, and the world will be ours." Her voice was strong and powerful, and Ikú felt her madness spreading to the others. She tried to fight off the invisible vines as they pierced her heart, but Arayé was both powerful and beautiful, and because of that even her madness was seductive.

Ofo smiled at the thought of piling loss on human beings, and Ano dreamed of a world filled with endless sickness. Iñá himself shook as he thought of a world filled with war, and Ikú—even her stomach growled when she thought of the thousands of lives passing through her at once. The fear Ikú felt melted. Lunacy's vines crushed them all as she spread among them; it was as easy to cover them as it was for the ocean to slip over the shore.

"We must be careful," said Ikú, wrapped in madness. "We must plan carefully." Even though her mind was tangled, she still retained her common sense. But not for long; the invisible vines of Lunacy thickened and tightened around her as Arayé spoke.

"There is no need to plan, sister," said Arayé, "for if we move together as one, quickly, no one will see us coming. We will win before they know they have lost!"

Madness is cruel, like a leopard, and when it leaps and catches its prey in its claws, there is no escape. Madness is contagious like a plague; in a group it spreads quickly. Among the five osogbos Lunacy roared, angrily. That night, for the first time, five of the world's sixteen osogbos were lost in her grip, and they were in agreement: they would work together and come down hard on the human world. Total destruction was their goal, the destruction of every mortal creature that walked, crawled, or crept on the earth.

Dark clouds rolled through the night, blotting out both the stars and the ethereal glow of the endless Milky Way above. In darkness their pact was made, and in darkness the earth trembled. Lunacy laughed among them; with five of the osogbos in her grasp, she had more power than she knew how to control.

The old man woke up as the earth trembled. Just minutes before dawn he felt his bed shake and he knew: *something wicked is coming for us all*. The old man was a diviner with senses sharpened by decades of divination, and those senses warned him of what was coming before even his diloggún hit the mat. As the sun broke the horizon he was out in the streets, banging on the doors of his two young students, both olorishas who spent their days training with him in the art of diloggún. "Something wicked is coming for us," he said, shaking. "And we need to make ebó before all of us suffer."

"How do you know this?" his oldest student asked, wiping sleep from his eyes. "We have yet to divine for the day."

"When you get to be my age and have as much practice as I do, you *know*," he said. "You *know* when something bad is about to happen."

And so while the rest of the village was just waking up, the three olorishas were already preparing ebó. To Elegguá they gave a black goat, catching some of the blood in a large jícara. When the sacrifice was done, they took that jícara to the village gates, and with it they laid out a jícara with blue water, a jícara filled with epó, a jícara filled with cool water, and a jícara through which the sacrificial cudgel had been driven into the earth. "This," said the old diviner, "is how we will save the world."

The younger olorishas looked at the meager ebó, the five jícaras sitting by the town's gates. They knew that all the osogbos were, after all, stupid but powerful creatures—they always entered a town through its front gates or a home through the front door; never did they sneak in through the back. That was just their nature. And while the goat to Elegguá had been a huge ebó in itself, these five gourds sitting by the gates seemed so small. Silently, not wanting to upset their elder, they whispered to themselves.

"How can such a small ebó save the town if a great evil is coming?" asked the younger olorisha.

"I don't know. But the old man's wisdom is great. Let's hope his wisdom is great enough to fight whatever is coming for us. Better yet, let us hope that his feelings are wrong. Has he ever been wrong before?"

"Never," said the younger olorisha.

After that they were silent, walking home behind the old man. Finally, the eldest reminded the younger, "We've seen him work miracles before. I trust that he is about to work a miracle again. The old man has never failed us before; the entire town is prosperous and happy because of his work."

That night, just to be safe, the old diviner insisted that his two apprentices sleep at his house. In part it was out of fear, for he was afraid. But mostly it was because if something awful were to happen in the village that night, the three of them together under one roof had a greater chance of survival together than if they were alone. While the old man pretended to sleep in his bed, his two students unrolled mats on the floor in front of his orishas. They, too, lay awake all night but not feigning sleep; their eyes were wide open and their ears were listening for strange sounds in the night.

Despite the old man's wisdom, they were afraid.

That day, everyone in town knew that their priests were by the village gates making ebó, and somehow word had spread: *we are all in danger.* When the sun set that day, there was no one in the streets. Everyone was at home behind their own locked doors with the drapes drawn.

As midnight came, there were great screams from the town's gates. The old diviner still feigned sleep, unmoving in his bed and unsure that his ebó would work. His two apprentices huddled together in fear. The townspeople, locked away in their homes, hid in darkness and prayed. Mothers kept their children close and fathers stood beside their doors with machetes drawn, waiting for an unknown evil to come crashing through at any moment. Everyone prayed that night; they prayed that the orishas and Olódumare would keep them safe.

And safe they were. For when the osogbos came to the town, the first thing they saw was the ebó that the three priests had left for them by the town gates.

Lunacy burned inside Ikú. Throughout the day it became more than a fever; it was a hot furnace that roared in her stomach like the flames of a forge. Her throat burned and her lips were parched. She saw the gourd of blue water sitting on the earth; she reached for it and drank it. "What are you doing?" asked Araýe. "Don't you know that water could be poisoned? It could be an ebó!" She reached out to smack the blue water from Ikú's hands, but Ikú whipped around and turned her back to Araýe.

"Let me be," said Ikú. "We have traveled for miles and I am thirsty." In one large draft, she emptied the gourd. While Araýe glared at Ikú furiously, Ano smelled the blood that was in the second gourd, and before Araré could see what Ano was doing, she picked it up and drank it down. Some of the congealed goat's blood dripped down her chin and stained her gown; she didn't care. Ofo and Iñá saw the remaining two gourds, and when Araré heard Ano give a huge belch from drinking the blood too quickly, she turned just in time to see Iñá drinking the jícara of fresh, cool water and Ofo lapping at the one that held the red palm oil. Araré realized that she, too, was thirsty, and she reached for Ano's gourd—it was empty. Lunacy, infecting all five osogbos, was unable to control the power they had—it was too much for her. Araré, overwhelmed with madness and thirst, trembled with anger as she realized that none of her siblings had left her anything to refresh herself with.

It was then that she saw the final gourd with a cudgel thrust through it.

"Greedy, ungrateful idiots!" she screamed. "You are all so selfish. Did you not think that I, too, might be thirsty after our long journey?" With both hands she grabbed the cudgel and pulled it from the earth. "Maybe I should drink *your* blood instead!"

Lunacy could not stop what was about to happen, nor did she care to stop it, because madness cares not who suffers its wrath. Those in her grasp, the lunatics, only care that others suffer, and they destroy, leaving misery and anguish in their wake. Araré broke that night, and since she was the only one with a weapon, the four osogbos, Ikú, Ano, Ofo, and Iñá, were powerless as she bore down on them like an angry beast. When she was done, she crouched on the earth like a leopard and began lapping their blood from the earth. And when her thirst was sated, she stood, holding her cudgel high, prepared to destroy the town with her own ashé.

But none of the osogbos noticed that standing by the town's gates was Elegguá. He stood alone, and alone he watched. Elegguá watched Araré as she took down her brothers and sisters one by one with her own angry hands. He applauded as he told her, "That was a job well done, Lunacy—you infected your aunt, Aro, and you made your own mother, Ano, sick. You even caught Ikú in your madness and forced Araré to do what no one else has ever done: you killed death. And you,

Arayé, were quite the willing hostess to your niece. I thought you were smarter than that. But now you need to leave. Neither of you have any power here."

"But power is all I have!" It was Lunacy herself who screamed with Arayé's voice, and she lifted the cudgel high, shaking it at the heavens. "I am Lunacy *and* I am Arayé; I am madness *and* I am the soul of all things wicked, and I feed on the wickedness living in every human heart. My power is supreme, and I will kill everyone, starting with this town!"

"There can be no death without Ikú," said Elegguá. "There can be no sickness without Ano, no loss without Ofo, no war without Iñá." Elegguá crossed his arms over his chest, smiling. "Without your siblings, you *are* wicked and you *are* crazy, but, more dangerous still—you are making *me* crazy! With just my bare hands I can rip you to shreds, and without Ikú, you can never die. So I can do it over and over and over again."

Arayé froze; the madness lifted as Lunacy realized her defeat. Still, Arayé held her ground.

"Take just one more step toward this gate," said Elegguá, "and you will discover how powerless you are before me. For I am Elegguá, and I will make you wish you were dead!"

Arayé dropped her cudgel and fled. Like the wind, she ripped through the forest, and the town was safe.

Elegguá blew his breath on the blood and flesh remaining on the earth. It bubbled, and soon it boiled, and from the gore rose four hideous forms: Ikú, Ano, Ofo, and Iñá. "Once you were all beautiful," said Elegguá, "once you were all seductive, but now you are repulsive. You have Ano's child, Lunacy, and your sister, Arayé, to thank for that."

They wailed, a collective cry so depraved that even Elegguá covered his ears, and then they were gone. Elegguá knew—he just knew—that they were searching for Arayé and Lunacy, and he knew that never again would they let themselves be fooled into working together again.

"Are we safe?" the youngest olorisha asked his brother. "That cry—it was so evil."

The old man had risen from his bed when the second cry shook the earth. Weary, he walked into his orishas' room, where his two students sat huddled together on their mats and sat on the floor. "We are safe," said the old man. "Our ebó worked. There is still osogbo in the world, but for now it is not coming for us. I can feel them running after one another."

Exhausted, the three of them lay on the mats and slept.

Ikú, Ano, Ofo, and Iñá spread out through the night, not trusting one another, but all four looking to destroy their sister, AraYé, and Lunacy, one of Ano's own children. Even now they seek revenge. And whenever any misfortune plots against us, we consult with the orishas, and they, in their wisdom, teach us how to overcome the osogbos that rise against us.

HOW ELEGGUÁ SAVED WISDOM FROM ARAYÉ
From the Odu Oché Metanlá (5-13) *

It was late in the land of Intelligence, and the king, Baba Domá, the father of wisdom, slept, lost in his dreams, while his two younger brothers, Baba Dogun, the father of war, and Baba Dòtá, the father of adversity, walked through darkened halls. In shadows they crept with only the light of a lamp to guide them, and they nodded to the guards as they slipped outside the palace walls, into the dark forest that lay beyond the town gates. The moon was full, casting an ethereal silvery glow that blanketed the woods. Into this they walked until they were deep in the trees and bush, in a place the moon could no longer touch. There they stopped and rested. When they were sure the only sounds in the forest were those of the trees swaying and settling against the midnight breeze, they whispered among themselves.

"We live in our brother's shadow," said Baba Dòtá. "There was a time he sought our counsel, but now that the kingdom is in peace he won't even consider the thought of war and expansion. He only needs

---

*I again give my thanks to Joseph Pagan, who translated a fragmented version of this story. In the version he translated for me, the original Lucumí names were preserved, and by studying those Lucumí names I was able to discover additional subtle layers to the story that I would have otherwise missed.

us when things are bad. In peace, he feels he needs only himself."

"We should rule, together," said Baba Dogun. "You and I live as his subjects and not as royalty. And never once has he taken up a machete. Never once has he taken up an arrow. Never once has he ridden into war. He diffuses his enemies with words, and instead of growing our kingdom by conquering our neighbors, we remain a small land with untapped potential. We should rule this world, not just this small corner of it."

"It is time to remove him from that throne and then *we* can rule. We are his brothers. We have as much right to it as he!"

"I agree," said Baba Dogun. "But how?"

"Do you not know?" Baba Dòtá asked. "His most loyal followers are small in number. There are the guards who guard him each night while he sleeps. There are the servants in the castle who work for him. But beyond those, the people of this village care not who leads them. All they care about is that their larders are full of food and their children are safe and healthy. As for the rest of the army—if he were gone, his loyalists would follow us, no questions asked." Dòtá reached into his dark robes and pulled out a flask. "I have some poison. It works slowly. We can poison his loyal guards and staff with their morning meal, and then, while our brother eats his own breakfast, he will see his people fall over, dead. He, too, will die not long after he eats. He will suffer first, watching his loyalists die, and then he will die. With him gone, we can take over the land."

"Where did you get that?" asked Dogun. The flask was made of clear glass, and by the lamp's light he could see the dark fluid, viscous and thick, swirling into itself.

"I got it from Araye," he said. "She told me that with this medicine I could destroy all who were loyal to Domá, and then the kingdom would be ours."

"It's so simple a plan," said Dogun. "Almost too simple. Are you sure it will work?"

"Araye is a powerful witch," Dòtá said. "It will work."

They slipped back inside the compound, making their way to the kitchen. As they were brothers to the king, no one challenged their entrance. The morning pots were already laid out for breakfast. A few drops of the poison went into each pan. "Just make sure you eat nothing this morning," said Dòtá. "By the time they serve breakfast to our brother, as he is taking his first bites they will begin to die." He smiled, and in the shadows it was a wicked sneer. "The kingdom is as good as ours."

The next morning, Baba Domá was seated at the head of the dining room table, as he always was, and his brothers, Dòtá and Dogun, sat on either side. Normally refreshed, Domá couldn't help but notice the dark circles under their eyes. "Did you sleep well, brothers?" he asked.

"Not so well," said Dogun. "I had much on my mind. The safety of our kingdom, for example."

"We have enemies everywhere," said Dòtá. "Enemies who would stop at nothing to destroy us. In this world, it is kill or be killed."

"Wisdom can overcome any adversity," said Baba Domá. "That is why we prosper in a world filled with war and turmoil. We live in peace because we live with wisdom, and that is how it should be."

A weary chambermaid shuffled to the table, bringing bowls and spoons. Instead of setting them gently on the table, she let them down hard. The bowl she sat in front of Domá cracked. "My lady, are you alright?" asked Domá. "You look fatigued."

He motioned for a guard stationed by the door to come help her, but he saw that the guard's eyes were half slits and he was rubbing his belly.

"I need to sit down, sir," said the chambermaid. "I do not feel well. I have not felt well since breakfast this morning." She barely made the chair, and her body slumped over the table. There was a great crash from the kitchen, and then the guard, who was moaning silently, fell over on the floor.

Baba Domá jumped up from the table. Fear slipped into his eyes; they were wide with terror. Dòtá and Dogun sat back, their arms crossed over their bodies. They watched Domá with smiles on their faces. "Poison!" he cried. "You have all been poisoned!"

"But not us," said Baba Dòtá. "We were the ones with the poison."

Domá ran from the room, cutting through his own kitchen where the bodies of his servants lay writhing on the floor. Some lay still while others convulsed. "Guards!" he heard his brothers yell from the next room. "Guards! Seize our brother before he escapes."

Dogun looked at Dòtá and seethed, "The poison worked too quickly, or you used too much. Domá never took so much as one bite."

"That stupid chambermaid," he said, "she broke his bowl before he had a chance to even lift his spoon!"

Being the father of wisdom, Baba Domá, unbeknownst to his brothers, was prepared for emergencies inside his own walls. He dashed to the back of his palace and ripped a mat up from the floor. Beneath it was a trap door no one knew about, not even his brothers. It snapped open easily and he jumped inside, pulling it shut behind him. The door was reinforced with heavy iron beams, and on the inside was a latch and a lock. Years ago, without his brothers' knowledge, he had had this secret passage built for emergencies. He locked it behind him and ran down the tunnel that would take him to freedom. It would take the guards hours to smash through the iron and find the tunnel. And when they did, Baba Domá would be long gone.

The tunnel ended at Baba Domá's private stables, and there he mounted his horse. As quickly as he could, Baba Domá rode north, to Oshogbo, the land where his orisha, Oshún, lived. He rode all day and half the night before he stopped to rest, and then only briefly. By the next morning he was at Oshún's home, and the orisha was surprised to see him.

"Baba Domá," she said, touching his shoulder lightly while he put his head to the ground before her in obeisance, "what brings you here to my land?"

Exhausted and dirty as he was, Domá embraced her. And then he told her the story of his brothers' treason.

"And you, the father of wisdom, the king of the land of Intelligence—why have you not used your own wisdom and intelligence to resolve this problem?" Oshún smiled. "Wisdom and intelligence overcome all adversity, Baba Domá. If I were coming to you for advice right now, what would be the first thing you would tell me to do?"

Domá sighed. "I would tell you to see the diviners."

"And that is what I'm telling you to do now."

Domá thanked her, and he sought out the wisest diviner he knew, Mofá.

Late at night, Arayé slipped into the land of Intelligence. No one saw her come; she was a shadow, as ethereal as a breeze slipping through the forest. Dòtá and Dogun were in the dining hall surrounded by their guards when she took form. She rose tall and mighty among them, almost a goddess among men. Wickedness flowed through the room, an ashé thicker than the air they breathed. It was stifling. It felt like chaos.

All the guards froze. Dòtá walked to her and tried to embrace her, but she stood back, her eyes dark and cold. "Do not touch me. You have failed me."

"We have not failed you, Arayé. The kingdom is ours now."

"But your brother lives."

"He escaped through a secret tunnel," said Dogun. "A tunnel we knew not existed. It was in the floor under a door reinforced by iron. It took us hours to break through, but we traced it to the stables. His favorite horse is missing, so we know he rides into the countryside. We have the army out in the woods looking for him even as we speak. Soon we will find him. Soon we will kill him."

"He should have been dead already," Arayé seethed. "As long as wisdom lives, I cannot reign supreme. I had my sights set on bigger things than just this tiny town."

Dòtá froze. He thought he saw fire in Arayé's eyes.

She gave a small flick of her wrists. The guards, who stood motionless, lifted their swords. "What are you doing?" said Dogun, alarmed when he saw his guards with their swords unsheathed.

"Put your swords down," Dòtá commanded them. He, too, was alarmed. "Arayé is our benefactor."

"No," she said, "I am your queen. Guards, take these two brothers to the dungeon. I will decide what to do with them later."

The guards took down the brothers easily, and with them kicking and screaming, they dragged them, by their hair, to the dungeon.

Arayé settled herself on the throne and crowned herself queen. With war and adversity locked up and under her control, there was still hope that she could rule the world.

Mofá was a simple man, preferring to live outside the bustling city to the north, where there were only thick forests and a fresh, running river close to his home. Fruit-bearing trees grew freely, and he knew every edible herb and berry that grew for miles around his home. He spent his days studying the wisdom of odu, and he devoted his time to learning medicine, the herbs that cured every ailment known to humans. When Baba Domá arrived by horseback both he and his steed were exhausted, and Mofá, being the best of hosts, offered both the king and his animal refreshment.

When they were settled he asked, "What troubles you, Domá? You are many days' travel from your home."

"My own brothers have stolen the kingdom," he said, "and through their treachery they have murdered everyone in the palace who was loyal to me."

"That is indeed a problem," Mofá said, inviting Domá into his divining room. "But as always, there is something that can be done. As long as one is not in the grip of Ikú herself, there is always something that can be done to save a man."

Mofá laid a mat on the floor and sat with his back against the wall. Carefully, he counted sixteen cowries from a red and black bag, putting five on a plate that sat beside his mat. He invited the king to sit on a low stool before him. Rapidly and indecipherably, with words that seemed to blur into one another, he chanted, and then he let the cowries roll out on the mat twice. Oché Metanlá was the odu that fell that day.

"Yes, you are the victim of greed," Mofá said. "It was Arayé herself who made your brothers rise up against you. And Arayé has won. No longer is your kingdom known as the land of Intelligence. Soon everyone in the world will know it as the land of Adversity and War, and its new queen is Arayé herself. You can never reclaim it. But there is another land to which you must go, a land in which you will be well received and do much good. It is to the land of Elegguá that you must travel, and Elegguá himself will keep you safe from all harm."

"My kingdom? It is gone? Forever?" Baba Domá was not one to cry, at least not since he was a child, but there at the mat his tears came freely. His family had ruled the land of Intelligence for centuries; they were descendants of the mighty Odua himself. In one act of treachery the entire kingdom had been lost. The tears that came at the mat were hot, burning his eyes with their salt. "But my people—I love them! I devoted my life to making that land prosperous!"

"Humans are notoriously ungrateful for the good we do, Domá. You devoted your life to them and gave them prosperity. You gave them leisure. And now your reign there is over. But in this new land to which you will go you will be received again as a king. Instead of having enemies at your side, you will have Elegguá with you. Elegguá himself is a king, but once you arrive with your limitless wisdom he will accept you as his equal, and together the two of you will rule more than a kingdom—you will rule the world."

Domá put his head on the mat to the old diviner, Mofá. It was an act of obeisance, an acknowledgment that the diviner's wisdom through odu was greater than his own worldly wisdom. Gently, Mofá touched his shoulders and blessed him. The king stood and then helped Mofá to rise, for age had made his legs weak. Still standing on the mat, the two men embraced.

"Don't worry so much, Domá," said Mofá. "Things might seem dark now, but there are greater forces in the world than the osogbo Arayé. She might be all things seductive and wicked, but the orishas have ashé greater than hers. And your destiny lies beyond that tiny kingdom. Wisdom will swathe the world, and the misfortunes of life will pale in comparison with your ashé. You will see. Odu never leads us astray."

With reddened eyes, Domá mounted his horse. Thankfully, it seemed that his steed knew the way to Elegguá's kingdom, and he was just along for the ride.

Araýe wanted to leave nothing to chance. She, too, mounted a horse and raced through the countryside, a mad specter bringing fright to all who saw her. She was a terror in the day and a nightmare at night, but no matter how hard or fast she rode she could not find Baba Domá.

The world was trembling beneath Baba Domá's feet when he arrived at Elegguá's palace. Elegguá was outside his front door, alone, when he slid off his mount.

"The world trembles, Baba Domá," he said, "for at this very moment Araýe rides through the world like an angry beast looking for you. And your kingdom, the land of Intelligence, has fallen into disarray. How did this happen?"

Domá offered no words; instead, he prostrated himself on the ground, putting his head at Elegguá's feet. Smiling, the orisha blessed him and lifted him. The two embraced, and Domá felt strength flowing into him from the orisha.

Finally, he spoke. "My brothers—they betrayed me. They betrayed me to Araýe, and poisoned my most trusted servants and guards. I escaped with my life, but barely. I went to Oshún for help, but my own orisha turned me away and sent me to the diviner, Mofá. Mofá read for me, and told me to seek refuge here." Again the tears came, and this time they came more freely. "My family has ruled the land of Intelligence for centuries with peace and wisdom, and my younger brothers, they betrayed me to an osogbo." He could say no more; in shame, he turned away from Elegguá.

"Osogbo is seductive, Domá," said Elegguá. "Araýe herself is the senior of them all, and most find her wickedness beautiful and desirable. She is a very seductive creature." Elegguá crossed his arms over his chest. "Don't be so sad. Araýe cannot be trusted. Just as she deceived your brothers into betraying you, so she has betrayed them. They don't rule in your place. She does. The land of Intelligence has become the

land of Adversity and War; your brothers are in prison, and soon Ofo
and Iñá will come to rule by Arayé's side."

And that is the story of how Wisdom came to rule at Elegguá's side. And,
of course, we know that Elegguá's kingdom is the world itself. It became
his kingdom because with Domá (Wisdom) in his spiritual court, there
was no wisdom *not* at his disposal. Herein lies a great secret, the reason
why Arayé is unable to outright destroy anyone who comes to Elegguá
for help or advice. Wisdom itself cannot be an effective ruler, for a good
king has not only wisdom at his disposal, but also strength and ashé to
make all things possible in life. Elegguá benefited from the wisdom he
gained that day, and Arayé, no matter how hard she tries, cannot remove
wisdom from the world as long as Elegguá owns and protects it.

And what happened to the land of Adversity and War, the kingdom
once known as the land of Intelligence? Adversity invites many enemies,
and war itself cannot be sustained forever. In time, the kingdom crumbled. Baba Dogun and Baba Dòtá were forgotten in the dungeon; they
died because no one *wanted* to feed war and adversity, and the osogbos
Arayé, Ofo, and Iñá were forced to wander the world, never again having a place of their own to call home. Such is what happens when greed
is the core of one's character.

OSÍA'S AFFLICTION: ARAYÉ
From the Odu Odí Irosun (7-4)*

"What can I do?" Érínlè asked Orúnmila as he sat across the table of Ifá
from him. "Every night it is the same. I come home from work. I want
sex with my wife. And every night my wife, Oba, turns away from me."
He frowned. Orúnmila listened but offered no advice. "She tells me she
is tired. She tells me that her head hurts her. She tells me that her body
aches, or that I ask too much of her all the time."

---

*Although I suppose it is an unusual thing to do in a book, I would like to dedicate this
story to my goddaughter Maria, who is Oba's daughter.

Still Orúnmila sat silent. His silence was unnerving.

"Not so much as a kiss!" Érínlè said, his voice coming back at him from Orúnmila's walls. "I'm a man. I have needs."

"Do you love her?" Orúnmila asked.

"You're the diviner. You tell me."

"Do you love her?" Orúnmila asked again. "It's a simple question, and you're sitting right here. I do not need to divine what stares me in the face."

"I came to you for advice, Orúnmila. Impartial advice—which is what you say you give. What can I do about my wife? Is there some medicine I can give her to make her . . . better?"

Poor Oba, thought Orúnmila. *All she wants is love. All Érínlè wants is sex. A simple question—'Do you love her?' Still, he cannot answer . . .*

"If this is how things are," said Orúnmila, "there is no medicine to make Oba want to have sex with you. If Oba does not want to make love to you it is because she is not happy. You must find out what troubles her and make her happy. And if you are not capable of making your wife happy, then you should leave her. The way you live with her and your daughter does all of you more harm than good. Perhaps then she will have the freedom to find someone who will make her happy."

Érínlè heard Orúnmila's words but did not understand them; he heard only what he wanted to hear. What he heard the diviner say was "You should leave her." On his way home, he twisted Orúnmila's words to "You should get rid of her." When he got home, what he wanted those words to mean was "You should throw her out *tonight.*"

Without a word, Oba packed a bag, and then she packed a bag for their daughter, Osía. *Barely five years old,* Oba thought, *and already she is homeless, as am I.* Then again, the two of them, Érínlè and Oba, were barely making it in the world.

They were both young when they had wed, and Érínlè, being but a poor fisherman, took Oba away to his one-room shack where the river met the sea. "You live here?" Oba had asked.

"I am a fisherman," said Érínlè proudly, "and I must live where I work."

"But it is so small," said Oba as he carried her inside. It was one room, no more.

"But our view—have you ever seen anything like it?" he asked.

Oba looked out the one great window that opened onto both the river and the sea. One half showed her the infinite waters of the ocean, rolling out before her until the horizon stole it from view. The other half showed the river and the mysterious forest that stood on its other side. A gentle breeze blew in; it smelled fresh and salty and was both warm and cool. She shivered. "It's beautiful," she agreed. Oba had been sheltered all her life; she had seen little beyond Obatalá's walls.

"One day we will build a great house," Érínlè promised. "But for now, we have each other."

Soon they had Osía, yet still they lived in that one-room house.

That was the reason Oba no longer wanted to have sex with her husband, Érínlè. Osía was too old to see such things and too young to understand them. Érínlè cared not; he simply wanted sex.

"Where are we going, Mother?" asked Osía. Memories and regrets—it was all Oba had, all except the young girl who tagged along at her heels. Oba peered down at her daughter.

"The only place we can. Someplace wonderful—we're going to my father's house."

Osía frowned. She didn't know her mother had a man she called Father; she only knew her own father, Érínlè, the man her mother called Husband. And she knew what husbands did to their wives.

It was a confusing time to be a child, and it was an even worse time to be a young girl out wandering the world. Osía knew this, but she didn't know *how* she knew. It was a feeling, like fear.

She didn't want to see her mother around another man.

Far behind them, Arayé tracked their path in the world. She slipped through trees and in shadows, Osía's fear drawing her close.

Oba had grown up in Obatalá's palace, and unbeknownst to him Érínlè came to see her every afternoon when he took his morning's catch to the marketplace. She always knew when he was coming for her—the smell of fish caught in the afternoon breeze would find its way to the palace. He would stop, they would talk, and then Érínlè would go off into the town to sell his day's catch. On the way home again he would stop to visit, but briefly, his pockets either bulging with cowries or his hands filled with his evening purchases. Oba always thought Érínlè a rich man, when in truth he spent every bit he earned.

One night when Érínlè was returning home very late, his breath smelled of liquor and stale tobacco. He gave Oba her first kiss, and the young girl's heart melted. She ran away with him that night.

Obatalá had been insane with worry until Olófin himself told the orisha, "Your ward, Oba, has run off with Érínlè."

"But they aren't meant for each other," said Obatalá. "She was meant to be with Shangó!"

"Fate has a strange way of working out, Obatalá. Be patient."

Patience was all he had.

By the time Oba came home to Obatalá with a child in tow, his patience had worn thin, but when he saw his daughter with her own daughter, his heart softened. "And who is this?" Obatalá asked.

"This, Father, is my daughter, Osía." Obatalá's eyes narrowed when he saw a hint of fear in the young girl's eyes, and for a moment he thought he saw something there, some trauma and a hint of madness. But it was gone as quickly as it came, and Osía was no longer fearful. She was only shy.

"Hello," she said from behind her mother's legs. She wrapped both arms around them; little did she know she was trying to keep them closed. Her movements were protective but instinctive.

"It is good to meet you, young lady," said Obatalá as he made a futile attempt to bend over. Osía peered from around the side. "My back," he said to Oba, looking at her. "My back is not what it used to be." He straightened. "Young lady, make yourself at home, but be good. Your mother and I have much to speak about."

As Obatalá and Oba retired to the next room, Osía stood in the great entryway and trembled, her eyes closed; she was afraid to open them, or to even move.

She knew something was coming for her.

And Arayé sniffed out the child's fear—she knew not where she was, but she knew where in the world the child had been, and like a bloodhound she tracked that scent.

When the door was closed, Obatalá stifled his urge to yell. "What has happened to that child, Oba?"

She was nervous in front of Obatalá. Five, almost six years apart, and instead of embracing her, he was angry with her. "What do you mean?" Her voice was weak, wispy.

"Osía is afraid of men, or haven't you noticed?"

"Osía has never been around any man."

"Not even your husband?"

Silence; it was so thick Oba could not move. When she found her voice, shaken, she said, "Of course she has been around my husband."

"And you?"

"Of course she has been around my husband and me. And she has been around us together. Why would you ask such a question? It's ridiculous!"

"Because something has traumatized that child!" His voice rose in anger and the walls shook. Obatalá remembered that Osía was in the next room and lowered his voice. "Her eyes show me pain. Her eyes show me fear. And as quickly as they show me that pain and fear, it is gone, hidden. What has she seen you and your husband *do*?"

Oba sank to her knees; she clutched Obatalá's feet in her hands and wept into them. "We lived in a one-room house. I didn't know, Father. I didn't know." Obatalá looked away from her; he looked up and wished his room had no ceiling so he could cry into the clouds and scream to Olófin.

But the child was in the next room.

"As soon as I knew she was too old to be around such things and too young to understand them, I put a stop to it. I swear—when I saw her look at us with fear in her eyes, I pushed my husband away from me and I haven't let him touch me since."

Never had a heart ached as Obatalá's did then. Obatalá knew that

Arayé was close to the child, but until she was in the grip of Arayé there was nothing he could do. He was powerless to stop her from tracking Osía in the world.

"What can I do?" Obatalá asked Olófin. It was night and he was dreaming. He often dreamt of heaven and what he had left behind to come live in the world.

"What is done is done," said Olófin. "But unless Oba has a stable place to live where the child can feel safe again, she will never heal from the trauma." He paused and let the words sink into Obatalá's brain. "Already the seeds of madness are in that child's mind, and Arayé, she follows those in whose souls madness grows, and she feeds off the wickedness growing in their hearts. Fear—it has a scent all its own, and Arayé tracks that smell. Still, Osía is young. If no more damage is done, eventually she will forget. And she will heal."

"I cannot bear it, Olófin," said Obatalá. "I raised Oba to be good, to be thoughtful in deed and action. How could I let this happen?"

"Life just unfolds," said Olófin, his hand on Obatalá's back. "Let it unfold. All you can do is guide them to the right place. And remember—Érínlè himself has a sister who is a powerful sorceress, Abata. The time will come when you will need her help if that child is to heal. Remember that."

When Obatalá awoke, he had but one thought in his head: it was not of Abata but of Shangó. Shangó was a noble man—he could provide a stable home for Oba to raise her child. His son, Shangó, was her destiny. *How easily we miss what orí has chosen for us,* he thought. *Perhaps I can still make things right for her.*

Of course, when Obatalá told Shangó that his daughter Oba, and her daughter, Osía, were coming to live with him, Shangó agreed. He was the new king of Oyó, and his own palace needed a woman's hand.

Oba's heart did not belong to Shangó; even now, she yearned for Érínlè and the freedom of both the river and the sea. Free from the one-room shack, however, Osía seemed lighter and happier, and with her own

room and the many rooms of the compound to explore, she was no longer fearful. Osía even seemed brave.

And Arayé had all but lost her scent.

It took months, but Oba, too, became brave. Without her daughter
clinging at her heels, watching her every move, her old desires returned.
The warmth she once felt in her loins for the delicate man Érínlè burned
now for Shangó, and one night, in silence, she crept to his chambers and
knocked on his door lightly.

For the first time in years Oba felt free to ride a man like an animal,
and ride Shangó she did. With such passion and vigor did she cry out
that Shangó, too, realized that Oba was the woman he needed. Night
after night, long after Osía had gone to bed in her own room, Oba crept
down the hallway to Shangó's chambers, and he, in turn, taught her
how to make love recklessly.

One night, while there was a storm brewing on the horizon, he
taught her the forbidden arts of sodomy and oral sex. For Shangó, nothing pleased him more, and Oba, wanting to please him, took his lessons
gladly.

Fear—the coming storm brought fear to Osía's heart. Its scent was
strong, intoxicating, and Arayé picked up on it easily. She followed that
smell to Shangó's palace. Inside the palace walls, Osía was easy to find.
Arayé sniffed at the air until the scent of innocence and fear reached her
nose; she stood outside the child's door, and like water flows through
the reeds of a basket, she slipped under her door.

Osía woke up when the first crack of lightning lit her dark room,
and when thunder rolled through the skies, she shivered. Arayé was all
around her, but children understand not the spirit of misfortune, that
it surrounds us but cannot hurt us unless we give in to it. She felt fear,
and like the frightened child she was, she threw off the covers and ran
down the hallway to her mother's room.

Her fear doubled when she saw Oba was not there. She reached
for her covers and pulled them back; she was about to climb into
her bed and wait. *Mommy has only gone to the bathroom, or to get a*

glass of water, she thought. But as she threw her leg over the mattress and tried to pull herself up, another roll of thunder shook the walls, and Arayé pushed her out of her mother's room and toward Shangó's.

It was then that she heard her mother's moans and cries. It came from behind Shangó's doors, the one room in the entire palace that she was forbidden to enter. *Why is she in there?* Osía thought.

Find out, Arayé whispered. It felt like a breeze against Osía's neck; the baby hairs there stood up. Then came the man's voice, Shangó's voice. It sounded mean, guttural; it was a grunt that was anger and pleasure and violence and need, just like her father's, and without knocking, Osía threw the great door open.

Arayé pushed her into the room just as lightning flashed through the open windows. The windows blew the white curtains in; they billowed like spirits, boiling in the night. And she saw her mother's head between Shangó's legs, Shangó pushing her head down every time she tried to get up. She heard her mother gag; she heard her mother choke; and still, Shangó pushed her head down further and further.

Osía screamed; her mind snapped, and Arayé slipped inside her. Oba screamed as she saw, even in darkness, her daughter's body slump on the floor.

In fear, Oba forgot her own nakedness and clutched her daughter to her breasts. Osía's eyes were vacant, devoid of rational thought. Instead, the fires of madness burned inside, and Oba knew she was looking into the eyes of a lunatic.

Wrapped in his own white sheets, Shangó stood behind her. He cursed.

Back in his own palace, Obatalá was dreaming of heaven as the great storm rocked Oyó. Again, he was with Olófin. "It is time," the old man said.

"Time for what?" Obatalá asked, confused. He thought he heard thunder, but storms rarely raged through the spiritual world unless something was amiss in the physical. And then he heard the thunder again. Something was wrong on the earth.

"It is time to call Abata," said Olófin. "Osía—she has suffered a great fright. Even now she is locked in a nightmarish world, unable to sleep but unable to awaken, and there, between life and death, she hangs because of what Oba and Shangó have done."

Obatalá's wrinkles deepened on his black face. They looked like great canyons across his forehead. "What have my children done?" he asked.

"They forgot that Osía is but a child. And now her mind has snapped."

A great crack of thunder woke Obatalá from his dream. For a brief moment, his room lit up as if on fire, and then thunder rolled across the sky again. *Oba,* he thought, *how could you do this . . . to your child . . . again?*

When the storm broke and the sun rose the next morning, he sent his messengers out into the world. They had to find Abata, Érínlè's sister. They had to find her quickly. And they had to send her to Shangó's palace, where he knew Osía lay near death.

For the first time in centuries, Obatalá prayed. He hoped Olódumare heard him.

It took days for Obatalá's messengers to find Abata. She often wandered the world but was always near brackish waters, and while there were few places where the river met the sea, they were far apart. "I have a niece?" she asked them. *How many years has it been since I have seen my brother?* she thought. *I didn't even know he had a wife. And what mischief has he created now?*

"Obatalá says your niece is in danger. She is in the grip of Araýe. He says you will understand when you see her, when you see Oba, when you see Shangó. But under no circumstances are you to leave that child there. You must take her away to someplace safe. And safety means far, far away from both her mother *and* her father, Érínlè."

Abata gathered her things that afternoon, and with a horse given to her by one of Obatalá's messengers, she made her first trip to the kingdom of Oyó.

Abata arrived in Oyó during a great celebration. To all his people Shangó announced his impending wedding to Oba, and although the kingdom rejoiced, Abata felt something evil simmering within the palace walls. She arrived in her royal blue gown with a shimmering blue veil that seemed diaphanous, almost made of air and swirling about her like a gentle breeze. Approached by such ashé, the guards stood back and let Abata walk unchallenged into the courtyard. She found Oba well protected, but weeping.

Before the future queen the guards insisted she put her head to the earth in obeisance, but Abata stood proud and unmoving before Oba. "You do not know who I am, sister-in-law?" she asked.

Oba's mouth fell open; it was shame and rage. "I am a single woman. I have no sister-in-law. Guards, seize her!"

Abata held both hands up and to her sides. With a quick flick of her wrists, the guards went flying off into all directions. They hit the ground hard and were unable to move. "Do not play with me, Oba. You are already a married woman. You are married to my brother, Érínlè." Oba fell to her knees, her mouth still open. "And you have a child by him no one in the kingdom knows about, Osía." Oba's body trembled. "With another man, Shangó, you were adulterous; your marriage to Érínlè has not yet been dissolved. And your child, Osía, has gone insane. She saw you and Shangó having sex."

Broken, Oba fell to the earth, her head at Abata's feet. "I did not mean . . ." she stammered. "I did not know she was there. It was the storm that broke her. It was the storm!"

Abata offered no blessing as she pulled Oba to her feet and held her at arm's length. "It was not the storm, Oba. It was you and Érínlè, and then it was you and Shangó. And now she lies locked in a nightmare from which she cannot escape. Araye has her. Obatalá sent me to take her away from you, away from Shangó, away from Érínlè. He has sent me to take her far away where she will no longer be traumatized, and where I can heal her."

Oba was limp in Abata's arms. "Do you not *hear* me, Oba? I am here to remove your child from this cursed place. She will not live another day inside these palace walls."

Dazed and confused, Oba moved slowly as Abata followed. Afraid of Abata's ashé and thinking it sorcery, the guards ran to find Shangó and told him, "A witch is here to steal Oba's daughter." No one in the kingdom outside Shangó's compound knew that his future wife had a daughter, and Shangó, convinced that it must be a witch, ran to Osía's room with his sword brandished.

He found Oba in Osía's room, lying in a fetal position by the door and crying. He saw a regal black woman sitting on Osía's bed, her great blue veil wrapped around them both. He raised his sword when he saw a great black shadow rising from the bed; it screamed, and the walls of the compound shook. "Araýe," Shangó whispered.

He put down his sword. The young child wrapped herself around Abata, crying. His face flushed with shame when he heard the child tell the woman what she had seen. Abata's eyes burned; she focused on Shangó as Osía whimpered. "You should be ashamed of yourselves, both of you," said Abata as she walked away with Osía held tightly against her breast. She walked away unchallenged.

Shangó's sword fell from his hand as he knelt beside Oba. Her eyes were red with something that seemed like madness, and she said over and over, almost a chant, "Osía . . . my child . . . Osía . . . my child . . ."

Another great storm fell over the kingdom of Oyó that day.

THE DANCE OF ARAÝE
From the Olodu Unle (8)

It came to pass that Unle wanted to have a great party, a night to celebrate all the good he had created in the world. Carefully, he handpicked his guest list. Iré, the spirit of blessings, was the guest of honor, since Unle's kingdom was truly the most blessed. He invited the most powerful men and women from his land to attend.

Not a single osogbo was invited.

The night of Unle's party, Araýe sat in her chambers staring into her mirror. She was enraged, and so hot was her anger that her breath steamed its glass. *How dare he honor Iré!* she said to herself. *And not a single one of us is invited to his party. Did we not make a pact years ago? Were it not for misfortune, Unle, the simple diviner, would have never become rich; he would have never become a king; he would have never built such a prosperous kingdom!* The mirror cracked and then shattered, glass spraying Arayé but only tickling her skin. *And when pacts are broken, they are broken—for good!*

Arayé pulled a red dress over her lithe body. Glass crunched under her bare feet but left them unscratched. She would teach Unle the value of a pact.*

It was late when the woman in the red dress arrived at Unle's party; with a red mask on her face, she stepped into the ball.

The room went silent.

First, they noticed her hair: it was woven into a thousand thin braids carefully piled on top of her head, but still, they cascaded around her shoulders to her waist. Then they saw her dress—it was tight, seductive, not the modest robe of a noblewoman but instead like the thin undergarment a worldly woman would wear to her lover's bed. Finally, they saw her feet: they were bare, but clean, too clean to be feet that had walked even a single step on the earth.

No one thought it strange. The woman in red was too beautiful, too seductive, to be criticized or questioned.

The drummers broke the silence with a single beat of a drum, and Arayé moved her hips. The room sighed, and the drummers beat again, slowly, as Arayé moved through the room. She greeted the women with a slight curtsy; she pushed her own body into each man's and kissed everyone on the lips, but lightly. Matching their own excitement, the drummers beat the drums more frantically, and the woman in red came to dance before them. Unle, in his thoughtlessness, had not lifted the

---

*To understand the role that the osogbos played in Unle's success, read the patakí titled "Unle Builds a Home" in my book *Teachings of the Santería Gods.* A subtle pact was made between the olodu Unle and the sixteen osogbos, a pact that Unle later broke when he chose to honor Iré without giving Osogbo equal respect.

consecrated drums of Añá to play; instead, he had invited drummers from the street.* With nothing to fear, Arayé danced behind the drummers, kissing them lightly on the backs of their necks, and then she danced right up to Unle himself.

She stopped. The drummers stopped. And everyone at the ball fell down dead.

Unle was in shock when Arayé caressed his shoulder, removing her mask.

"How dare you," she whispered. Her voice was almost a light breeze against his skin, and he was afraid to move. "How dare you honor our brother Iré and not invite any of us! How dare you not invite me, the oldest of all the osogbos on the earth! Since humans were first born there has been wickedness on the earth, and I have been here, even before you were born, feeding on their wicked hearts."

Unle looked to his right where the guest of honor, Iré, was seated—only now he gone. There was only an empty chair. "Without us, there can be no blessings. Without Osogbo there can be no Iré. You broke our pact."

"I did not think . . . ," stammered the old diviner.

"You did not *need* to think!" Her voiced echoed off the ballroom walls. Before only a breeze, it was now a gale, a hurricane, and everything in the room seemed to spin and clatter around Unle and Arayé. "Even Olófin himself saw the balance between us. Without misfortunes there can be no blessings, and without blessings, osogbo is all that remains, and I am the only one here with you now. I will be the only one with you always. And everywhere you go in the world, no matter how much good you do, when you leave I will be the one who remains in your place."

There was a great crash as the room settled; the wind ended as abruptly as it began, and everything stopped. Bodies, chairs, tables, food, the drums—it was all chaos and death in Unle's palace. And for the first time in his long, blessed life, Unle found himself alone.

For him, a lonely old man, there was no greater punishment.

---

*Añá is an orisha whose essence enlivens the drums; she is believed to be the voice of Olófin on Earth. When her drums are played, she drives osogbo from the room.

OBATALÁ'S INSANITY:
HOW ARAYÉ DESTROYED HIM

From the Odu Unle Ofún (8-10)

Arayé saw a great weakness in the orisha Obatalá: he cared too much about wickedness staining the world. At night, in the shadows, she came to him, showing him in his dreams every wicked thing that crept across the earth.

After years of this, Obatalá broke—he couldn't handle the nightmares anymore.

On the night he broke he awoke suddenly covered in sweat, his body shaking with rage and fear. Every night had been like this for longer than he cared to remember. He would lay his head on his pillow and close his eyes, weary from a day's labor, and as soon as his body went limp, his mind raced. He dreamed of all the pain and suffering existing in the world. He saw humans with bodies contorted and twisted in the most horrible shapes, afflicted with diseases that ate the flesh agonizingly and slowly. He heard mothers wail and fathers cry as their children died before their time. He saw entire countries rising against one another in war, murdering the innocent for no reason other than the color of their skin or the stain of their faith. He saw murder, rape, torture, arson, and every evil thing that humans do to one another in desperation. All that pain bore down on him like a crushing weight until he couldn't breathe. All that pain tormented his head, and he suffered. Sometimes he felt the world's pain; it was physical and it was intolerable.

One question burned his thoughts: *Why? In a world created by Olódumare's own hands, why does so much pain exist?* He reached out with his mind to feel every bit of it in the world; he wanted to know the torment of the human soul and the anguish it encompassed. Like a tsunami, despair swept him over, ate him up, and pushed him to his limits.

It was then that Obatalá went quite mad.

In his madness, he robed himself in black cloth, grabbed a machete, and rode out into the night. Like a sinister shadow he swept the globe, wailing like an osogbo and beheading everyone who stood in his way. The more he killed, the more wanted to kill, and like an insatiable force of nature he pillaged, he plundered, he avenged every horrible act in the world with brute strength. A great cry rose to heaven that night, because in his insanity Obatalá murdered not only the guilty, but also the innocent, for all human hearts contain wickedness.

Olófin heard their cries, and he took form on the earth to stop Obatalá.

The orisha was about to murder an innocent woman when Olófin stood between them. He held his arms out to the orisha, offering an embrace. "My son," Olófin pleaded, "you are not well. The world is afraid of you. Come here, to me."

Obatalá stiffened; rage boiled his blood. "*I* am not well? The *world* is not well! I can fix it—I can destroy everything and start it up again." His eyes were bloodshot with madness.

"Obatalá, look around you," Olófin pleaded. "You are murdering the innocent along with the guilty." He pointed to the woman Obatalá was about to behead: "She is a mother with eight children. If you take her, they have no one."

"Look inside her heart, Olófin." Obatalá's voice was gravelly and rough. "She is a thief. She robs people who work hard for their livelihood. And she is a prostitute. She is vile; she must die!"

"Look deeper, Obatalá," ordered Olófin, his voice calm but firm and unyielding. "Look deep inside her, and see why she does this."

Obatalá touched her head, wanting to crush it, but with Olófin watching, he was restrained. He closed his eyes and looked inside her head. He saw flashes of her youth: an alcoholic father and an abusive mother. She saw her husband raping and beating her. He saw the husband abandoning her for another woman, leaving her and her eight children to fend for themselves in the world. He saw her pain, her anguish, and how her heart broke every time she robbed, every time she turned a trick. But it was how she fed her family.

Obatalá trembled, just a hint of sanity returning to his eyes. "Olófin?" Tears came. "What have I done?"

The orisha collapsed into Olófin's arms, and together the two fell to the earth. For hours they sat there, Olófin comforting Obatalá, and Obatalá sobbing uncontrollably. When Obatalá's eyes closed from exhaustion, the mighty Olófin raised an arm to heaven, and a strong, swift wind carried them home.

No one ever saw insanity in Obatalá again. It is said that he lives in Olófin's palace, and Olófin, afraid of what he might do in the world if released, keeps him restrained, but comfortably so. And for now, the world is safe. We are safe. But the osogbo Arayé—she still plots . . .

7

Other Stories about the Osogbos

If our sufferings do not fill a basket, our blessings will never fill a cup.

FROM THE OLODU IROSUN (4 MOUTHS)

Writing this volume was a process of discovery and redesign. When I began working I had an image in my head of a book filled with nothing but patakís. Each osogbo has more than a single story to be told; each has a life to be explored and examined. But as I wrote the book, it took on a life of its own; it became philosophical in tone, and instead of just telling stories I explored the concept of osogbo and what it brought to the world. Through those earlier chapters I wove stories from the dilog-gún to illustrate my points; however, when it came time to sit down and write each misfortune's individual stories I had only so many words left for this book, so I had to choose thoughtfully.

Ikú, being the most misunderstood and most feared of all the mis-fortunes, demanded a chapter to herself. And Arayé, being the senior osogbo in the world, needed to be explored deeply through her sagas. That gave me room for one final chapter, one last collection of patakís to illustrate the flawed characters of these spiritual entities. I chose to speak of Ano's child, Lunacy, in the story titled "Ochosi's Confusion." Iñá, the osogbo War, is a complex character, and I chose two tales to illustrate his nature: "The Taming of Ogún" and "Iñá in the Kingdom of Unle." Eyo, Tragedy, is a major affliction in everyone's life at some time, therefore I felt the story of Eyo's birth, "The Good Brother and the Bad Brother," was essential to this collection. Of all the odu that ever walked the earth, Unle was the one who did the most work to try and banish the osogbos from the earth, so "Unle Builds a Home" made the final cut. The last two stories, "The Birth of Cholera" and "Ikú, Ano, and a Mother's Child" fleshed out this chapter. To me, all these stories speak of our inner strength, our will to live; they teach us that when things seem darkest, often we are closer to the light and to salvation than we know.

OCHOSI'S CONFUSION
From the Odu Okana Oché (1-5)

Ochosi sat alone in the dark, his hands covering his ears. He rocked back and forth, muttering to himself, trying to drown out the voices' onslaught. Ano's child, Lunacy, was after him, and although she is but a single creature she mimicked a legion of voices. "Do this," some voices demanded of him, while others insisted, "No, Ochosi, don't do that. Go out and do this instead." Often they came at once, a cacophonous roar, and he screamed in desperation, a primal roar that shook the walls of his home. "You shouldn't scream so loudly," warned one voice, "or the neighbors will think you are mad," while another voice countered, "But if you scream, we might go away." Finally, unable to handle the voices any longer, Ochosi stood up and spoke to the darkness, "Enough! None of you know what you want. None of you make any sense. Just go away!"

It was quiet inside his head.

Ochosi grabbed his crossbow and walked into the forest. Silently he trod through the undergrowth. In the distance he saw a deer. It was beautiful, with horns that reached proudly toward the skies. Carefully he aimed, one deadly arrow poised for the kill. "Don't kill that animal!" the voices screamed at him. "No, kill it—its meat will be tender!" The voices continued to plead with him while his hands shook.

"No, don't aim there; aim higher."

"No, not higher, lower."

Each voice was talking over the other until they were lost in a cacophony. Ochosi ignored them, focusing only on the hunt and the deer whose life he meant to take. He shot his arrow. Silently it ripped through the air and plunged deep into the animal's heart. Without a sound, it fell down, dead.

Calmly, Ochosi told the voices, "He who tells me how to hunt is like a man telling a woman how to give birth to her child. Be gone; I need no one's advice on what to do with my life."

Lunacy fled and never came back.

THE TAMING OF OGÚN
From the Odu Ogundá Oché (3-5)

The war was over, but Iñá wanted more. He had the orisha Ogún in his grip, his thirst for war pounding the orisha's body with every beat of his heart. Ogún stood above the rubble, his onyx-colored, muscled form slicked with sweat and gore. Yet his destruction was not done; Iñá's ashé was hot in Ogún's blood, and he brandished two machetes above his head with his thick, powerful arms. A deranged, primal scream poured from his lips, as much a warning as a threat. Earth stood still; darkness descended. Those who could ran, others hid, and some just cowered before his wrath. Like a rabid beast, Ogún descended on the town's survivors, slicing any who dared breathe. Blood flowed, and death was quick to all in his path.

Oshún Ibú Yemú trembled in the shadows. Her frail body, weak with age and exhaustion, could barely stand upright, let alone face the wild warrior orisha. But in the city she had many children, several of them priests, and she could not sit by idly while Ogún, in Iñá's grip, wiped out her followers. Smearing honey on her lips, she stepped into his path, holding both arms up to heaven, singing, "Gbajure aye e! Okonrin gogorogo ti ngbojuto iyade!"* For a moment, Ogún wavered as he saw the elderly Oshún before him; the words had barely reached him, but the challenge of the old woman touched him. Again Oshún Ibú Yemú sang, her words more insistent, more earnest, her words rising to heaven, more a prayer than a song, but sweet all the same. Ogún wavered. He trembled. The fog lifted from his brain as he looked around, and his eyes opened to the great evil he was causing—the needless death of those who once had nothing but love in their hearts for him, the patron of iron-workers. His heart stood still, and Iñá, who had him firmly in his grip, lost control. Ogún shook off the osogbo like a loose shawl.

Ogún, exhausted, fell to the earth in tears. Oshún Ibú Yemú came to him slowly, and carefully she knelt beside him, her ancient knees complaining as she bent over him. With love, Oshún cradled him against her breast.

For now, her people were safe.

THE GOOD BROTHER AND THE BAD BROTHER
From the Odu Ogundá Merindilogún (3-16)

Eyo and Tetura were brothers, twins, born from the same womb and at almost the exact same time. Eyo had come first; he looked at the world and saw it was safe. Then his brother, Tetura, came out. In life, as in birth, Eyo always ran before Tetura. He was the tempest, the storm, the bad that swept the land, while Tetura was the calm, the sunlight, the goodness that tried to undo what his brother had done, for Eyo was nothing but tragedy in the world, and Tetura spent all his time clean-ing up the chaos his brother created. When they were grown and their mother died, Tetura kept the family home, while Eyo decided to go out into the world alone. "You should not leave me," Tetura pleaded, "for I do not know how to live without you."

---

*Loosely translated from the Lucumí, "You are a great warrior in the world; your size does not let you come without knocking down the door!"

"You are too weak," Eyo replied. "You know not how to have fun and you kill all my joy. This is my time to be free. This is my time to know the world."

And know the world he did. Everywhere he went, Eyo created tragedy and left chaos in its wake. Without his brother to restore the balance and create harmony, soon the whole world knew that Eyo was nothing but trouble.

While he was away, Tetura went to see the diviners. "Do not let anyone stay in your home," they warned him. "No one, not even your own blood, not even your own brother, for he is a vile creature. He is Eyo—he brings tragedy and leaves destruction in his wake."

While Eyo walked the world alone his powers grew, and he knew, "My destiny is to destroy." And destroy he did. It was not long before the world sought justice, and everyone Eyo had harmed came together to destroy *him*. It was a lynch mob that scoured the countryside looking for the osogbo, for he was, indeed, a misfortune. And when Eyo discovered the world had turned against him, he went running back to his ancestral home.

"You cannot say here," Tetura said, his heart sinking when he saw his brother: he was hungry, he was thin, he was dirty, and his clothes were tattered.

"But the world is out to destroy me and I have nowhere else to go! You are my brother. You are my *twin*. We shared our mother's womb."

Tetura's heart was broken when he let his brother inside. He hid him in the cellar.

Unbeknownst to Tetura, the king had put a bounty on Eyo's head, so now the entire kingdom was looking for Eyo. Everyone wanted the reward. Because everyone *except* Tetura was out in the streets looking for Eyo, they all knew he was hiding in his brother's house.

The mob came to Tetura's home, their eyes glazed with madness. It was late at night when they arrived, and they encircled the house, lighting up the night with torches. They beat on the doors. They beat on his windows. They demanded, "Send your brother out so we can kill him. The king wants his head!"

But Tetura, being all things good and kind in the world, could not bear to send his brother out to the mob. He pulled a rug over the door that opened to the cellar beneath the floor and over this he dragged a piece of furniture so heavy that the mob would neither see nor find the entrance. Tetura opened his front door to meet the horde of humans, to tell them that his brother was not there, but before he could open his mouth they pulled at him and threw him into the street. They threw their torches in the door and through the windows, and soon Tetura's house was on fire. It burned with Eyo locked deep inside the cellar, and when the fire and smoke reached him Eyo began to scream.

The crowd cheered. Tetura cried.

Eyo died that day in the cellar; he died from the smoke and fire. Yet death only freed him from the flesh. When Ikú came for him she realized that he was one of their own. "Come with me," said Ikú, "and I will teach you what your ashé is. You are Eyo, Tragedy, and you will do great wicked things on the earth."

Since the day Eyo was set free from the flesh he has run through the world unchecked. And Ikú's word was true—his ashé was great. Everywhere he went he created great tragedy, sometimes in the lives of humans, other times in the world itself. Tetura, who was, in truth, the odu Ogundá Merindilogún, spent his life fighting Eyo's machinations in the world, but Tetura was a mere mortal. When he died, Eyo was left in the world with no one to bind him, no one to stop him, no one to clean up his messes. Since that day he has been an osogbo to be feared.

UNLE BUILDS A HOME
From the Olodu Unle (8)[1]

After years of wandering and serving his elders, Unle was no longer a young man. His body was old, his energy fading. He knew it was time to build a home of his own and cease his travels. Wanting to live some-place serene and quiet, he searched the coast of West Africa until he came to a small village.

It was well populated, but not overly so, and Unle noticed that the people who lived there were the saddest, most miserable humans he had ever seen. *I can help these people with my work,* he thought. With his earnings as a diviner, Unle hired the strongest and most skilled of the villagers to build a modest home, and although it was modest it was still grander than the homes of his neighbors. They became envious.

When his home was done, Unle moved in, and he divined for himself. Eight mouths opened on the mat. Unle said, "Death, Ikú, held me and left me. Sickness—the sisters Aro and Ano—embraced me and fled. I have survived the evil plans of my enemies." He marked ebó for himself; he made ebó, and the orishas told him that he was to offer all manner of food, drink, and kindness to any strangers who came to visit him. Unle vowed to prosper in his chosen home, and he resolved to do all that the orishas had told him.

Little did Unle know that the land he had claimed as his own, while outwardly serene and beautiful, lay in the middle of the sixteen osogbos who chose to settle on the earth. It was for this reason that the villagers were sad and miserable—because misfortune plagued them all the time. Ikú, Ano, Aro, Eyo, Arayé, Iñá, Tiya-Tiya, Ona, Ofo, Ogo, Akoba, Fitibo, Égba, Oran, Epe, and Ewon each owned a plot of land, and together these sixteen plots of land encircled the village like a vise grip. Each osogbo also owned an equal expanse of forest around one central plot. This land in the center was the most beautiful and fertile, while the sixteen plots around were almost equally so, but to avoid fights about who would have the absolute best, the sixteen osogbos had decided to keep that land in the center neutral. And as humans sought new places to conquer and live, the osogbos were glad to let them settle in their midst, as the misery they brought those humans brought joy to their hearts. But they could sense that Unle was different. He had ashé. And while the osogbos weren't yet sure what that gift entailed, they sensed it could loosen their grip on the world.

Unle was a skilled diviner, and people from faraway lands sought him out. They would travel through the abodes of the osogbos on their way to visit Unle and make ebó, and there, at the mat, Unle would know the osogbo whose land they had traveled through, and he would mark ebó so the osogbo could no longer hurt his client. Quickly they would make ebó, and this would only anger the osogbos more, for when the visitors would travel back through their lands, the osogbos were powerless to touch them.

One night, Ikú, Ano, and Aro met in the darkness. The night was cold, and they lit a fire against the chill. Some time passed awkwardly as they warmed themselves. Finally, Ano spoke: "Unle is an arrogant man. The world is a huge place, yet he chose to settle in our midst. I will drive him out. I will visit him tonight!"

"And what will you do? Give him a cold?" taunted Aro. "Unle may be elderly, but he's an extremely healthy man. Any illness you give him will be fleeting, easily cured." She gazed into the fire and smiled. "No, let me go tonight. I will visit him and make his remaining existence miserable."

Ikú frowned. "So you give him a lasting illness, Aro? And make him weak? He's already an old man. He is weak. And while he suffers from your visitation, he will still remain in our midst. He will wither for years, and we will have to put up with not only him, but also his brothers and sisters and godchildren as they make their way to pay their respects and nurse him back to health. And let us not forget that the other odu and diviners are powerful; even if you vex him well, there is still a chance that one of them might have the power to destroy us. No, let me visit him tonight. Death is the only way to be rid of him. Not even the orishas can bring back the dead."

The three osogbos came to an agreement: Ikú would be the one to visit Unle, for death was the only way to remove the old man from their midst. Each supplied Ikú with their power. Ano gave her all the fleeting illnesses of the world to use against Unle, and her sister, Aro, gave Ikú all the lasting, terminal diseases she had at her disposal. Ikú hid all these under her cloak; it swayed and billowed with their evil, as if whipping in an unfelt wind. Blessed with all the gifts of the two sisters, Ikú stole away, invisible to the world, to Unle's house.

As Ikú scraped at the front door, seeking entrance, Unle felt her presence. He called out into the night, "Who is here?" as he opened his front door in welcome, remembering his own divination from when he came to this place. "I can't see you, but I can feel you; I know that a powerful spirit has come to visit me tonight. Show yourself, and let us know each other."

Unle knew that it was Death herself who had come to visit him, and he knew that Ikú only came when it was time to die. Yet Unle was a wise odu, and he knew many ways to thwart death for a time. Ikú, surprised at the warm welcome by the naive man, called together a disguise; she presented herself as a middle-aged woman, pleasant to gaze at but worn from years of toil. As her disguise coalesced and congealed, Unle was surprised. He had expected a fearful specter but instead found Ikú to be warm, almost inviting. Still, Unle was not ready to die, and he intended to stretch out his time on the newly created earth.

Before Ikú could strike, Unle offered her a place to sit and rest her weary feet. Quickly he offered her food and drink, bringing out all the already-prepared foods he had from that day. As they spoke, Unle busied himself in the kitchen, and before Ikú could remember why she was at his house, the odu presented her with a wide array of yams, fruits, meats, and desserts. Unle continued to distract the osogbo with warm conversation while she gorged herself on the food before her—she was so full that she was lazy. And while Unle chatted on, Ikú thought, *I can't ever remember a victim who has fed me so well!*

Then she rose to strike, only she was so gorged that she could barely move. Unle, sensing danger again, brought her a huge share of liquor and encouraged her to drink. So quickly did she drink, and so quickly did she become drunk, that she could no longer hold a coherent thought. She soon forgot why she had even come to Unle's house. When Ikú was beyond intoxication, Unle gasped and said, "Why, it is nearly morning and we have been up all night eating and drinking. I have a long day ahead of me, and I must have at least a few hours' sleep." He helped Ikú up from her chair where she was all but passed out. "Before you leave, my friend, let me offer you this, the fattest chicken from my coop. I am sure you have a large family yourself and will need to feed them, too, when you get home." Ikú was so drunk, so full, so tired, and so confused that she could only thank Unle for his hospitality, and with the night slowly melting as sunrise approached, she left.

It was morning when Ikú stumbled back to the embers that remained of the osogbos' fire. She was visibly drunk and gorged, and the two sisters were angry when they saw she had returned without Unle's soul. Aro hissed, "Why did you not kill him like you promised? He still intrudes on our land!"

"You dared taunt me, Aro, because all I could do was give him a cold? And you, Ikú, I had images in my head of you slicing and dicing him to pieces with your scythe. Instead, it seems you had a merry time with the old man. Kill him indeed! Only way to get rid of him indeed! You are a disgrace! At least if I'd gone, he'd be drowning in his own secretions by now."

Ikú, shaken and dizzy, mildly offered, "Perhaps we should just leave him alone . . . ?" She was still sated on Unle's kindness.

"We will finish what you could not do!" screamed Ano as she took back all the misfortunes that she and her sister had piled on Ikú. "You are useless. We will gather the other thirteen osogbos, my sister and I, and tonight we will rage on Unle's home like a storm from heaven. We will do what you could not!"

The sisters left Ikú there by the fire, and soon she fell asleep.

Later that day, after Unle had rested, he divined for himself once more. The diloggún told him that he was facing osogbo again, and so he quickly made ebó with a goat, a ram, and sixteen roosters. With these he prepared a huge feast and set his table for sixteen guests. He also laid out sixteen bolts of cloth as his divination demanded. Then, exhausted, he sat down to rest and waited for his divination to fulfill itself.

It was at sunset that the fifteen remaining osogbos decided to assault Unle and his home; with them they had brought Eshe, all the general afflictions of the world that they did not control among themselves. Because Unle had already proved with Ikú that he could see them regardless of how they appeared, they came in their full power and normal forms, assaulting his home from without, seeking entrance.

Unle heard them as they scratched at his walls, and remembering how he was told to entertain all strangers that came to his home, he threw open his door and called out into the night, "Friends, it is cold outside and warm within my walls. Come inside and let us know one another."

Aro called to the other osogbos, "This is too easy. To be invited is to guarantee one's own destruction. Follow me!"

All the osogbos rushed inside Unle's house, and the modest man was aghast at the nakedness of his guests. Before any of them could raise their hands against him, Unle gathered up the sixteen bolts of cloth and presented each osogbo with one. "Clothe yourselves," he offered, "for it is not seemly to be traveling naked."

Such was Unle's surprise and modesty that each osogbo blushed before him, and quickly they each wrapped themselves with the cloth offered. As they dressed, he ushered them to his table where the feast had been prepared. It was then that Aro understood how Ikú had been thwarted. "Old man," she hissed, "someone has told you our weakness. You know that we cannot harm those who offer us random kindness."

"No one has told me anything," insisted Unle.

"Someone must have!" The other osogbos, comfortable in their new clothing, were feasting, oblivious to Aro's growing frustration.

"I merely divined and did what divination told me. I made ebó to the orishas, and then laid out this feast and waited for the guests I was told would come."

"You are a diviner? There is a diviner living in the midst of our kingdom?" Suddenly Aro knew why all those they had afflicted had been saved, and why they remained powerless to destroy them after that. "Now we will lose all our powers in our own kingdom."

"No one knows your secrets. I myself did not know, not until you told me just now. I only did for you what the orishas told me I must do to avoid misfortune: I received strangers with kindness. And now that I seem to know your greatest secret, I will do for you what I do for everyone who confides in me as a diviner: I will keep your confidence. Unfortunately, I must continue to help those who come to me for divination; those, I am afraid, will be saved from your evil if they choose to make ebó. But don't worry—not everyone who comes to me for divination makes ebó. Even if I continue my work, which I assure you, I will, you will still have plenty of victims to prey upon."

Aro stood, confused, angry, and hurt. She had not yet put on the cloth, and she was cold. She had not yet touched the food, but hunger overwhelmed her.

"Come, lady—clothe yourself. And eat. The night is still young, and there is much to discuss, is there not?"

Aro smiled as she dressed herself. "It was Ikú herself who came to see you yesterday, and it is your kindness that kept her from killing you the moment she walked through the door. I am Ano, sickness, and it is your kindness now that keeps me from laying waste to you. No human, orisha, or odu has ever granted us such kindness. We will not harm you today. We won't harm you tomorrow. And, definitely, we won't harm you the day after that. But watch yourself, Unle; always remember us. For it is the nature of life to wither and die, and one day, while we won't come to you as an enemy, we will come to you again. It is what we do."

But that night, for once, all the osogbos were Unle's guests; he tended and treated them all well. And when the sun rose the next day, they parted as friends. True to his word, Unle remembered each of them with kindness and never betrayed their secret. And since not all his clients who came for readings made the prescribed ebós, the osogbos still had their fill of human misfortune.

This is how Unle thwarted all the osogbos of the world with his wisdom and lived to a ripe old age, even in a land surrounded by misfortunes.

IÑÁ IN THE KINGDOM OF UNLE

From the Olodu Unle (8)

The spirit of Iñá moved silently in the night, making his way to the ocean. It was a moonless sky, but Iñá's eyes loved the darkness; for him, beauty lay in murky shades of black in the shadows. At the shore he stood, ice-cold water washing over his feet, the sand beneath them shifting and sucking his toes in the muck. It was low tide and the ocean seemed calm. "Olokun," he whispered to the orisha who rules the ocean, straining to hear over the waves. "Olokun," he called again, with still no answer. Finally, "Olokun!" he roared. His voice was so powerful it stirred up the very ocean before him.

Olokun rose from the sea.

At first he was just salt water rising like a waterspout. Then the water washed away, and with only the light of stars Iñá could see a dark male body, darker than even the night air. Olokun walked in the ocean toward him, his body bulging with rippled muscles and a chest that looked at once both female and male, with its breasts a bit too big for a man but too hard and defined for a woman. Soon the two stood at the edge of the ocean face-to-face, Iñá's back to the sand and Olokun's back to the ocean.

"What business have I with you, osogbo?" Olokun asked. "I don't like to be bothered with your kind." His voice roared with all the power of the sea.

Iñá smiled; it was a wicked grin that chilled even Olokun. "The kingdom that stands on your borders is soon to be without a king," he said, pointing to the edge of the cliffs beyond which the kingdom's borders lay. "For tonight the king himself lies dying in his bed, and the old man Unle holds vigil over his wasted flesh." When Olokun only glared, Iñá continued, "This is the same kingdom that for years has intruded on yours without so much as an ebó. The entire town lives by worshipping Obatalá, the very orisha who bound your kingdom and shrank your realm. And the king has no heir. When he dies, you could have your own priest reclaim that kingdom in your name. He could rule, and instead of worshipping Obatalá as supreme they would be forced to worship you as the orisha of their town."

"Obatalá protects that kingdom, and he is a powerful orisha, Iñá."

"As are you," he replied.

"And to wrestle that kingdom away from Obatalá's worship, it would take a war."

"I am the spirit of war, and I am at your service."

"You serve no one but yourself, Iñá." Olokun turned and had begun to sink back into the ocean when Iñá's hand reached out to grab him by the shoulder. Olokun felt heat from Iñá's fingertips, and then he felt something hot flood his body—anger. He turned and struck the osogbo with his fist, sending him flying through the air and landing in the soft sand with a thud. The anger Iñá put into Olokun pierced his heart and clouded his mind, and in a rage he roared, "I will have my priest destroy everyone who stands between him and that throne; and I will have him destroy the worship of Obatalá and replace it with my own. When the king dies, he will gather soldiers and they will march. My priest will take the palace by force, and I will kill any man, woman, or child who stands in his way!"

High tide began rolling up on shore, a furious rush of water that sounded like a thousand maniacs laughing.

Iñá's work was done. Soon there would be war. And soon Iñá would feast on the blood-soaked earth.

Sadness lay across the land like a thick quilt the day the king died. He had been already an old man when some of the town's elders had been in their youth; he had attended the burials of many as they passed. "He is blessed by Olófin!" his people had agreed, and there were those who thought him immortal, forever frozen in the fragile frame of an old man. Still, flesh is weak even when blessed by the orishas, and the day came that the king could no longer rise from his bed without assistance. Soon, he could not sit up at all. And one morning his attendants walked in to find him still sleeping, but burning with fever.

"It's old age," the royal physician said. "The time of his passing—it's near."

Since his youth, Unle had served as the old king's diviner, and Unle was there at his bedside, an old man himself but not quite so ancient as the king. "I will sit with him," he vowed to the doctor. "I will not leave his side; he will not die alone." For days Unle sat there, unmoving. After many days the monarch's breath slowed, and when his chest fell for the last time it was a soft sigh, a gentle, mournful release that let Unle know: *he is dead*. He put his head on the king's chest and wept.

This was how the royal physician found them both when he made his afternoon rounds.

"How long?" he asked.

Unle looked up, not rising from his master's bedside. "Hours, perhaps," he said. "I've been praying for his soul since his last breath."

"I'll make the preparations for his funeral." Gently, the young physician touched Unle's shoulder. "You need rest. You've sat vigil at his bedside for days."

Gently, Unle let himself be led to his own chambers. Sleep came, dreamless and deep.

After the funeral and days of mourning, the town's elders pushed back at the sadness engulfing the kingdom. There was work to be done. "He died with no heir," said the eldest of the elders. "He had no wife, and he had no children; the kingdom was his family. And now there is no one to rule in his place."

"But he did have one man he looked up to more than any other," said the youngest. All eyes were on him when he said, "Unle." They were silent. "Unle served him faithfully for decades. The king never made a decision without consulting his diviner, and in the end, no matter what the people wanted, he did what the orishas wanted. That's why we have been prosperous all our years."

The eldest man stood up. "Would Unle, then, make a good king? Could a diviner rule?"

It was another elder who answered him, an aged priest of the orisha Obatalá. "In a sense, he already did. If our king presented all our troubles to Unle for divination, and if divination gave him the answers by which to rule, would not a diviner be able to rule wisely? Especially since it was the same diviner that our king trusted all his life?"

For the first time anyone could remember, the elders' idea was put to a vote. Unanimously, the town decided that Unle would be their new king. He, of course, accepted.

Unle's wisdom, acquired from a lifetime of study and servitude, was unmatched in the world. So loved and respected was he by mortals that when their king died they installed him as the new ruler. He accepted the crown not for himself, but for his friends, and vowed to do all he could to improve their lives in the village. Tirelessly he worked, and very quickly the small village became a prosperous town; everyone enjoyed the abundance and riches brought by Unle's leadership.

Even Unle's enemies enjoyed the newfound wealth, for Unle did have enemies.

Iñá went to the home of Olokun's priest with the orisha's blessings, and as the man slept, lightly he touched him over his heart. The heat of war entered his soul. The young priest awoke, Iñá's ashé rushing through his blood, and he said, "This kingdom—it should be mine!" No one was there to hear him, but he swept his feet over the edge of the bed and stood. Had someone been in his chamber, they would have shrunk back in fear. His eyes narrowed, his dark features sharpened, and he raved in the darkness. "Unle is not fit to be king, and Obatalá is a weak orisha. I am young. I am strong. And it is Olokun who owns this world. I will kill Unle, and while I bathe in the blood of my enemy the town will crown me king. Then the temples dedicated to the orisha Obatalá will be torn down. Shrines will be built to my orisha, Olokun. We will dominate this earth." He remained awake all night long, planning, and during the day, stealthily, secretly, he gathered rebel forces to overthrow Unle and take over the kingdom Unle now ruled. He planned war, with the spirit of Iñá, who *was* war personified, at his side.

After months of planning, the priest had sufficient strength and numbers, and together they rose up at the town's gate and began making their way to the palace. Unle's advisors came to him in fear. They warned him of the impending revolution, and Unle, knowing he didn't have the strength to fight, fled.

He fled to the home of Mofá, the wisest diviner in his kingdom.

When Mofá opened his door to Unle, concern darkened his ancient face. Unle was an elder, and a strong elder, but the man who visited that day looked tired and weary. His brows were furrowed, his eyes red from tears, and his body was stiff with exhaustion. "Unle?" asked Mofá. He wasn't sure if it was really his king.

Unle pushed his way inside Mofá's home, closing the door behind him, and he rested his back against the entrance. "Mofá," he said, "I am afraid for my life." He shook, his entire body quivering as if bracing against a chill. "Olokun's priest is angry that I was crowned king and not he, and he has gathered an army strong enough to rip the kingdom from me. I think he wants me dead." Unle closed his eyes, trembling.

"The orishas have a solution for everything. Let us see what the solution to this is."

Mofá divined for the diviner that day, and as Unle's signature odu fell on the mat, Mofá frowned. He continued to question his diloggún and found that the osogbo of war, Iñá, was on the old man. He took a deep breath. "If you want to save your own life and remain king in your own kingdom, you must offer a sacrifice to Obatalá: a white, female goat." Mofá looked at Unle as he listened to make sure he understood. "But this is most important, and I want you to understand this: the way that you offer the sacrifice must change."

"How so?"

"A kingdom can have only one king, just as a body can have only one head. You are both a king and a head. But right now both are in danger. Your kingdom is under attack. Iñá is there and he wants one thing—your head. When you sacrifice this goat, you are to clean yourself with it. Throw the entire body into the ocean, but save the head. Find a safe place to hide in the rocks on the shore. Keep the head with you; do not lose it. As this situation plays out, it will all make sense . . . in time. And just wait there until you are found."

While Unle was sitting on Mofá's mat, the evil priest and his rebels were storming his palace. When they found it empty they assumed he had fled in fear, and a great cry rose to heaven—victory! Because the town was still under Obatalá's protection, the rebels made a sacrifice to him, a single white goat. But Olokun's priest was already planning how to tear down the temples dedicated to the orisha, and on the cliffs overlooking the ocean he was planning a huge house to store the sacred implements of Olokun. Then he would force everyone to dedicate themselves to the worship of his orisha, not Obatalá.

"What should we do with the head?" one of the rebels asked the priest. He looked at the head of the sacrificed goat thoughtfully.

"Throw it into the ocean from high off the cliff," he said. "That is the place where soon I will build a temple to my orisha, Olokun. But give Olokun the head as a symbol that now the head of his priest rules this town. Once we are settled in we will plan a huge series of sacrifices to properly honor my orisha."

As he was told, the rebel went to the edge of the cliff and threw the head into the sea for Olokun. It was swallowed up by the ocean's waters, and it made its way to the bottom, where Olokun lay waiting. When the head settled at his feet he knew that his priest was the new king. *Soon the town will be dedicated to me,* Olokun thought. He was pleased.

Neither the rebel nor Olokun knew that just beneath the cliffs, Unle hid in the rocks holding the head of a female goat. But Obatalá knew—he had received Unle's offering, and at that moment he was preparing to descend to earth to make sure *his* child, Unle, remained in power.

As the day's celebrations continued among the rebels, they moved their party to the shore. It was a big festival that day as they roasted their goat. As they cooked, Obatalá made the great trip between heaven and earth.

When Obatalá appeared among them, at the edge of the shore where water and land fought with the rising and lowering of the tides, Olokun's priest prostrated before him and waited for the orisha's blessing before rising. Obatalá offered none; instead, he demanded, "What is happening here? Why do I feel a great evil spreading on the earth?"

Olokun's priest remained on the sand and looked up at the mighty orisha. "Father," he said, "we are having a celebration. Unle fled the kingdom today, and the people are installing me as their new king."

Obatalá knew the evil in the priest's heart; he knew everything in the hearts of humans. His ancient eyes narrowed, and as he touched the man on his shoulders he felt the heat of Iñá still running through his veins. Wordlessly, with a light touch of his fingers, he bid the priest to rise. As the priest sought to embrace Obatalá, the orisha put his hand on his chest to hold him back—the heat of Iñá made the orisha's head throb—and he said, "To celebrate the coronation of a new king in this kingdom, it is Olófin's law that you must make sacrifice to me. What offering did you give?"

"Father, to you we offered a female goat." Obatalá saw the meat roasting over an open pit. Beside it were the animal's body parts. The orisha began counting them.

"I have two arms, two legs, a sternum, the left and right sides of the stomach, a liver, two kidneys, and a heart. There is the chest, spinal column, pelvis, and tail. There is the neck and the ring. I have the first two vertebrae, and here is the skin."

The priest was proud as Obatalá counted all the parts. Then, confused, Obatalá asked, "Where is the head? Is the head not mine as well?"

The priest's face turned red; he had instructed his followers to give the head to Olokun, and he had not another one to serve to Obatalá. "Father," said the priest as he tried to retain his composure, "of course the head is yours. It is but an oversight. I will have another goat sacrificed to you immediately to be in compliance with Olófin's law."

"There is a head in the boulders on the shore," said Obatalá. "Since the head is mine, and since the head rules the body, the one with the head will rule this town forever." Quickly, the rebels ran to the rocks, and there, with Obatalá in their midst, they found Unle hiding, holding the head he had kept from his own sacrifices.

That day Obatalá used his ashé to banish Olokun's priest from the town, for though he was an old man he was powerful, the king of all the orishas, and no one, not even Olokun, could fight against his word. And it was because Unle had saved the head of his sacrifice for Obatalá, as Mofá had instructed, that Unle had remained the head, the true king, of Obatalá's earthly kingdom. There, just beyond the cliff that overlooked Olokun's realm, he lived his life out, ruling with knowledge and wisdom. And Olokun, as angry as he was, could not touch Obatalá's kingdom because it stood higher on land than his power reached.

Unle ruled there for many years, and it was the most prosperous kingdom on the earth.

THE BIRTH OF CHOLERA
From the Odu Unle Ogundá (8-3)

At the moment of death, my elders taught me, the soul of the deceased escapes with the body's last breath. It isn't a normal breath, they said, but a sigh from deep within the belly. When Aro, sickness, came to our village, my two elder priests were the first to so sigh. I was the last priest left to my people. Some said they were the ones to bring osogbo to our town. Now I must be a healer, a doctor, but at this I am a failure. While my patients lay dying, I console them as well as their loved ones. The sick fight death; they struggle against the pain and the weakness as their bowels unleash an unholy flood of rice water, their eyes sinking in their sockets while once-healthy black skin ashens, turning bluish in the extremities. They flatten with death as water leaves from their behinds, but their loved ones don't care. They hold the dead close and wail, unafraid that their own time might come soon. Then I am forced to be a mortician, wrapping flat, stiff corpses with white sheets before the stronger men of our village pile the bodies on carts.

They all smell like dead fish.

Each body is a failure, my failure, sealed in white cloth.

Together, with thick ropes biting into our shoulders, we pull the carts into the forest. We are silent, and under the strain sweat drips down our faces, our muscles aching from working so hard under a hot summer sun. Our noses know we are near the iroko trees before our eyes do; the stench there is thick from dozens of bodies exposed under the roots of the trees.* Most men cover their mouths, but the smell no longer bothers me. I say a prayer for each before we tip the cart—and, yes, we tip it because we can no longer bear to touch the hard, flat

---

*Until the olodu Odí (7 mouths) and Odí Meji (7-7), the bodies of the dead were not buried. Corpses were wrapped in white cloth and laid to rest under trees in the forest.

corpses filling it. They roll onto the earth, a mass of dead wrapped in white. When the plague began, further north, we lay the first ones ceremonially, my elder priests included, and with the proper rites—we lay them carefully against the tree trunks. But now those older bodies poke through shredded cloth, the elements already doing their job and taking human flesh back to the earth.

One corpse looks like the next; in death, all are equal.

It's a nightmare, I think. *If only someone would touch me, or pinch me, or shake me . . . so I could wake up.*

"Obeyono?" A man standing to my side grabs my shoulder; I don't wake up. The nightmare is real. I try hard to remember his name but I can't. He is young, tall, and wiry. *Someone this young should not know so much suffering,* I think, *but how old am I? Twenty-six.* All this sickness makes me feel old, as young as I am.

"Obeyono?" he says again. "Is there nothing we can do?" I see another young man in our group sprinting south, guarding his abdomen with one hand while the other seals his mouth. Vomit runs between his fingers. *We have another one,* I think.

"We need help," I say. "Maybe if I go see Olófin, maybe he can help us."

While that one young man falls behind a tree, retching and relieving himself, the young man next to me has a glimmer of hope in his eye.

We carry the sick man back to town in one of the carts; no one is willing to touch him or help him except me. Still guarding his stomach, he crawls into one of cleaner carts, balling up in the only corner he can find not soiled with human waste. He lies there shivering as we pull him back from the forest. We enter the village. Normally on a day like this the marketplace would be filled with women hawking their wares while their men look on protectively, and children would be screaming and shouting under the darkening shadows of a setting sun. But today is quiet except for the wails of women over their newly sick or dead husbands and children. There are lamps and torches lit in memory of loved ones, and their fires light up the shadows as the sun slips from view. My own wife tends the sick under a makeshift tent set up in the village square, bedrolls and blankets being all that separates their bodies from the earth.

The smell is horrible.

I find her showing a woman how to change her husband's soiled sheets without lifting him; she rolls him from side to side as the wife cleans his backside, putting a new cloth between him and the bedroll. "Obeyono, there are more sickened," she says. Even though she has not bathed in days, she is still the most beautiful woman I've ever known, my only happiness in the wake of so much osogbo.

"I am going to Olófin's," I say, my voice firm.

"Obeyono, no. We need you here." Her eyes are pleading with me.

"Olófin is the wisest among us, and if anyone knows how to stop this epidemic it will be him."

"Can't you make ebó?"

If only she knew how often I've made ebó, how many times I've opened my own odu on the table of Ifá and chanted my heart out for the orishas. My prayers have gone unanswered. "I've made ebó. But I'm missing something." Then, more quietly, so no one else can hear, I whisper to her, "I don't know what else to do. I am too young and untrained."

She moves close to me, her head touching my chest lightly. She smells of earth and sweat. I take her scent in deeply; it is fresher than the other smells of the square. "I will pack for you," she says. "But for our sake, husband, be swift."

While the sick moan and their caretakers sleep fitfully at their sides, I mount my horse and slip out of town.

The last time I traveled this path I went with my elders. The day had been young, the sun barely over the tops of the trees, but it was hot and we stopped frequently to water our horses. Now I travel at night, and there is only the moon, full and pale but high enough in the sky that the forest glows with silver light. It is just enough for me to see a few feet ahead, and I know my horse's eyes can see much farther. With nightfall comes cooler air, and although I travel slowly through the shadows I know I will make it to Olófin's house much faster than the last time I came this way. There will be no stopping to rest the horse, no need for frequent watering. His gait is fast and steady. Soon, I relax on his back and let my body rock in time with his.

There were three of us on my last trip, myself and my two elders. Olófin had called for us by messenger, and his message was cryptic. "Olófin feels that something isn't right in his life," the young man told us, "and he wants the three of you to come to his home and divine for him."

"Us, divine for Olófin?" I asked. Olófin was the wisest man in the land, the closest person to Olódumare we knew. "Why would Olófin need a diviner?"

"You are too young to understand these things," said the eldest priest. "Everyone comes to the feet of Orúnmila in time." He stood quiet for a moment, letting his words sink in deep. "We will go," he said to the messenger, "and we will divine for Olófin. Go ahead of us while we make preparations and tell him we will be there soon after your arrival."

The messenger left as he was told; we packed. Before too much time passed we were on the road, and within two days we were at Olófin's house.

We wasted no time there. We sat before the table of Ifá. Because I was the youngest, the freshest, my elders demanded that I be the one to make the prayers and work the *ikin,* counting them by hand and then marking the figures in the sand on the table. I was nervous, my fingers fumbling with the palm nuts while my elders frowned and Olófin looked on. But soon I found my rhythm, and I was counting the palm nuts and marking lines in the dust on the wooden board. Soon there were several lines marked, a complete series, and I put the ikin back in the container.

My elders smiled. "Ogbe Ogundá!" said the middle babalawo, the odu after which I was named. "Maferefún Orúnmila! What troubles you, Olófin?"

Olófin frowned and took a deep breath before speaking. "I woke up yesterday with the feeling that something . . . wasn't quite right." There was silence. This was what the messenger had told us, and my godparents were waiting for more. "So I called for you. Something has changed in my life. I want to know what it is and what to do about it."

"There is nothing new in your life!" said the eldest babalawo. "As always, you are Olófin and you know your place. You have all the blessings Olódumare has to give!"

"As said my brother, there is nothing new under the sun," said the middle bobalawo. "You have the blessings of Olódumare and all of the orishas. Your life is as it should be."

They looked at me, my godparents and Olófin, all three of them waiting for me to speak. I sat there trembling, looking at my own pattern in the dust, worried. This was my sign in Ifá, the odu under which I was born. And when I was made a priest, both of my godparents had told me how blessed my own life would be. Not two months later, my first and only child died. *Cholera,* one of the village women had called it; she was a healer, an herbalist, and before she could treat my child, my little son was dead. I no longer felt that my odu was much of a blessing.

I had watched when the last breath left his body; it was, indeed, a great sigh that came from deep within his belly. Whether or not his soul left with it, I have no clue.

"This is my odu, Olófin, and it is a very dangerous sign."

My elders were annoyed. "He is too young. He knows nothing," the eldest said. The other priest agreed.

"Everyone has a right to speak here," said Olófin. "Young man, continue."

"This is my odu as a babalawo," I said. "Everyone told me it was blessed, that my life was as it should be. But not two months after this odu fell, my son died. One of the older women in the village said it was cholera; he couldn't be saved."

"Did you not make ebó?" Olófin asked.

"I made ebó when my odu came, but when my child got sick things happened too fast. There was no time," I said.

"Olófin has no children!" said the oldest babalawo. "There is no child to die!"

"Agreed," said the other babalawo, "because this odu speaks nothing of children." He looked at Olófin sternly. "Please, Olófin, pay no attention to him. He knows nothing about odu. And he is so young. There is nothing wrong with your life."

"Everything is as it should be," said the eldest priest.

With those words, they closed the odu.

We were sent home, and three days later the messenger returned. I greeted him at my home, but as before he wasted no time with his message. "Olófin sends for your elders," he said. "Have them make the trip immediately. You are to stay at home."

A few days later they returned, their skin ashen and gray, smelling of rotten fish. They weakened quickly, while others in our town also began to get sick. "Those two priests brought back a great osogbo with them," whispered the wise woman, the same woman who was there when my own son died. Before long, it was a plague. And it took the old woman with it.

By sunrise, alone, I arrive at Olófin's home. I tie my horse to a tree and quietly approach the front door. *It is too early,* I think, gently tapping on the wood frame. The same messenger who had come to our village many times opens the front door. "Obeyono," he says, "Olófin said you might come." He points to a stand just outside the door that holds fresh water and black soap. "Wash your hands well before you come in and remove your shoes. You must be clean when you come inside this house."

I wash, and after I wash the messenger pours another jícara of fresh water over my hands. My shoes come off and sit outside the door. I walk into the morning gloom; Olófin's house is usually light, airy, and well lit. Today it seems a home in mourning.

The messenger seats me while he disappears deeper into the house. It was here that we sat and read the table of Ifá. It was here that the odu Ogbe Ogundá opened in the powder. It was here that we told Olófin nothing in the world had changed. I shudder, for surely the world has changed. People are dying and it seems that there is no way to stop it.

Shadows in the house shorten as the day grows brighter. It is perhaps noon before Olófin comes in to greet me. In reverence, I kiss my fingers and touch the dust on the floor. Olófin offers no blessing; his eyes seem empty, full of sadness.

"I know what brings you, Obeyono," he says, his voice a whisper. "Of the three of you who read for me that day, you were the wisest. I should have listened to you." With his arm on my back, he gently leads me through his house, to his back door. He pushes it open and shows me the woods that lie just beyond his compound. "Out there, deep in the woods, lies the body of my son. My only son."

I have no words, only shock, and I listen as Olófin speaks.

"When the three of you came to see me that day, my child, my only child, lay sick in bed. No one knew I had a child. But you seemed to know." He is silent. And then he tells me, "Well, maybe you did not know I had a child, but you had experience with this odu, and you yourself lost a child. Your elders should have let you speak, and I should have listened more carefully. But they . . . they were trained by Orúnmila himself, and I trusted their wisdom. It was not a trust I should have so easily placed.

"After the three of you left, my son died. I mourned. I sent my messenger back to your village to ask for just your elders. I wanted them to come see what they had done—that they had refused to let you speak, refused to let you save my child with your ashé. But now I know there is no way to save someone from this illness. It can only be prevented.

"So filled with grief was I when they came to my house that I had part of my son's body stewed, and since they failed to see death in my house, I fed them death in my house. It is that same death that they took back with them to your village."

Now I understand the horror Olófin feels. His own son, dead; the babalawos he trusted most, dead. And there is no coming back from death.

"But now, Olófin, we all suffer," I tell him. "The elderly. The young. The weak. The strong. We all die, and we die in great numbers. Is there no way to call back what you have unleashed?"

"I will teach you a great secret, Obeyono, and never again will anyone criticize you for your youth." I am silent. I wait. "Ano is a creature of filth. And while she can be spread on the earth, in the air, or in the water, most often we spread her by our own hands. This is why I had you wash your hands before you came into my house. You came from a place filled with sickness, and that sickness you carry with you on your very own hands."

It takes me a moment to realize what Olófin is saying. I look at my hands. I turn them over. How many sick people have I touched? How many corpses have I carried? The number is too high to count. The thought that Ano can be spread on my hands makes me feel ill.

"But I've not washed my hands before, Father," I say. "My wife, she has never washed her hands. There are many in the village who do not wash their hands, yet they tend to the sick and they don't get sick."

"Olódumare was wise when he created the world," says Olófin. "Even though Ano would like nothing better than to make the entire world sick so that Ikú can gorge herself, there will always be those on the earth with the ashé to fight off any plague that comes. Were it not for that, life would have ended centuries ago. The first case of smallpox would have wiped the world out; instead, it gave birth to Babaluaiye's priesthood, those who are immune to his scourge."

"Olódumare is wise."

"That he is."

I put my head on the floor in obeisance to Olófin. Gently, he blesses me and lifts me. As he embraces me I feel his ashé; it is like warm water flowing into me, soothing me. I don't deserve his blessing, but the old man is so kind he gives it despite my shortcomings. When he holds me at arm's length and lets me go, I want to reach out to him, to grab him and fall to my knees and beg his forgiveness. As if he is reading my mind he says, "There is no need for that. But you must go back to your village. You must teach them how to wash their hands. Those who have tended the dying since the plague first began are the strongest among you; they will not get sick if they have not yet. The bodies of your dead—take them far away from your village, for the disease can sink into the earth. Take them far away from your rivers, because it can travel in the water. Do these things and the epidemic will slow, and then it will end. This I promise."

I am crying when Olófin leads me to the front door. "Obeyono," he says as he opens the door, "there is no need for tears. You are blessed. The world is as it should be. And you will be remembered in history as the one who knew the secret to ending the great plague."

So I take Olófin's wisdom home to my village. Those of us who cared for the sick in the beginning continue to care for the sick until the end. We clean them; we change them; we feed them and give them cool water. And we wash our hands well and change our clothing before going home to our own loved ones. The great caravans of cadavers are no longer taken to the iroko trees at the edge of town; instead, they travel at least two days into the depths of the forest, and those who take them wash their hands and change their clothes when they leave that place.

It only takes eight days; eight days and the plague that sought to destroy us all leaves us.

And since that time, whenever Ano comes to visit our village, we follow the words and wisdom of Olófin: we wash our hands whenever sickness is around. And we live. My son did not live; Olófin's son did not live; but we—we live.

IKÚ, ANO, AND A MOTHER'S CHILD
From the Odu Ejila Shebora Meji (12-12)

It was late morning when the young mother woke up. *Such a deep sleep,* she thought. *The baby has not slept this well in months.* She stood beside his crib, looking down; his face was flushed. Lifting the baby carefully, she felt how his clothing was damp, his body limp. The baby barely moved. She put her moist lips to his brow and felt fever. She rubbed one hand over his chest and belly; a wet cry escaped his lips. "Husband!" she screamed. The tiny boy was barely moving. "Husband! I need you!" Instead, her teenage son came into the room. "Where's your father?" she asked. "The baby's sick. We need a doctor."

"He left early to work in the fields," he said, rubbing sleep from his eyes. "What's wrong?"

The panic made her voice shake; it made her body shake, with the baby barely moving in her arms. "The baby is sick. We need the doctor. Run into town and bring him."

He dressed and ran off toward the village. He had never seen his mother looking so worried.

It was early evening when Mofá arrived at the young mother's house with her teenage son at his side. The door was ajar; they let themselves in. The woman's son found her standing over the baby's crib, her hands folded just below her chin and her eyes closed as if praying. Her face was ashen; tears like crystals dried on her dark cheeks. The young man stood in the doorway and cleared his throat softly. Her eyes snapped open; they were red.

"You brought him?"

"He's in the front room," he said.

"Watch the baby." She all but ran to the front room, and when she saw the wise old physician standing there patiently, she all but fell into his arms, embracing him. "My baby son is dying," she whispered. "He barely breathes. He barely moves."

She led Mofá by the hands to the infant's crib. Mofá looked down on the child. His breath was all but still in his belly. He put his head against his chest, careful not to disturb him. "He is all but at death's door," he said, his brow furrowed deeply. "I think he is beyond any medicine I can prepare. Maybe we should divine instead. There might be ebó . . ."

It was dark when the diviner spread his mat on the hardwood floor, and the young mother lit a lamp against the darkness. Together they sat facing each other, he on the mat and she on a low stool. Mofá prayed while rubbing the shells on the mat, his deep voice and his clicking cowries keeping time with one another. When he rolled the shells out on the mat twice, he frowned. "Ejila Meji," he told the young woman.

It meant nothing to her, of course, and Mofá kept chanting and casting. Finally he looked up and told her, "Elegguá says Ano, sickness, is with your child, and even now she is calling for Ikú, for your baby is strong and fighting her and she cannot hold on to him for long. But Ikú is coming for your child tonight. She is close. We have to make ebó if we are to fight off Ikú before she can get into this house. Have you any okra?"

"I do," she said, her voice soft.

"I need it. And two buckets. Olófin willing, Ikú will not be feasting tonight. And Ano is losing her strength. Your baby is too strong. If we can keep Ikú away, he will make it through the night and live."

He had the young woman kiss the mat before rising, and he did the same. She gave the diviner the two buckets and the okra he had asked for. Mofá put half of the okra in each, breaking each bean into two parts as he did. To the very rim, he filled each bucket with water.

"Go to bed. Get some rest," he said, straining to carry one bucket to the front door. "You need to keep up your strength for your son. The rest is up to me." He set the bucket down by the front door with a groan and went to take the other to the baby's bedroom door. He set that bucket down with a grunt.

The young mother kissed Mofá on the cheek, the same kiss she usually reserved for her child. Then instead of going to her own room she walked into his. *There is no rest for a worried, weary mother,* thought Mofá. But soon he knew she was asleep; he heard the deep breathing of mother and son in the small, silent house.

Beside the front door, with his first bucket of okra and water, Mofá waited, fighting against sleep. *It's going to be a long night, waiting.* He looked down; a thick slime was forming in the water.

Ikú came that night for the little boy. She entered the front door where Mofá stood watch, and as she took her first few steps toward the child, Mofá cast the first pan of slime on the floor. In shock, Ikú took a step back; she slipped, fell down, and broke her leg.

"Wicked man!" she hissed, standing on her one good leg.

Mofá ran to the baby's room where the second bucket stood outside the door, and with a great grunt he dashed the water from the second pan at Ikú's feet. Again she slipped, breaking her other leg.

In pain, Ikú howled, "I have not the strength to take the little boy tonight, but death cannot be thwarted forever. One night, I will return." She shrank into the shadows and left the house that night.

By morning, Ano had lost her strength, and she too fled the house. The mother was relieved when she woke to the cries of her baby. Gently, she held the little one to her chest so it could suckle. The baby ate hungrily.

As powerful as Ikú was and still is, it was the humble okra that saved the little boy's life that night. And the mother rewarded Mofá greatly for his help.

 # Afterword

> *Let us not engage in the world hurriedly. Let us not grasp*
> *the rope of wealth impatiently. That which should be*
> *treated with mature judgment, let us not deal with in a*
> *state of anger. When we arrive at a cool place, let us rest*
> *fully; let us give continuous attention to the future; and let*
> *us consider the consequences of things. All this remember,*
> *for we shall eventually pass.*
>
> FROM THE ODU UNLE MEJI (8-8) IN THE DILOGGÚN

While I was finishing this manuscript, Rebecca was still alive but not well. Aro held her with an iron grip, and every time her ovarian markers came close to normal levels, the remaining cancer cells became resistant to treatment. Because the drugs used in ovarian cancer therapies are metabolized by the kidneys, her renal function declined, and every infusion meant to heal her became a threat to her health. In December 2012, after the Chanukah holiday, Rebecca sat me down and told me, "No more. I'm done." She was tired of the drugs that left her bedridden, her stomach tight with nausea while her body felt like it was on fire. She had decided the fight was not worth the cost. Rising cancer markers, abdominal bloating, pain, and social isolation—all of it had taken the fight out of her. She was ready to give up.

Cancer, as a manifestation of Aro, is a subversive creature. In the odu Ofún Meji (10-10) of the diloggún, the osogbo made a pact to walk hand-in-hand with her sister, Ano; together they afflict us not only with long-term illness, but also with daily sufferings that can crush the human spirit. They make us *want* to give up, to invite death in. In the odu Ejioko Metanlá (2-13), they both acquire the ashé to enter the human body, and Aro acquires a special ashé—to enter and hide, undetected, until the day comes that the human body is weak and the spirit broken. Then, while we are at our lowest, she rises up like a leopard and tries to consume us. That is what osogbo did to Rebecca: Aro hid; Aro rose up; and now Aro was consuming her.

From the beginning I watched Rebecca lose everything as she fought for her life. First it was her job, and then it was her house, and then, one by one, she lost most of her possessions to foreclosure and, unfortunately, theft (by one of her own long-term "friends"). Her communal ties and friendships were strained to the point of loss, as watching someone you love wither away is difficult, and few can handle it. The impending death of a loved one reminds us of our own mortality, and as mortal creatures our instincts tell us to run and hide when Ikú is near. Rebecca moved in with me, and for a time, while in her brief remission, she was self-sustaining as she tried to build up a private practice as a licensed mental health therapist. But when the cancer came back she was too weak to work. All but the strongest of her long-term friendships faded, and those friends who remained at her side were overpowered by her suffering. Her ex-fiancé, her life partner, and myself banded together to make sure all her needs were met, everything from food to shelter to medications and medical care. Although I was the one at her side on a daily basis, keeping a roof over her head and providing for her comfort needs, others were involved in providing for her medical insurance and special nutritional needs. Ultimately, it is the loneliness and isolation that Aro brings that kill our spirit even before the body dies, and in all but the strongest families and friendships, those who are dying die alone. Fortunately, Rebecca had a strong family (by both blood and spirit), and she had a small handful of friends whose devotion was unshakable.

She also still had her faith—or so I thought. In January 2013,

Rebecca sat on my mat for her annual reading, a custom many ilé ocha have, in which an odu is marked that sets the tone for the coming twelve months. At that point she was ready to give up, to let the cancer run its course; her cancer markers were rising beyond belief and her oncologist had told her it was time for hospice. But Eleggúa assured her, "This is not your year to die," and if she did *everything* her doctor told her to do and made frequent *adimús* (offerings) to the orishas Shangó and Yemayá, she would survive the year, and then . . . next year we would see what would come.

"But my doctor says hospice is my only option," she argued.

"Then for now," I told her, "hospice it is. In the meantime, start cooking for Yemayá and Shangó." I gave her my recipe book for the orishas. She set it on her television stand, and there it sat, unused.

A week after the reading her oncologist called: there was a new treatment for ovarian cancer that many were claiming was an almost "miraculous" cure. She needed blood work run to make sure her renal function was sufficient to handle the chemotherapy. She did so, and she was cleared for the treatment. On February 1, 2013, she started the new regimen. At $22,000 a dose it needed to be miraculous, but even more of a miracle was that her insurance carrier agreed to pay most of the costs, and I made the copays for what insurance would not cover. Payment was not demanded with each treatment; payment in full was demanded up front. It drained a huge part of my life's savings—but the life of a friend, of family, is always worth the sacrifice. Instead of weekly trips to M. D. Anderson for infusions, this treatment required only a monthly trip to the cancer center. Three days after each treatment she would become active, almost hyper, from the combination of chemotherapy and steroids, but then, as more days slid by, she would become lethargic and sleepy. After two weeks her mouth would fill with sores, her hands and feet would become red and bruised, and her body would be in pain.

But her cancer responded; test results showed the cells were dying.

It was late June 2013 when Rebecca had her meltdown. I remember it as though in slow motion. We were sitting in the living room watching television; she was propped up in the recliner wearing her pink Snuggie while I lay on the sofa. Her cell phone rang, and as she listened her eyes filled with tears. When she hung up she struggled to get out of her Snuggie and the recliner, and I followed her to her room, where she pulled out the big red plastic tub in which she stored her medications. She pulled out eight unopened bags and two bottles of pills that were almost full. "I need to start taking my pills," she said. "I stopped taking my pills." She was shaking.

"What pills?" I asked her.

She held out two bottles of pills that had been opened. "I was supposed to take these every day. They were part of my therapy." One was an oral chemotherapy drug I'd never heard of, and the other was metformin, a drug used to treat diabetes but found to be effective in the long-term survival of ovarian cancer patients. I looked at her, and before I could stop myself the words came out: "Elegguá said you had to do *everything* your doctor said, meaning *take your pills.*"

"But they were making me sick. I didn't want to feel sick."

We both sat on the bed and cried together that afternoon.

Her July appointment with the oncologist did not go well. Rebecca refused to take the other two pills again until she spoke with her doctor, and although she had asked for an earlier appointment, the medical system being what it is in the state of Florida, she couldn't get in to see the doctor until the date of her infusion. Instead of giving her an infusion, her oncologist told her, "It's at the point where we're no longer helping you. We're not healing you, we're killing you." She stopped the infusions and came home with an in-home consultation scheduled with hospice. We were at the end, and she knew it. My godfather offered to see her, to consult Elegguá for her, but Rebecca lost her will to fight for good that day. She chose hospice care and a palliative dose of the ovarian cancer drug Hexalen to manage her symptoms, but even that harmed her more than it helped her, and by early August that treatment was discontinued. On August 23, 2013, the inevitable happened. While she was on her way to the bathroom, something inside of her felt like it had popped. It was late that Friday evening; I was in bed reading when she screamed for help. I pushed open the bathroom door and there she sat, soaked in blood. I remember the last conversation we had in our home; it is frozen in my mind, a tape that even now I can replay.

Rebecca asked me, "What are you thinking right now?"

"I'm not. I'm panicking inside."

"Why?"

"Because this is bad."

"If I was your patient, what would you be thinking?"

"Don't ask me that. I can't think like you're my patient. You're my best friend. I couldn't even think about you in clinical terms."

"Breathe. Calm down. If there was a patient sitting here instead of me, what would you be doing?"

"I'd be standing right beside you like I am now, letting you lean against me in case you were too weak to be holding yourself up. I'd be rubbing your back like I am now, comforting you, and I'd be thinking, *Where's that goddamn RN when I need her?*"

"And as your best friend, what would you be doing now that you aren't doing?"

"I'd be holding your hand and crying."

And that's exactly what I did until she started to faint. When the hospice RN I had called knocked on the front door, and when I heard the sirens in the distance, I was carrying her to her bed, her life's blood flowing like a river, soaking my clothes. That was our last conversation in our home.

It's amazing that even though she was the one dying, she was the one comforting me.

On September 6, 2013, Rebecca Brown passed away peacefully at an in-patient hospice care unit, surrounded by her family and loved ones. Her family and friends dropped everything—stopped their own lives—and came to her side to support her through the dying process. She passed from this world painlessly and on her own terms. And after she died, as we went through her possessions, we found letters she had written to each of us, some finished, some not. Each letter expressed her love and gratitude for those of us who had stood by her side. We all knew we were loved, as did she.

Hindsight is a horrible thing. Ovarian cancer is one of the most misdiagnosed cancers in women. Most doctors were taught decades ago in their initial training that it is rare, and even when women have early stages of the disease they are usually asymptomatic. For this reason most doctors falsely believe that there is no way to detect or even diagnose the illness until women are in advanced stages, at which point the cancer is untreatable. Now we know that there is pain with even stage 1 ovarian cancer, and the most obvious misdiagnosis of the disease is ovarian cysts. Symptoms are often mistaken for those of other diseases—in Rebecca's case, irritable bowel syndrome and Crohn's disease, which are not uncommon misdiagnoses, especially if the patient has autoimmune diseases such as multiple sclerosis. The toxin secreted by early-stage ovarian cancer causes thickening of the intestinal walls; a misdiagnosis is likely unless the physician knows what he's looking for. When Winter Park Memorial Hospital diagnosed a simple cyst on her ovary in October 2010, more than likely that is when her cancer was just starting, and more than likely at that point it was stage 1. If the physicians had looked more deeply into the pain and abdominal inflammation she was experiencing, they would have found it, they would have treated it, and instead of living in a hazy world of chemotherapy and narcotics before dying an early death, she would be happy, in remission, living a full life.

Divination and ebó can take us only so far, my friends. If I can leave any aborisha, olorisha, or diviner with one strong message it is this: we need better education in women's health issues, and not only must we be better educated on the lore, patakís, proverbs, and meanings of the odu, we must also be educated as people. We have to realize that while ashé can accomplish much, ashé is not only found in our heads and in our hands; ashé permeates this world, even the world of modern medicine. If we are to heal, if we are to be of benefit to the clients we serve, we have to find a way to meld the preventive practices of divination with common sense and not be afraid of Osain's other manifestations in our lives—the practice of modern medicine—or Érínlè's and Abata's workers in the world, the doctors, specialists, nurses, alternative therapists, and clinical and patient-care technicians who dedicate their lives to the arts of healing. And even those who work Érínlè's and Abata's ashé from a worldly standpoint need more education themselves. It must be an ongoing process.

Ebó, natural medicine, and modern medicine: we must be attentive to each. We must use the potential of each. And we must realize that in the end all we have in this world that matters is our health. If Rebecca's story and this book about osogbo leave you with no other message it should be this: Be proactive. Take care of yourselves. Take care of your families. And take care of your friends. More importantly, make your time with your loved ones count, because when Yemayá Ibú Achabá makes that final eggshell cross on our forehead, when we are truly in Ikú's grasp, neither medicine nor ebó will save us.

Aro: for lack of a better word, she is a bitch, as are all the osogbos we face. But tragedy is that which gives life meaning, and death—it's not the enemy. The only blessing worth having is to live a full life, and the only true tragedy is to die before one's time. I pray that you all lead the happy, healthy, full lives Olódumare has planned for you.

ÓCHA'NI LELE
SEPTEMBER 20, 2013

 # Notes

CHAPTER 1.
THE PHILOSOPHY OF ORISHA WORSHIP

1. Lele, *Sacrificial Ceremonies of Santería,* 28.
2. Lele, *The Diloggún,* 212.

CHAPTER 2.
THE CONCEPT OF OSOGBO

1. Balogun, "The Nature of Evil," 1.
2. Bewaji, "Olódumare," 11.
3. Ibid.
4. Ibid., 1.
5. Kola Abimbola, quoted in Balogun, "The Nature of Evil," 10.
6. Ibid.
7. Balogun, "The Nature of Evil," 2.
8. Ibid., 3.
9. Ibid., 3–4
10. Ibid., 9–10.

CHAPTER 3.
THE CONCEPT OF ORÍ AND DESTINY

1. Ramos, *Obí Agbón,* 122.
2. Ibid., 123.
3. Ibid., 124.

4. Ibid., 134.

5. Balogun, "The Nature of Human Person," 2.

6. Ademuleya, "The Concept of Orí," 212–13.

7. Balogun, "The Nature of Human Person," 1–2; and Ademuleya, "The Concept of Orí," 212–13.

8. Ademuleya, "The Concept of Orí," 213.

9. Balogun, "The Nature of Human Person," 5.

10. Ibid., 5–7.

11. Ibid., 4.

12. Ademuleya, "The Concept of Orí," 214.

13. Balogun, "The Nature of Human Person," 3.

14. Banacek Matos, informal conversations held in Brooklyn, N.Y., January 2012.

15. Clayton Keck, informal phone conversations, October 2010.

16. Ademuleya, "The Concept of Orí," 215.

17. Ibid., 215.

18. Ibid., 215–16.

19. Sanchez, http://ifalola.blogspot.com (accessed Feb. 6, 2012).

CHAPTER 4.
OSOGBO, ORÍ, AND ELEGGUÁ

1. Balogun, "The Concept of Orí," 118.

2. Ibid., 120.

3. Ibid., 119.

4. Ramos, *Obi Agbón,* 127.

5. Ibid., 122.

6. Ibid., 123.

7. Ibid., 125.

8. Kola Abimbola, quoted in Balogun, "The Nature of Evil," 7.

9. Ramos, *Obi Agbón,* 125.

10. Ibid., 125.

11. Lele, *Teachings of the Santería Gods,* 209–11. This story first appeared in that book.

12. Ramos, *Obi Agbón,* 125.

13. Balogun, "The Nature of Evil," 7.

14. Joseph Omosade Awolalu, quoted in Balogun, "The Nature of Evil," 8.

CHAPTER 5.
IKÚ, THE SPIRIT OF DEATH

1. Lele, *Teachings of the Santería Gods,* 32–37. This story first appeared in that book.
2. Ibid., 37–42. This story first appeared in that book.
3. Ibid., 169–72. This story first appeared in that book.

CHAPTER 7.
OTHER STORIES ABOUT THE OSOGBOS

1. Lele, *Teachings of the Santería Gods,* 152–58. This story first appeared in that book.

# Glossary

Lucumí, like the original Yoruba from which it evolved, is a tonal language, like Chinese. Because the Afro-Cubans had neither the time nor the opportunity for formal education during the period of slavery, many of these words are not spelled consistently. While I have tried to keep my own spellings consistent throughout my books, my spellings will differ from those of other authors in the field. However, the pronunciation is still the same. For any Lucumí or Spanish term that does not have an accent mark, the proper emphasis goes on the second-to-last syllable in the word. To facilitate proper pronunciation, I have included the appropriate accent mark for all words that vary from this pattern. Vowel sounds for all non-English words will approximate those of the Spanish language.

Keep in mind the following points when pronouncing words:

- The *ch* sound is used in Lucumí and Spanish words; these languages have no *sh* sound.
- The *ñ* character (*enye* sound) is used in Spanish words only, not in Lucumí words.
- The *y* sound in Spanish has a slight edge to it, so that it sounds more like the English and Yoruba *j* sound. I have used *j* here whenever possible.

Note that in each glossary entry one or more words may be italicized. The italicization of a word indicates that a definition of that word can be found in the glossary as well.

abokú: One freed by death.

aborisha: One who worships the *orishas* of the religion *Santería;* an aborisha has taken at least the initiation of the *elekes* and *warriors.*

adele: The *cowrie* shells in an *orisha's diloggún* that are not read in a *divination* session; for most orishas, there will be only two adele since the complete diloggún is made of eighteen cowrie shells. For *Elegguá,* however, there will be five adele since his diloggún has twenty-one shells.

Aganyú: The *orisha* of volcanoes. He is also known as the father of *Shangó* and is the ferryman who carries people across the river.

ajagbalá: A location at the front of the neck, at its base, just above the dip in the collarbone; ajagbalá connects us with the future—our future and our descendants' future—and it leads us to the possibilities that lie before us.

Ajala: An avatar of *Obatalá* responsible for sculpting the *orí* of both animals and humans.

Akoba: The personification of all things not good.

akunleyan: Free will.

Alabalashe: A praise name used for both *Obatalá* and *Olódumare;* it means "the prosperous one who wields the scepter." It is also the name of an avatar of Obatalá responsible for teaching the secrets of the 256 *odu* to *orisha* priests.

aleyo: One who follows *Santería* but is not initiated as a *priest* or *priestess;* a noninitiate or outsider.

apere: Perfection.

ara: The material element; the human body.

Arará: Present-day Benin.

Aro: The personification or entity of durative illness.

ashé: A very dynamic universal force; the spiritual power of the universe. It has many meanings, among which are "grace," "life," "fate," "power," "talent," and "wisdom"; the meaning intended depends on its context. Most *santeros* agree that life is ashé, and that ashé is life.

asiento: The major initiation ceremony of *Santería,* in which an *aleyo* becomes an *iyawó.*

atarí: The crown of the head.

avatar: Many *orishas,* including *Obatalá, Yemayá, Oshún,* and *Elegguá,* have different avatars, also known as "paths" or "roads," which could be thought of as different incarnations of the same spirit. Each avatar is related to one of an orisha's many incarnations on the earth (many orishas have spent mortal lives among humans). Only those incarnations of significant religious, historical, or political importance are remembered specifically and become avatars, or paths of that orisha.

ayé: The material world.

babalawo: An initiate of *Orúnmila*. A babalawo is always male because only men may enter Orúnmila's mysteries. Also known as "father of the secrets."

babalorisha: Literally "the father of the orishas." It is an honorary term used for olorishas who have initiated other priests and priestesses into the Lucumí faith.

Babaluaiye: This *orisha* originates in the land of *Arará,* which is present-day Benin. He is the father of smallpox, disease, and afflictions of the skin.

composite odu: A combination of two *olodu,* such as the combination of Unle (8) and Obara (6); this forms the composite odu Unle Obara. Some refer to these composites simply as *odu.*

cowrie: The type of shell that is used to create the *diloggún* of an *orisha.*

derecho: A religious fee, a monetary offering.

diffused monotheism: The belief in one God interacting with humans through various emanations of him/herself. In the *Lucumí* faith, God is known as *Olódumare, Olorún,* and *Olófin,* and the various emanations are known as *orishas.*

diloggún: The system of *cowrie divination* by which a *priest* or *priestess* of *Santería* learns the will of the *orishas;* also, the eighteen or twenty-one cowrie shells that contain the soul of an orisha; also, the set of sixteen shells a diviner casts to perform divination. The exact meaning of the word depends on the context in which it is used.

divination: The act of uncovering the will of the *orishas,* the desires of *egun,* and the trends of the future. The *Lucumí* faith employs three systems of divination: *obí, diloggún,* and *Ifá.*

diviner: One skilled in the art of *divination* who knows the secrets of *obí* and *diloggún.*

ebó: An offering made to an *orisha.*

ebó de entrada: "The ebó of entrance," a divination of cleansing done before the postulant goes to the river for his or her initiation.

eemi: The force causing us to breathe.

efun: A loosely packed, powdered chalk made from crushed eggshells. Sometimes it is used as an *ibó* in *diloggún.*

Égba: The personification of paralysis.

egun: The many ancestral spirits related to one through one's blood relatives or one's spiritual relatives.

eledá: A spark of God, *Olódumare,* enlivening the heads of all living creatures.

Elegguá: He is often portrayed as the personification of fate, a young child, and an old man. Elegguá is the messenger of all the *orishas* and the first and last to be honored in every ceremony performed. Without his goodwill, nothing in the religion of *Santería* may be done. In *Ifá,* it is said that there are 256 paths of Elegguá, one for each *odu.* Each of these paths is known as *Eshu* and has its own specific name, such as *Eshu Ayé, Eshu Bi,* and *Eshu Laroye.* In *ocha,* there are 101 paths of Elegguá (each also known as Eshu). In many *ilé ocha,* when an initiate receives the *warriors,* he is told the name of Eshu that his Elegguá enshrines.

elekes: Beaded necklaces given to both *aleyos* and *santeros.* The bead color denotes not only the *orisha* to whom they are consecrated, but also the path of that orisha. In the initiation of the elekes, an aleyo will generally receive four elekes (the elekes of *Obatalá, Yemayá, Oshún,* and *Shangó*) unless the *diloggún* specifies otherwise. Sometimes the eleke of *Elegguá* is also given.

Elerí: The union of *iporí, orí, eledá, gbogbowan olodó,* and *orisha* in the consecrated *olorisha.*

emi: Breath.

eni-ayan: A chosen one or a chosen head.

eniyan: Human beings.

Epe: The personification of curses.

Érínlè: An *orisha* envisioned as a beautiful, androgynous youth; he is the patron of homosexuals and fishermen. At one time he was mortal, but *Yemayá* was so taken with his beauty that she made him immortal and stole him away to the bottom of the sea. There she tired of him, yet he learned all of her secrets. Yemayá removed his speech by cutting out his tongue, and then she set him free to walk among the rest of the *orishas.* To this day, Érínlè will speak only through her. He is also seen as the great physician, the one who can cure any illness with his extensive knowledge of medicine.

Eshe: The personification of general afflictions; though listed as an *osogbo,* Eshe's ambiguous nature makes him but a shadow among their ranks.

We count him as an osogbo, but he is so minor that he is not given a ranking of importance among the others in the list.

Eshu: An alternate name for the *orisha* known as *Elegguá*. While *Ifá* lists one Eshu for each of the 256 *odu, ocha* has only 101 paths of Eshu. Some examples of Eshu that are shared by both Ifá and ocha are *Eshu Ayé, Eshu Laroye,* and *Eshu Bi.*

Eshu Ayé: This *avatar* of *Elegguá* is said to walk on the shoreline where waves lap at the sand. This *Eshu* works closely with the *orisha Olokun.*

Eshu Bi: This *avatar* of *Elegguá* is both a young child and an old man; he is forceful and stern. It is said that this *Eshu* walks with the first two Ibeyi, the twins who were born of *Shangó* and *Oyá* (some lineages believe they were born of Shangó and *Oshún*). He is the protector of twins and also of small children.

Eshu Laroye: This *avatar* of *Elegguá* works closely with *Oshún* and is her constant companion; he is often referred to as the "little talkative one." He is one of Elegguá's most important and popular paths, being the one addressed and refreshed before any invocation or prayer to the *orishas.*

eshu ni pacuó: A *Lucumí* phrase denoting the back of the neck.

Ewon: The personification of imprisonment, especially false imprisonment and kidnapping.

Fitibo: The personification of sudden death and cardiac arrest.

gbogbowan olodó: A secret artifact that the postulant brings home from the river ceremony before consecration as an *olorisha.*

houngan: A priest of Vodun (i.e., Voodoo).

ibó: Tools used by the *diviner* when reading the diloggún.

Ifá: A system of divination used by *babalawos* exclusively. It consists of 256 *odu.* Only the priests of *Orúnmila,* the babalawos, may use Ifá.

igbodu: The sacred room where *orishas* are born and initiates are crowned.

ika eniyan: "Wicked people."

Ikú: The spirit or personification of death.

ilé: A *Lucumí* word meaning "house" or "land."

ilé ocha: The spiritual house of *ocha* or of the *orishas,* headed by either a priest or a priestess who has many years of experience in the *Lucumí* faith.

Iñá: The personification of war.

initiate: One who has been initiated to the level of priesthood in the *Lucumí* faith. It may refer to an *iyawó, priest,* or *priestess.*

ipakó: The base of the brain stem controlling the body's animal functions;

through it we connect with not only our past but also our family's past, and their past mistakes.

ipin: Destiny.

iporí: Our perfection; our spiritual pinnacle of existence.

iré: Any type of blessing or good fortune that can befall the client as he sits for a session with the *diloggún;* also, when capitalized, the entity or spirit of blessings.

ìwa: Character; our natural tendencies in life.

iwajú: Comparable to the third eye in Eastern mysticism.

iyawó: A *Lucumí* term for the new *initiates* of an *orisha.* It translates as "bride," no matter the initiate's sex. For at least a year after one's initiation, the rest of the initiates in one's *ilé ocha* will refer to the novitiate by this term.

jícara: A dried gourd that is cut open to resemble a bowl. It is used to give offerings and to pour libations to the *orishas.*

lavatorio: A ceremony performed by *olorishas;* literally, it is the washing (and spiritual birthing) of a new *orisha.*

Lucumí: A contraction of various *Yoruba* words that translates into "my friend." The Lucumí were at first the physical descendants but are now also the spiritual descendants of the Yoruba slaves brought to Cuba. This word also refers to the corruption of the native Yoruba tongue that is now used in *Santería.*

misa: A spiritual mass.

ñame: A type of yam, a root used frequently in Latin American cuisine.

oba: A *Lucumí* word that denotes a king.

Obatalá: An *orisha* considered to be the king of all the orishas of heaven; the creator of the human form. Obatalá has both male and female *avatars.*

obí: The system of divination based on the coconut; also the coconut itself.

Obí: The man who became an *orisha* and then fell from grace because of his own pride, becoming the coconut used in *divination.* Despite this, Obí is still an orisha and treated with respect in the *Lucumí* religion.

ocha: A shortened form of the word *orisha.* It also denotes the *Lucumí* faith.

Ochosi: An *orisha;* one of the *warriors* and said to be the patron of both the hunt and justice.

odu: The many patterns that can fall when using the divination system known as the *diloggún.* There are a total of sixteen *parent odu* and 256 *composite odu.* Each of these has its own proverbs, *patakís,* meanings, and *ebós.* The word *odu* is both singular and plural in *Lucumí* and *Yoruba* usage.

Odu: The name of the *orisha* who governs all 256 sacred *odu* in the corpus of *Ifá* and the *diloggún.* It is an orisha sacred to *babalawos,* and she (for Odu is female) is the source of all sacred, spiritual knowledge.

Ofo: The personification of loss.

ogbón: Our unconscious selves.

Ogo: The personification of maleficent sorcery.

Ogún: One of the warrior *orishas;* the patron of ironworkers, civilization, and technology.

okán: The heart.

Okana: The name of the woman upon whose life many *patakís* of the *odu* are based. It is also one of the sixteen *parent odu* of the *diloggún.*

olodu: The sixteen *parent odu* that give birth to all sixteen *composite odu* in each family.

Olódumare: A *Yoruba* contraction that translates into "owner of the womb." This is the supreme deity of the *Yoruba* and *Lucumí.*

Olófin: It is said among the *Lucumí* that Olófin is "God on earth"; he is the eldest *avatar* of *Obatalá* and can be received only by the priesthood of *Orúnmila,* the *babalawos.*

Olófin Ayé: A praise name for *Olófin;* it means "the supreme ruler on earth."

Olófin Orún: A praise name for *Olófin;* it means "the supreme sovereign ruler who is in heaven."

Olokun: The androgynous *orisha* who rules and owns the ocean. In most *Lucumí* homes, Olokun's primary manifestation is male.

olorisha: A *Lucumí* word denoting an initiate of an *orisha.*

Olorún: A *Lucumí* contraction of two words: *olo,* "owner," and *orún,* "the sun." It means "owner of the sun," a name for God, his symbol being the sun in the daytime sky.

oloshún: An iniate of the orisha Oshún.

omiero: Any number of herbal waters made by *initiates* of *Santería;* it is used in bathing the *iyawó* and giving birth to the *orishas.*

Ona: The personification of afflictions.

onise ibi: "Workers of osogbo."

oniyemayá: A term denoting an initiate of *Yemayá.*

opolo: The brain.

Oran: The personification of moral or legal crimes.

orí: A *Yoruba* word that means "head" or "consciousness"; it is used to refer to the spiritual consciousness of humans. Also, it denotes a special faculty or a talent, and it represents the first and highest point of that special skill.

oriaté: An expert not only in the reading of the *diloggún*, but also in all the ceremonies of the *Lucumí* faith.

orí-inu: The inner head; similar to what Carl Jung called the *collective unconscious.*

orisha: A *Yoruba* contraction that means "select head"; it denotes any of the myriad spirits in the pantheon of *Santería* that are an extension of *Olódumare's ashé.*

orún: Heaven.

orún burukú: The "bad" heaven.

Orúnmila: The *orisha* of *Ifá* and its priests, the *babalawos.* Only men are called to his priesthood. Orúnmila does not speak directly through the *diloggún;* however, certain *composite odu* indicate that he would like the one at the mat sent to his priests so he may speak directly.

orún reré: The "good" heaven.

Oshún: The *orisha* bringing love, sweetness, money, prosperity, fertility, conception, and all the things that make life worth living. She is the sister of *Yemayá* and one of *Shangó's* wives. In some lineages, she is referred to as the mother of twins.

Oshún Ibú Akuaró: One of *Oshún's* many *avatars.* She is found where the river and sea meet, in their brackish juncture. Because of this, she has a close association with both *Érínlè* and *Yemayá.* Note that this Oshún was married to Érínlè; however, she left Érínlè to be *Shangó's* consort. In the process, she lost all of her riches.

osogbo: The spiritual principle of misfortune or negative influence; any of the evils that may be predicted for a client through the oracle known as *diloggún.* When capitalized it refers to the living, spiritual entity of misfortune in the *Lucumí* faith.

otá: A smooth black pebble through which the *ashé* of the *orisha* is connected to his *orí.*

Oyá: This female *orisha* is the patron of forked lightning. She is the gatekeeper to the cemetery, *Shangó's* partner in battle, and the lady of the marketplace. She is also the orisha of fast change and tumultuous cycles. Some also see her in the action of the tornado. She is Shangó's third wife and his favorite, even over *Oshún.*

Oyó: The capital of the ancient Yoruba empire, established in the fourteenth century, which became the most politically important state in Africa from the mid-seventeenth to the late eighteenth century.

parent odu: The sign giving birth to all sixteen *composite odu* in a single family; *olodu.*

pataki: The many sacred stories and legends found in the *diloggún;* some of these are about the *orishas,* while others are about the actions of historical/mythological humans who lived and died in both Africa and Cuba. All patakís teach spiritual truths found in *odu,* and many are considered historical texts, although oral.

priest/priestess: One who is initiated into the mysteries of an *orisha.*

Santería: The name of *orisha* worship as it developed in Cuba; the English translation from the Spanish is "worship of the saints." The name derives from the syncretizing of the Catholic saints and the orishas of the *Yoruba.*

santero/santera: A priest or priestess of *Santería.*

Shangó: The fourth king of ancient *Oyó* and the *orisha* of storm, thunder, and lightning.

tambour: A drum party dedicated to the *orishas.*

Tiya-Tiya: The personification of gossip.

Unle: The name of the mortal on whose life many of the *patakís* of this odu are based; also one of the *parent odu* of the *diloggún.*

warriors: The four orishas that are received together in one initiation: Elegguá, Ogún, Ochosi, and Ósun.

Yemayá: Born when *Olokun* was chained to the bottom of the ocean by *Obatalá,* Yemayá arose to become mother to the world and the *orishas.* She is the patron of motherhood and the fresh waters of the world.

Yoruba: The native Africans who originally settled in the southwestern parts of the area known today as Nigeria. Their deities, the *orishas,* form the basis of the *Lucumí* faith. The word *Yoruba* also denotes the language shared by these peoples, the native tongue that, mixed with Cuban Spanish, became known as Lucumí.

yubon/yubonna: A priest or priestess who assists his or her godparent in the rituals of the *elekes, warriors,* and *asiento.*

Bibliography

Ademuleya, Babasehinde. "The Concept of Orí in the Traditional Yoruba Representation of Human Figures." *Nordic Journal of African Studies* 16(2) (2007): 212–20, www.njas.helsinki.fi/pdf-files/vol16num2/ademuleya.pdf.

Balogun, Oladele Abiodun. "The Concept of Orí and Human Destiny in Traditional Yoruba Thought: A Soft-Deterministic Approach," *Nordic Journal of African Studies* 16(1) (2007): 116–30, www.njas.helsinki.fi/pdf-files/vol16num1/balogun.pdf.

———. "The Nature of Evil and Human Wickedness in Traditional African Thought: Further Reflections on the Philosophic Problem of Evil." *LUMINA* 20(2) (2009): ISSN 2094–1188, http://lumina.hnu.edu.ph/articles/balogunOct09.pdf.

———. "The Nature of Human Person in Traditional African Thought: Further Reflections on Traditional Philosophy of Mind." *Afroeuropa* 3(2) (2009): ISSN: 1887–3456, http://joural.afroeuropa.edu/index.php/afroeuropa/article/vreafile/147/132.

Bewaji, John A. I. "Olódumare: God in Yoruba Belief and the Theistic Problem of Evil." *African Studies Quarterly* 2(1) (1998): ISSN: 2152–2448, http://v2i1a1.pdf.

Lele, Ócha'ni. *The Diloggún: The Orishas, Proverbs, Sacrifices, and Prohibitions of Cuban Santería.* Rochester, Vt.: Destiny Books, 2003.

———. *Diloggún Tales of the Natural World: How the Moon Fooled the Sun and Other Santería Stories.* Rochester, Vt.: Destiny Books, 2011.

———. *Sacrificial Ceremonies of Santería: A Complete Guide to Its Rituals and Practices.* Rochester, Vt.: Destiny Books, 2012.

———. *Teachings of the Santería Gods: The Spirit of the Odu.* Rochester, Vt.: Destiny Books, 2010.

Ramos, Miguel. *Obi Agbón: Lucumí Divination with the Coconut.* Miami, Fla.: Eleda.org Publications, 2012.

Sanchez, Ifalola. Blog at http:ifalola.blogspot.com.

Index